GERALD DU

'If you have ever enjoyed Geral
this book. Edward Whitley is a b
funny and very serious at the same time. If you really want to understand the world conservation battle – and enjoy a fabulous book – buy *Gerald Durrell's Army*.'

DAILY MAIL

'This book gives a memorable portrait of Gerald Durrell, a unique insight into conservation work, and a down-to-earth and often hilariously funny account of Edward Whitley's adventures around the world.'

THE GOOD BOOK GUIDE

'A fascinating book of great importance.'

DAILY TELEGRAPH

'Evocative, funny and often hard-hitting – a valuable contribution to the conservation of wildlife and the future of the planet.'

MARK SHAND

'An intelligent, perceptive and very funny view of the trials and tribulations conservationists face while trying to save what is left of our lovely world.'

GERALD DURRELL

'A Noah's Ark of a book, full of the oddest things imaginable: muggers and ticks, giant jumping rats, and ganja-eating rodents, the Irula Tribesmen Snake-catching Co-operative and a man who committed suicide by jumping into the lions' cage during feeding time. Hilarious yet pessimistic, moving and sad, Edward Whitley is a wonderful writer, as good as O'Hanlon or even Durrell himself.'

WILLIAM DALRYMPLE

Edward Whitley was born in 1961 and read English at Oxford University. Whilst there he won a Blue for Modern Pentathlon, and wrote *The Graduates* a book of interviews with Oxford graduates including John Betjeman, Iris Murdoch, Indira Gandhi, Bob Hawke and Dudley Moore. Published in 1986, it was chosen as his book of the year by Richard Ingrams, who remarked, 'It contains the funniest interview I've ever read.' *The Spectator* wrote, 'Mr Whitley has a lively unprejudiced mind, insatiable curiosity, cheek, and ability to laugh at his own gaffes and bloomers, a disrespectful enjoyment of words displaying itself in bold new coinages, outrageous similes and felicitous transcriptions of accents.'

Edward worked as a banker for Rothschilds before leaving in 1989 to become a writer. He has been widely published as a freelance journalist, notably in the *Daily Telegraph*, the *Daily Mail* and *The Spectator*.

He is a committed conservationist and advises a number of charities. He assisted WWF with a Debt for Nature Swap in Guatemala, and he is a Member of Council of the RSPB, the Wildfowl and Wetlands Trust and Gerald Durrell's Wildlife Preservation Trust on whose behalf he has raised funds for the unique International Training Centre – the subject of this book.

GERALD DURRELL'S ARMY

EDWARD WHITLEY

PAN BOOKS
LONDON, SYDNEY AND AUCKLAND

First published 1992 by John Murray (Publishers) Limited

This edition published 1993 by Pan Books Limited
a division of Pan Macmillan Publishers Limited
Cavaye Place London SW10 9PG
and Basingstoke

Associated companies throughout the world

ISBN 0 330 32832 8

1 3 5 7 9 8 6 4 2

A CIP catalogue record for this book is available from
the British Library

Printed by Cox & Wyman Ltd, Reading, Berkshire

To my Wife
Araminta

CONTENTS

Illustrations by Bryan Hanlon

ACKNOWLEDGEMENTS

I would like to thank Gerald Durrell in an all-embracing way for setting up the International Training Centre next door to his zoo in Jersey. In so doing, he has not only provided the world with a growing number of trainees to fight for their countries' conservation – 300 trainees from 70 countries to date – but has also provided the idea and material for this book. As I visited 26 trainees from 10 countries, there is scope for at least 7 sequels on the subject.

I would also like to thank Gerry in particular for inviting me to join him on an animal hunt in Madagascar where he sent me off on a fourteen-hour train journey with ten lemurs, wrote a poem to my wife Araminta in which he scraped up some improbable rhymes and introduced me to the giant jumping rat, the hissing cockroach and legions of sweat bees – experiences which I am now delighted to enjoy with hindsight.

The Jersey staff helped arrange my itinerary – Jeremy Mallinson, Simon Hicks, John Hartley and David Waugh – and were most tolerant of me trespassing all over their fields of expertise.

The Jersey trainees, the subject of this book, showed me around their jobs and projects with great enthusiasm. They are the unsung heroes of conservation and their commitment and dedication in the face of appalling circumstances are inspiring.

Finally I would like to thank Rod Hall, an engineer with British Airways. In his spare time Rod has set up 'British Airways Assisting Nature Conservation' which arranges for people, animals and equipment involved in conservation to fly around the world in otherwise empty seats or storage. In the process of researching this book, I flew British Airways free of charge to each country I visited. Rod's idea is a prime example of the sort of lateral thinking which can help the world at no extra cost – a small gesture by something which flies at 30,000 feet that has a dramatic effect on the ground below.

INTRODUCTION

GERRY'S KITCHEN TABLE

Gerald Durrell writes his books at the kitchen table. He writes in long hand, and his manuscript piles up between empty glasses, bowls of fruit and jars of mayonnaise and curry powder. The kitchen cupboards around him are bright mandarin orange, the sort of virulent orange which flared up in the 1970s before the onslaught of anonymous shades of pastel.

'I agree it's not ideal,' Gerry admits. 'In fact the orange gives me a piercing hangover every time I look up. So I have to keep my head down and concentrate on what I'm writing, which at least means I get more done.'

The view from the window is a further distraction. The kitchen overlooks an obscure part of his zoo in Jersey, a backyard where the Celebes apes live.

'They set an appalling example. Look at them. They may not be up to much now, but they're usually engaged in an orgy of mind-boggling depravity. The observation notes of a highly distinguished academic researcher who came here to study them read like *Up Pompeii*. It's hard enough to cook in this kitchen, let alone write.'

As well as writing and cooking, Gerry also supervises the operations of the zoo from here. The zoo staff come up and sit around on low chairs, their chins just off the kitchen table. Their conversation is not what you would expect from zoo staff. Jersey Zoo is a unique zoo in that it only holds animals close to extinction. It tries to breed sufficient numbers to guarantee their survival in captivity, and then reintroduces them back into the wild. A key part of this work is to ensure that there is enough wild for them to go back into. A good deal of time is spent out in the countries where the animals come from. There the Jersey staff do field studies of the wild animals and join forces with the local governments to try to safeguard their future.

'By definition a zoo is international,' Gerry said. 'It is a collection of exotic animals which people come to see because they cannot afford to go to Borneo or Brazil to see them there. You go to a zoo and you get them all in one package. One minute you're standing next to an orang-utan, the next you're looking at a golden lion tamarin from Brazil. Not even Thomas Cook can transport you like that. And any zoo worth its salt must educate you about these animals. This used to be just a notice saying "I'm Guy the Gorilla", but now they have information boards showing where they come from, what's going on in their country, what they eat and so on.

'There has been a good deal of criticism of zoos. But if we don't take animals into captivity, they will be wiped out while all the animal liberationists sit around wringing their hands. Animals have always been my starting point. I love working with them and think that we can learn a lot from them. I use them to win people's attention. If they're interested in animals, I can show them everything else which is going on in the world.'

Gerry has several criteria in choosing animals.

'I only look after animals we can breed here. So that rules out things like rhinos or elephants or polar bears. We just couldn't do them justice. Jersey is a sanctuary where these animals breed while we try to repair the damage in their country. Then with luck there is somewhere for them or their offspring to return to.

'And I only choose animals where Jersey can take a clear leading role in their conservation. So again that rules out working with the African rhino, for instance. There are so many organizations running around East Africa that nobody knows who's calling the shots, let alone firing them.

'When we've chosen the animal, the St Lucian parrot or the angonoka tortoise or the Mauritius kestrel, we take a good deal of responsibility for it. We liaise with the government at every stage of the process as we capture them, breed them in Jersey, study them, re-introduce them and use them as a symbol of the country's conservation. We print posters and sponsor an education campaign based on saving these animals from extinction. And of course for every tortoise or parrot saved, countless other things are inadvertently saved alongside it.

'And lastly we have to be geographically comfortable. We cannot spread ourselves too thinly. If we're going to support a project for twenty years, which is what we do, then we have to be involved and visit it and bring people over here and exchange animals. So Jersey has concentrated on four main areas – Brazil, the Caribbean, Madagascar and Mauritius.

'We work in Brazil because Jeremy Mallinson, our Zoological Director, is obsessed with lion tamarins. Absolutely obsessed. I've sent him to several psychiatrists but there's no cure. Then Simon Hicks, our Trust Secretary, supervises our projects in the Caribbean. He solemnly assures me that the most endangered species are there and he keeps finding the world's rarest iguana or snake to add to our work, but I suspect it's just the rum and sunshine going to his head. My wife Lee is an expert on all things Malagasy and can almost pronounce the names of our two trainees out there, and John Hartley, my personal assistant, is the world expert on Mauritius.

'Because we have concentrated in these areas, we have built up contacts and developed other projects. In Mauritius, for instance, we started with the Mauritius kestrel. We've now expanded to the pink pigeon and the echo parakeet and we're advising the government on the creation of their first national park. All this started from breeding a handful of kestrels.

'The beauty of being a small team is that we can move quickly. When St Lucia was hit by a hurricane in 1980, I sent our curator of birds out on the next plane with a chain-saw to help clear up the reserve. We were the first outsiders to get into the country. The Prime Minister got to hear about it and never forgot it. Nine years later he came over here to pick up two Jersey-bred St Lucian parrots to start a captive breeding programme in St Lucia.

'All of this work led me to the idea of the Training Centre. We increasingly found that whilst we could breed animals here, when it came to putting them back where they belonged, there was less and less forest. And we could only do so much ourselves.

'Although you know what is right for a country, you can't just tell the people what to do. Well, you can but no one listens to you. They just wobble their heads ambiguously and go on destroying everything. I can go into a village and stand there and tell people what's going wrong, but they'll just think that I'm mad or drunk. No one will understand what I'm telling them any more than an English village would appreciate an African witchdoctor telling them to do a rain dance every day. To make conservation succeed, there have to be people on the ground explaining the process, and they should be people of the country.

'So fifteen years ago I suggested that we set up a training centre here. I wanted to teach people from anywhere in the world how to look after their countries. We were sitting around this table. All the staff said I was mad. Well, they should have known better. When I was six I told my mother I wanted to have a zoo though all I had was a matchbox full of wood-lice.

'I decided that the first trainee should come from Mauritius. I've always had a close bond with Mauritius – it was the home of my favourite bird, the dodo, which is the symbol of Jersey Zoo. So I went there and met a promising young man in the Forestry Division called Youseff Mungroo. I told him all about the world-famous International Training Centre at Jersey where he could learn the secrets of conservation. Poor chap, he wasn't to know that it didn't exist. Amazingly, he agreed to come.

'Youseff arrived in Jersey during a freezing cold winter and stayed for eight months. It was so cold that he lived in the reptile house for the first two months as it was the warmest place on the island. He must have learned something because he's now the Conservation Officer of Mauritius and together we have saved two birds, the Mauritius kestrel and the pink pigeon, from certain extinction.'

Over the next four years, a trickle of trainees came to Jersey and the course gradually took shape. In 1980 the farmhouse next door to the zoo came on to the market. It was bought and converted into a proper training centre with a library, a lecture theatre, laboratories and accommodation. Ten years later over 300 trainees from 70 different countries have been trained in Jersey.

'So what started off as one freezing Mauritian cowering in the reptile house is now a proper International Training Centre. We bring together people from all over the world. A forestry officer from Mexico will sit down next to a vet from Malawi; Arabs, Africans, South Americans and Indonesians all talk with each other. God knows what about, certainly not cricket, but they all see they're dealing with the same problems.

'Each year we train thirty students on the basic programme which lasts sixteen weeks. Then we've built a diploma course on top of that at Kent University. And next year we're running a policy-makers' course for senior people in conservation. This is to show the people at the top what can be done. The problem is that you get a fifty-year-old bureaucrat who's appointed Minister of Forestry just before he retires; people are bribing him to let them log the trees, and he's just a normal civil servant who doesn't know the difference between a tamarin and a tapir and doesn't give a damn about either. Now how do you get him interested in conservation?'

Gerry doesn't like leaving rhetorical questions unanswered.

'I don't know. Nobody knows. So we get him over to Jersey and find out. And because the people we most want to help are least able to afford to come, we pay for them ourselves. You can't do this over fax machines or the telephone, even if they worked which they never do. You have to muck in with each other. An hour spent playing an absurd drinking game with a Nepalese forester is a much better basis for getting him to help you than any number of official letters. He knows what you're talking about, or at the end of the game what you think you're trying to talk about.

'People spout a lot of nonsense about the world becoming a "global village" as if they've just popped back from the post office in Bangladesh. Well, we've got a global training centre. And a global dining-room for that matter.'

The global dining-room at the Training Centre is unpretentious. There are four formica tables, a large fridge and a stone fireplace. Two clues give away the fact that this is not any old dining-room. The postcards along the mantelpiece are from an astonishing variety of countries – Uganda, Malaysia, Paraguay and the Philippines for starters. And on top of the fridge Daddies sauce, HP sauce and Heinz tomato ketchup stand alongside sweet chilli sauce from Thailand, Indian pickle and a red-hot Mexican sauce which should carry a government health warning.

Just as Gerry's kitchen is the hub of Jersey Zoo, the kitchen at the Training Centre is the hub of life for the trainees. It is presided over by Olwyn who cooks supper every night, a glorious celebration of English cooking – roast beef and Yorkshire pudding, pork and apple sauce, steak and kidney pies, followed by trifles, cakes and fruit pies.

'They like their food.' I was in the kitchen with Olwyn, watching her sprinkle out some flour to make pastry. She has rosy cheeks, blue eyes and a magnificent bosom, and is capable of producing vast quantities of food effortlessly. 'But sometimes they flavour it with their own sauce. They like strange things. I had one who ate nothing but mackerel and lemon curd; and one put peanut butter on everything. You see, they'd never seen it before.

'For most of them it's the first time they've left their countries. I look after them. They may feel ill or homesick. I'm used to that. Before I came here, I set up a YWCA in a Liverpool housing estate. I was by myself with these girls who had run away from home because they had been beaten up or were on drugs or pregnant. It was quite rough. Local boys used to put Molotov cocktails through the letter box.'

'Molotov cocktails?'

'Petrol bombs,' Olwyn said brightly. 'So these trainees are no problem. Some of them call me "Mama". One of them wrote to me last week asking whether he should get married. Even my own son never asked that.'

Olwyn produced steak and kidney pie with a blackbird bursting out of the top.

'I think we'll have ice cream amd meringues for pudding, with Jersey cream. They'll like that.'

They did. Over supper the conversation was a hotchpotch of English and Spanish. It was a typical week – there were trainees from Venezuela, Colombia, Mexico, Canada, Australia and the United Arab Emirates. As Gerry predicted, the conversation was not about cricket. It was about reptiles and how to incubate their eggs, how to feed a baby snake, whether to change a parrot's diet and how to win more money from the government. The Australian tried to explain to the Venezuelan the difference between ship, sheep, shit and sheet. I could see the potential for an absurd drinking game.

The trainees work for two weeks with each section in the zoo – large mammals, small mammals, apes, marmosets, and reptiles, and four weeks with birds. They then spend two weeks writing up a project which often concerns a problem in their own country. Throughout the sixteen weeks they have lectures and tutorials with David Waugh, the training officer.

'With so many nationalities it is difficult to know where to pitch the course,' David told me. 'They generally speak English but write it to a greater or lesser extent. Some of them are university graduates, others have had no further education.

'So they spend a fortnight with each zoo keeper. They learn a lot from them. The zoo keepers are no longer like the Johnny Morris type of keeper who wears a uniform and just chucks in cauliflowers. They do research, they publish papers, one of them is doing an Open University degree. So the trainees learn about hygiene, diet and breeding techniques. These are the basics which are crucial if you want animals to breed in captivity. They are also vital for a good healthy animal collection which people can come and visit and from which they can learn about their wildlife. If you have a couple of wretched chimpanzees in a ghastly cage without proper food, then nobody will respect them.

'I also give them a series of lectures. These discuss genetic inbreeding, the optimum size for reserves, record-keeping, hand-rearing, education and methods of study in the field. These are all areas in which a modern zoo should be participating. I find that the trainees are starved of the theory of zoo-keeping and conservation, but they're also the people who can really put these ideas into effect.

'And then there is the library. Generally they've never had access to a library before so it's important to let them read as much as possible. We've got videos and they can watch the nature programmes on telly. We take David Attenborough for granted now, but they're amazed by it. And everything works here. José who's here at the moment from Mexico wants to study wolves. We don't hold them, but I can telephone all the zoos which do and arrange for him to go and study them. For me that's not a problem, for him by himself in Mexico that's impossible.

'The trainees also keep us in touch with what's going on in their country. It's very easy for Westerners to issue a directive and assume that it gets through to the country concerned and that people there understand it and act on it. This is never the case. There are infinite misunderstandings about the simplest things. The trainees face enormous difficulties over things we take for granted. Take Itang Isangedighe, for example. He was a trainee in 1982. I received this in 1989.'

David handed me a letter. It read:

Dear Dr Wough,

Request for Favour

Here comes my hand. I hope you are doing fine. May I inform you that the cost of living in Nigeria is unbearable now. To survive is no longer easy. One has to try his hands on a number of things to keep going as salary is not enough for feeding let alone my children. School expenses for my children are beyond my financial capacity.

This is why I most humbly beg you to enquire, buy and send me by air the following few materials which can be easily parceled to me for casual fishing in the rivers surrounding us in Calabar. I have never personally seen these types of hooks but I strongly believe that you'll have them there:

i) Magnetic hook – this hook needs no bait, but it is said to get itself magnetised to any fish available within a certain radius from the hook.

ii) Lurer hook – this one is said to be designed in the shape, size, colour, attractiveness and nature of living things (although actually synthetic) in the form of a maggot, insect, rat, frog, worm, butterfly or larva or any other attractive thing but within which is embedded a suitably sized hook with which fish could be caught very trickishly. . . .

Hoping to hear from you soon,

Itang Isangedighe

'How can you expect someone to save wild animals when he can't afford to eat or educate his children? If I was him I'd be eating any crocodiles I could lay my hands on. People in the West never realize that you cannot just fire off directives to people telling them to save animals and expect them to do it.'

This book is an account of a number of visits I made to graduates of the Training Centre. It is one thing hearing Western organizations booming on about the need to save the rain forest or conserve this or that animal. It is another to visit a dry coastal forest in Brazil which is much more threatened than the rain forest, or to see a relatively well-paid forestry officer begging for magnetic fishing hooks, or to spend time working in the Wildlife Assessment Section, which is one of three sections in the Wildlife Division, which is one of six divisions in the Protected Areas and Wildlife Bureau, which is one of three bureaux in the Environment and Research Office, which is one of fifteen offices in the Department of Environment and Natural Resources in the Philippines.

I wanted to see what the problems are at the grass-root level. When we loosely talk about conservation, what we are really talking about is what these people do for a living. The Jersey trainees are the foot soldiers fighting on the front line and their perspective is very different from ours. Instead of talking in grand terms about global warming or the ozone layer, they look at what they need to do their job on a day-to-day basis. Often these are things which we find absurdly simple such as wire mesh, or a bicycle to patrol for poachers, or a pair of binoculars.

'Everything looks fine from the comfort of our own homes,' Gerry said, as we discussed my travels around his army. 'Or rather it looks terrible but we think "Gosh, isn't that terrible? Now, what's on the other channel? Shall we watch the James Bond film?" Everyone thinks they care about the world and indeed vast sums of money are raised in Europe and America.

'But at the other end it's all very different. Nothing is how you expect it. Once you walk off the jumbo jet and through customs, it's like going through the looking-glass – you'll have to run twice as fast just to get anywhere, you'll probably get attacked by a jabberwocky and you'll certainly have to believe six impossible things before breakfast.

'How are you going to organize your trips? You'll find the whole world is in the same mess so you could go anywhere. Let's meet in Madagascar which is about the most remote place you'll get to. Do you like frogs' legs? I'll have them ready for you at the Hotel Colbert.'

It was some time before Gerry and I met over frogs' legs in Madagascar. By then I had visited his army in a number of bizarre places. I had been in the last reserve of the black lion tamarin in Brazil, whose forest has been reduced by 98 per cent; I had joined a couple of stoned Rastas in Jamaica on a midnight hunt for the highly endangered *Geocapromys brownii* which eats their ganja (no more endangered as a result of our hunt); and I had met an engaging Ghanaian who runs his zoo on £100 a year and couldn't afford a bottle of schnapps for his sister's funeral. I had established that the only truly universal common denominators are brown bottles of warm fizzy beer, cockroaches and mosquitoes.

I arranged my trips in a pattern so that each trainee and each animal in the countries I visited would highlight a different aspect of what is now referred to as 'our global problem'.

The first distinction was whether the Jersey trainee was a government official or working for a private organization. An early warning sign that a country is in trouble is that no private organization is involved in conservation. The officials in the government department have scant pay or motivation and so precious little happens. Alpha Jallow, working in the Department of Wildlife in the Gambia, would be equally happy pushing paper in a tax collector's office. But the first step towards people taking responsibility for their own wildlife is when private organizations begin to be involved. Thus Ernest Lamptey, a government official in Ghana, has set up a private committee of local businessmen to raise funds for his zoo and, at the other end of the scale, Claudio Padua in Brazil has managed to set up a project in the government reserve which is funded entirely by private means.

Then I divided my visits between large land masses – Brazil, West Africa and India – and small islands such as the Caribbean, Mauritius and the Philippines. Madagascar falls outside these definitions, but then it falls outside most definitions. Islands are much more fragile than mainlands. They are destroyed more quickly and one can see the effects of this destruction much more clearly. They are like a quick litmus test.

And to complete the matrix I searched for a cross-section of small mammals, large mammals, reptiles, birds, and small and large birds of prey.

In Madagascar I joined Gerry and Lee on their first great animal-collecting trip since he went to the Cameroons in the 1960s. Gerry was after the mysterious long-fingered aye-aye and the alarmingly named giant jumping rat. After the promised lunch of frogs' legs we went off to search for the giant jumping rat. Lee and I finally confronted it in a moon-lit Malagasy forest. It bounced off into its diminishing woodland and we chased after it. The faster we ran, the faster it bounced away from us. It wasn't to know that it was bouncing out of space towards extinction. There are now five giant jumping rats in Jersey Zoo, the only ones in captivity in the world, and one of them has already produced babies.

When Youseff Mungroo lived in the reptile house in Jersey as the first trainee, there were only four Mauritius kestrels alive. They were going the way of the dodo. There are now over 200. Gerald Durrell's army has marched a long way from his kitchen table.

ONE

THE CARIBBEAN

GEORGE ANTOINE'S BOOTS – JACQUOT THE ST LUCIAN SUPERSTAR – OSWALD AND LUCY'S STRETCH LIMO – A WALK INTO THE FOREST – THE FLYING PARROT – A DEEP LAMBADA – GEORGE'S SUSTAINED MOMENTUM – MASHED UP IN KINGSTON – RHEMA KERR, HOPE ZOO AND THE CONEY – THE RASTAS' CONEY HUNT – MOBAY! MOBAY! MOBAY! HOW NOT TO REACH MONTEGO BAY – HYACINTH, MERLENE AND THE CONEY MAN – – THE CONEY FACTOR IN THE EQUATION OF LIFE – DWAAT – CELTGBA, A RASTA'S SOLUTION

I decided to start with the Caribbean. Compared with other places on my itinerary, such as Nigeria, Brazil or India, the Caribbean has some obvious advantages. If I couldn't find the animals I was looking for, there were always beaches, rum and reggae to be getting on with. I surreptitiously packed swimming trunks alongside my walking boots and tubes of jungle juice.

My first stop was the tiny Caribbean island of St Lucia where I was looking for the St Lucian parrot. I was then off to Jamaica to find the hutia, an obscure, brown nocturnal rodent.

'The hutia is fascinating.' Gerry had twirled a hand as if to imply something exotic, rare and mysterious. 'It just squiffles around doing nothing and vanishes into the forest. You'll never see one.'

'What about the parrot?'

'Much the same. Only it squawks around and vanishes into the forest. You might just see one of those in the distance. If you're lucky. But listen out for its call, it's very distinctive: "Pieces of eight! Pieces of eight!" And if you wear an eyepatch it'll swoop down and perch on your shoulder.'

The theory of evolution is now well known and accepted: each animal survives because it has evolved a unique way to exploit the rest of life around it. It occupies what television naturalists tell us in hushed excited voices is 'an evolutionary niche'. A humming-bird, a woodpecker, a lion, a herd of zebra, a tortoise – there are usually obvious clues as to how an animal has evolved to breed, eat and defend itself, so that even if we have never seen it in the wild or on television, we can guess what it does for a living.

This is not the case with the parrot. In our eyes, parrots occupy the evolutionary niche, or perch, of sitting on pirates' shoulders or in domed wire cages. I had seen so many of them looking at me through the bars with cold, inimical eyes and squawking abrupt obscenities that I could not imagine what they would do if left to their own devices in the forest.

Because parrots are the only creatures which can even remotely talk back to us, we feel that we have a special relationship with them. Perhaps if weasels or toads could answer back as well, there would be less pressure on parrots. As it is we feel we can relate to parrots in a way that we would never dream of with other birds. We call them jocular names such as Long John or Onan ('Because he spills his seed upon the ground') and since they are colourful and long-lived and can amuse themselves in tiny spaces, we assume that they enjoy being part of the family. It seems rather po-faced to point out that if a parrot enjoys a long and raucous life as a family favourite, it will not breed and so for all the good it is doing it may as well have been shot in the forest.

There is a further point. If we persist in seeing animals in the way that we see parrots, our perspective on the outside world grows increasingly warped. If animals are colourful and charming and show no objection to being caged, then we will look at them as pets. If they are brown, boring and nocturnal we won't be interested. And this spreads to the outside world. Even if we don't want animals as pets, we prefer to conserve the bright charming ones rather than the dull brown ones.

In the Caribbean I set out to look for both sorts. Although I had never seen a hutia, I had seen various other boring brown furry animals which snuffled around a good deal, so I could imagine one. But I had no idea what a parrot would do in the forest. I could not even imagine how it would fly – would it be like a magpie, or a pigeon or a duck? At the back of my mind I imagined it flapping around at shoulder height, showing off its gorgeous colours and muttering 'Pieces of eight' under its breath.

When I arrived in Castries, the capital of St Lucia, I telephoned George Antoine, the Jersey trainee who looks after the St Lucian parrots. We arranged to meet at the main square at noon.

'But George,' I just caught him before he rang off, 'how will I recognize you?'

'I'll be wearing boots.'

With that cryptic clue, George rang off.

I walked out into the street to catch a minibus into town. As I waited, I eyed people's feet. They padded past in training shoes, flip-flops, bare feet and shiny black school shoes. Goats and chickens scratched around. The road was scattered with loaves dropped from the towering breadfruit trees and pulped by the traffic. The open sewers were clogged with rubbish. It was midday. The lack of shadows made everything look oddly two-dimensional in the white light. The minibus swerved in and I crept inside.

'And where do you want transportation?' The large bearded Rasta asked the question in jamming time to the music he was playing. He agreed he was going into town and jerked a thumb to recommend a seat. A red, yellow and green knitted Rasta pendant obscured most of the view through the windscreen and swung wildly as we took the corners. Inside sat some twenty people, patient and quiet in the face of the music. The reggae changed to calypso and the disc jockey sang out something about Jacquot. I distinguished the words from the calypso clatter:

'When I look up and look down
And see the trouble on the ground
Parrots of the world unite!'

It was the current St Lucian hit. Jacquot is the St Lucian name for their parrot.

I was struck by something which impressed itself on me whenever I began looking for an animal in its own country. Although I had researched the St Lucian parrot (*Amazona versicolor*) extensively through scientific journals and knew everything about its esoteric nesting habits and diet and had seen it in captivity, nothing had prepared me for actually being in St Lucia and looking for it.

The calypso hit blasting over the national radio would be classified as nonsense by the scientific criteria of academic research. But a calypso about Jacquot will probably save more parrots in their home country than any number of research articles.

Jacquot was not always a celebrity. Throughout the Caribbean parrots have been hunted to supply the pet trade. Increasing banana plantations have also removed the forest so the parrots have progressively fewer places in which to live – apart from small wire cages. In the last thirty years the parrots of Martinique, Puerto Rico and Guadaloupe have become extinct. In 1975 a survey of the St Lucian parrot estimated that there were around 100 left. It was well on its way to joining the other Caribbean parrots in extinction.

Gerry heard about the survey and decided to try to save the St Lucian parrot. He had a high regard for the St Lucian Forestry Division which would be crucial to its survival, and the island was of a manageable size so it would not be too much of a drain on Jersey's finances.

'We thought we had a chance,' Gerry said. 'The remaining forest in St Lucia was small, so we could do thorough parrot surveys with a few men. We would quickly know whether the population was on the mend or not, which would save us wasting thousands of pounds.

'What was fascinating was that it was a classic conservation case. St Lucia is a small round island with people living around the edge and a forest on top of the hill in the middle. It's like a Christmas cake. The population is expanding and the farmers want to grow more bananas, but if they chop down all the forest, the water supply will suffer. It is a very simple choice – do they have their cake and eat it? In which case there will be nothing left. Or do they choose to keep it going? It's a metaphor for the world at large.'

Jersey made contact with the St Lucian Forestry Division and drew up a memorandum of agreement. Jersey would take seven birds out of St Lucia to breed them. These would be held as a satellite population so that if disaster struck and all the St Lucian parrots died, they would not be extinct.

'It was quite difficult,' Gerry remarked. 'Because everyone else just goes into the Caribbean for what they can get out of it, the St Lucian government didn't trust us at first. They suspected we wanted planning permission for some secret hotel deal or something. It took a while to persuade them that we were entirely charitable.'

With the blessing of the St Lucian government, David Jeggo, the curator of birds at Jersey Zoo, collected seven chicks from nests in the wild to start a captive breeding programme. These were the only St Lucian parrots ever to have been legally allowed outside St Lucia. They remained the property of the St Lucian government which was very important as it proved that Gerry was not just stealing parrots for his zoo.

It is extremely difficult to breed parrots, and for five years nothing happened. In the meantime Jersey funded a publicity campaign in St Lucia which taught St Lucians about their parrot. The Forestry Division organized visits to every school in the country. The name 'Jacquot' was coined and when St Lucia became independent in 1979, the parrot was declared their national bird.

'It was a fantastic campaign,' Gerry said. 'We provided posters and soon every child knew about Jacquot, their national bird. They knew that he lived in the forest so they shouldn't cut down the trees. They also knew that if the forest went and Jacquot went, then the water would go bad. And they knew they shouldn't eat Jacquot on Christmas Day, an old French tradition. Typical French – if you tell them about any rare animal, they always dream up a recipe for it.'

So when Hurricane Hugo hit St Lucia in 1980 Jacquot was well prepared. 'The hurricane destroyed most of the island. The forest was splintered and of course the parrots could have been wiped out, in which case Jersey would have had the only St Lucian parrots.

'I heard about it on the radio one evening and sent David Jeggo out on the next plane with a chain-saw. David helped clear up the forest and did a parrot survey. In fact the damage was less than had been feared and he estimated there were still over 100 alive.

'And because of the education programme around the schools, a number of baby parrots found wandering around in a daze were handed into the Forestry Division who put them back into the forest. If the hurricane had happened earlier, these would have been thrown into the pot.'

Later that year, the first egg was produced at Jersey. It was infertile. Nothing further happened until 1982 when another egg was produced and a chick hatched. Then in 1984 the chick died. Jersey had had the parrots for nine years without success. But in 1985 two chicks hatched and survived, and another in 1986. Jacquot had turned the corner.

By 1989 Jersey had bred fourteen St Lucian parrots. Gerry decided to fulfil a promise he had made fifteen years earlier and return some of them to St Lucia. He invited the St Lucian Prime Minister over to Jersey to pick up the birds. In November 1989 the Rt. Hon. John Compton came to Jersey to pick up Oswald and Lucy, two Jersey-bred St Lucian parrots.

When they arrived, Oswald and Lucy received the treatment usually reserved for American soap opera stars or West Indian cricketers. A reporter scaled the aeroplane, stuck his head into the flight deck and interviewed the pilot live for national radio about the two parrots he had flown over. Had they had a good flight? What did they think of the in-flight entertainment? A stretch limo flanked by two outriders whisked the parrots away. The Prime Minister formally handed them over to Gabriel Charles, head of the Forestry Division, to start their new life. Charles handed them over to the care of George Antoine, a Jersey trainee in 1988. It was George whom I had to recognize by his boots.

As I stood in the main square looking for somebody wearing boots, a man began walking up and down in front of me eyeing me aggressively. He kept waving a plastic bag at me. I began to look furtively around for help, wondering whether to move away, when he said:

'Mister Edward Whitley?'

I admitted as much.

'George Antoine!' he proclaimed and raised his knuckles to punch mine. 'My boots.' He swung up the plastic bag and opened it to reveal a pair of grubby boots.

'But George, how was I meant to see them?'

'You thought I'd be wearing them? You're crazy, man.' He flourished his feet under my nose. 'Too hot for nothing but these.' He was wearing bright white training shoes which I had noticed were *de rigueur* among young men around town.

We walked through town. Old ladies sat over wooden crates selling peanuts, chewing gum and single cigarettes. Closer to the market there were bowls of nutmeg and cinnamon. George seemed to know most of the town and waved and punched his way down the street acknowledging shouts of 'Hey! Jacquot!' and giving people strict instructions to 'Take it easy.' It didn't seem that anybody was going to argue with him. Various people wore T-shirts with the slogan 'To hell with work' or 'Take it easy St Lucia'. They spoke patois with sharp clicking sounds. St Lucia was swapped between France and England several times but became English in 1784. Despite an unbroken association with England since then, the patois has remained obstinately French in bias.

George took me along to the Forestry Division's office. It was a pink hexagonal building set back in its own private garden. The wooden walls were topped with a steep gabled roof, so the overall effect was of a dovecot. Inside was the sort of office I had always dreamed of having. The walls were draped with animal skins – leopard, jaguar and zebra. There were stuffed turtles and bottles of pickled snakes, scorpions and spiders. A stuffed iguana crouched on the mantelpiece. I realized that they were all endangered species, though bizarrely not all from St Lucia. A stuffed Arctic fox completed my sense of dislocation.

'A present from the Canadian government,' George offered, by way of explanation.

At the central desk by the window sat a large girl with tightly braided hair. She was sobbing into a handkerchief. She looked up at me and heaved her shoulders again.

'This is Hermina,' George introduced me.

Hermina sniffed a welcome and put her book down. She was reading *Captured Love*, a Mills and Boon.

'She likes her reading, dat right, Hermina?'

Hermina nodded tearfully.

'I don't know why,' George confided, 'it always makes her very unhappy.'

We went into the office to see Michael Bob, deputy head of the Forestry Division. George wanted to arrange a trip to the rain forest to see the parrots. I was expecting something faintly eccentric about a man whose surname rather than Christian name has been abbreviated, but found a fine-looking man lounging back on his chair, looking as relaxed and lethal as a West Indian fast bowler.

Caribbean protocol is such that the conversation consisted of a series of sidelong glancing shots, each moving imperceptibly closer to the issue in question.

'De forest, Michael.'

'Yea, de forest.'

'And de parrots, Michael.'

'Yea, de parrots in de forest.'

'Dat's right. Now Mr Edward like for to see de parrots.'

'De parrots in de forest?'

'Dat's right.'

'De parrots in de forest. Boy. Dat's gonna be hard.'

After some intense soul searching and head scratching we agreed that I would have to hire a jeep and drive George around to Soufrière, Michael's village, the next day. From there Michael would give us more explicit instructions.

When I came out of the office, Hermina had finished her book and was triumphantly describing the ending over the telephone.

'And guess what? He did get dat girl. No man, really . . .'

We went to rent a jeep. George led me to the Avis counter and introduced me to Hyacinth, who was also reading a lurid romantic novel, although not weeping. She filled out the hire agreement form in careful rounded long hand. George leaned over and asked what sort of discount she was going to give us. Hyacinth looked at me.

'Is he single or married?'

'Single,' George lied on my behalf.

'We can give him a 10 per cent discount,' Hyacinth said approvingly.

George and I took possession of a gleaming jeep which leapfrogged the traffic lights on our way down to the beach for lunch. George put a Forestry Division sticker on the windscreen. Its logo was a tree with a drop of water and the slogan '*La forêt c'est la vie*.' It was the first time I had heard the expression used dynamically rather than with a resigned shrug of the shoulders as another thing goes wrong.

We pulled up by a beach shack where the smell of fried fish was strong in the heat. We sat on a veranda and looked over the beach towards the sea. The view was pure holiday brochure stuff – groups of St Lucian boys played volleyball or football, and fat white tourists lay on towels and white plastic recliners.

'This is where all the money is,' George said. 'Without tourists we have no money in St Lucia. Plenty of bananas but no money.'

'You've got parrots,' I pointed out.

'Sure. We've just about got parrots,' he corrected me. 'But nobody like for to see the parrots. Parrots don't make St Lucia rich. Actually without the parrots St Lucia would be much richer as people would build more banana farms.'

'How many parrots are there in the forest?'

'De forest?'

'Yes, the forest.' I realized that I had broken Caribbean protocol.

'De parrots in de forest?'

'Yes, the parrots in the forest.'

'Well, we have two in captivity, that's Oswald and Lucy. And in de forest we now have 300. At least David Jeggo did a survey last year and that's what he reckoned.'

We left the tourists on the beach and went off to see Oswald and Lucy. They had a brand new aviary in the Forestry Division's premises four miles outside Castries. Originally this site was just some rows of seedling trees and a collection of confiscated animals. The Canadian government recently gave St Lucia a grant to build new premises for the Forestry Division and building had just started. Large airy offices, built from teak and mahogany, were almost finished. George's parrots were housed right outside the offices so that the Head of the Forestry Division could see the birds and remember his priorities. The birds in turn could see the gleaming teak offices but would not recognize them for their original habitat.

The aviary for Oswald and Lucy is sufficiently large for them to fly around in some comfort. George showed me around, then gave his own opinion on the matter.

'See these cages? They're wonderful, right, but there are still some problems. Jersey paid for them and Jersey have helped us save these parrots. Now that in itself is more than good.

'But we built the cages and the division should have consulted me on them. I work here all day so I know what I need. When someone like Mr Durrell has done the job so far, the government here should do it properly.'

'Like what?' I asked, expecting George to discuss the government's broad conservation efforts. His answer was a good deal more specific.

'Like the sinks here. I have to clean the dishes outside and the water runs away over the concrete to drain. Now I need a sink and a counter right in this building. What happens if a bird is sick? Where do we inject him? Where do I store my vitamins? The government should have consulted me and I would have told them about a sink and some taps. It is not good.'

Oswald and Lucy hardly looked endangered. They were lime green with blue heads and red throats and they sat on their perches like any other parrots I had seen. We walked inside and George approached Lucy with a slice of apple. She sidled along the branch, turning her head warily to watch him out of one perfectly round yellow eye. She finally took it with her beak and shuffled off ungraciously to gulp it down at the top of the branch.

We then approached Oswald who would have none of the apple and flew from side to side away from us. Although the aviary is around fifteen yards long, it was difficult to imagine him flying any further, he was really just swooping from perch to perch, so I was still in the dark as to how the parrots would fly in the forest.

'Born in Jersey.' George tipped back his cap and scratched his head to express wonderment. 'Born in Jersey and come back here. Lots of people visit them here. They are all very grateful to Jersey. Now we have our own national bird.'

I found seeing them in their new aviary less exciting as it did nothing to dispel the thought of pirates' shoulders and cages. Here were two parrots looking extremely comfortable.

I left George and returned to my hostel. The evening had quickly darkened and the Friday night music was just warming up in the distance. I went across the road to buy some mosquito coils.

Made in China, the coils were credited with the following qualities: 'No spraying, spilling and staining! Just light a coil and the fragrant smoke will make mosquitoes and sand flies swirl, swoop and swoon.'

The following morning my legs were mottled, measley and heavily mosquito-bitten. I went down for breakfast and found a Mr Clive Bacchus presiding over a breakfast table debate. As far as I could ascertain, Mr Bacchus and his two colleagues were in the government. They were certainly talking about the Prime Minister in first-name terms, and kept referring to their last meetings with him and other ministers. When I asked if they were politicians they laughed.

'No, but everybody knows everybody in St Lucia.'

The other person at the table was an Indian from Bombay, a doctor called Sanjay. He spent most of our breakfast on the telephone imploring someone to come and pick him up to take him to the hospital.

George arrived to take me off to see the parrots in the forest.

This time he was wearing his boots. He also had a knapsack. His broad grin split the atmosphere just as Mr Bacchus was shouting over Sanjay who was getting desperate over the telephone.

'I tell you there is an emergency come into casualty.'

'Are you ready to go, man?'

I stocked up with plasters, jungle juice and my water bottle and off we headed.

St Lucia is the shape of a tear drop with Castries at the neck. Mountains rise up in the middle and a road runs around the coast. The argument over the country's future centres around whether there should be a road cut through the middle. As it is, the banana farms are encroaching more and more from both sides of the island. The Forestry Division argues that without a forest in the middle the rainwater will run straight off the mountains and wash the topsoil away. The Agriculture Division seems blind to this argument and is keen to plant more bananas which are the island's only export.

Trouble will come for bananas with the removal of the European trade barriers. As part of the Commonwealth, St Lucia's bananas are subsidized. But as the rest of Europe can buy bananas from anywhere in the world, cheap bananas from Central America could come into Germany and then pass straight through into Britain and undercut the expensive Caribbean ones.

Caribbean bananas are expensive because their farms are small and hilly and it is not worth stopping at every little island to collect their fruit. Unhappily for St Lucia, the island has begun to rely on bananas to the extent that the farmers grow them exclusively and spray chemicals to prevent anything else growing in between the trees. The only hope is that St Lucian bananas are sweeter than the Central American ones, but it will take time to educate people that bananas are more than just a commodity. Until that happens, the farmers intend to grow more bananas to make up for lost margins. The only place to grow them is up in the high forest in the middle of the island. And that is where the water table is and that is where Jacquot is. If the forest goes, the water table will go and the parrot will disappear. St Lucia will eventually become a moonscape and even the tourists, who enjoy seeing a bit of greenery if only from the windows of the plane, will disappear. The St Lucians will have eaten their cake.

We drove off round the top of the island and down the left-hand side. The road is a spectacular and sustained piece of vivid tarmac sculpture. The hairpin bends were so acute and so steep that as we rounded corners, they would fill up one side of the windscreen. They looked impossibly high, but the jeep took them in its stride, climbing up the side and wallowing over the top. The pot-holes were random, frequent and deep. They sent us crashing forward or flying up to hit our heads against the roof. George loved it and never tired of yelling out 'And bang we go.' After the first hour, my laughter subsided into grim determination.

George's visit to Jersey was the only time he had been out of St Lucia. He had always loved animals and when he left school in 1979 he had worked as a carpenter. Although he could earn more as a carpenter, 70 East Caribbean dollars a day, he chose to work within the Forestry Division where he earns EC$40 a day – £12. He believes in the work he is doing.

'The children understand it. When they come round and look at my animals they understand it. They are the most important people to teach. They have only just begun to understand. But now they know the parrot is our national bird and they want to save it.'

George also explained that he now knew about medicines, food and hygiene. His parrots were going to be as well looked after in captivity as they would be anywhere. But he still found it difficult back in St Lucia. People resented the fact that he had been to Jersey.

'Some people are real envious. "Man! Why should that George Antoine go to Jersey? All he does is feed parrots all day. That's a child's job." But it shows that what I do is important. None of these builders gets to fly off to Britain to study how to build. And their houses will probably blow down in the next hurricane!'

We eventually bucked and bumped our way into Soufrière, halfway down the west side of the island. Fishing boats rode at anchor, palm trees leaned over at easy angles and a long cemetery stretched out between the road and the beach. The graves were raised mounds with wrought-iron railings around them. Many of them had wrought-iron hearts speared by a sword like a Valentine card. We asked two boys who were struggling along under a ghetto blaster where Michael Bob's house was.

'Michael Bob? We just seen him sitting out on the balcony with his lady.' Back we went, left, right and right again. The narrow streets were lined with blue and white houses. People sat outside sunning themselves. We found Michael Bob sitting with his lady who was wearing a red mini skirt and a black T-shirt.

'Everybody knows you're here, Michael.'

'Dat's right.' He tilted his chair back to a more comfortable angle.

George's behaviour changed abruptly. He shuffled his feet and fidgeted his hands almost in parody of someone ill at ease. He took off his cap and twisted it around. Michael Bob spotted this immediately.

'Now you got a problem, George?'

'No, boss. I'm fine,' George vehemently denied, adopting the offended air of an experienced sailor who has been accused of sea sickness.

Michael Bob examined him closer.

'You have got a problem, George,' he announced, moving in.

'No no,' George weakly denied.

'What is your problem, man?'

After further cross-examination, George finally revealed that he had no idea where to go in the forest to find the parrots. He had never seen them in the wild.

'Now is dat your problem, George?'

George hung his head and admitted as much.

'Well that's *no* problem, man.' Michael Bob dismissed it and proceeded to give us detailed instructions, delivered with some invective.

'If you go there you must see de parrots, man,' he concluded energetically. 'You must see them. You will surely see them. A 60 per cent outright chance. More than that. I say 70 per cent. I would go with you,' he added in all seriousness, 'but I have another engagement.'

George was still repeating directions to himself as we set off.

Past the cemetery a small cricket pitch was being prepared. A line of old men advanced across the outfield, trimming it down with machetes. A gang of long-legged boys scrambled over a roller on the wicket. The sea lay just beyond the palm trees which lined the far boundary. In the list of teams chalked up on the blackboard, the Soufrière captain was Michael Bob.

At the end of the village the road disappeared between pot-holes and banana trees crowded overhead. We passed the odd homestead with barking dogs and screaming children in the middle of the road. The scrub farmland turned into scrub forest and the road turned into mud. We drove uphill for half an hour without passing anyone. The track was now taking us through waist-high scrub up into the mountains; the patches of forest closed in. The track forked.

'Which way, George?'

George looked indecisively at a tiny map of St Lucia as if that might conceivably help.

'I don't rightly know. We have a problem. Maybe take the right-hand road but take it easy.'

We took it very easy indeed and the forest came closer and the scrub grew higher. The forest just seemed to have established itself, bright green and gleaming, when a clearing materialized. There was a hut in the middle with smoke coming out of the chimney. Two men were lying on the veranda. We stopped to ask them the way.

'Where you going, brother?'

'We want to see the parrots.'

'You want to buy some ganja?'

'No, see the parrots.'

'De parrots in de forest?'

'Yea, de parrots in de forest.'

The two Rastas collapsed weakly against the railings.

'You crazy, man,' was the last we got out of them as they subsided into hilarity.

'I reckon for we take the wrong road,' George concluded. 'Another reason why the forest is cut down is to grow ganja. The

Americans sometimes come over here to help our policemen stop it. But when the Americans are here, the amount of ganja around goes up.'

Back we went and found the junction. This time the track swerved sharply downhill. It was like driving over freshly made and crumbling cake. We came down another hill, the track falling to pieces under the wheels, and went through pure rain forest until another clearing opened out in front of us and we saw some dilapidated old sheds.

'This is it. This is the research station Michael Bob was describing. This is where we walk. Just a couple of hours.'

We left the jeep and walked into the forest. Within moments we were surrounded by silence. Birds called in the distance but everything else had grown quiet at our approach. The trees towered over us, their trunks shrouded with creepers. The forest floor was bare and muddy. The air was clammy, the light gloomy. I was surprised by how clean the forest floor was. George explained that it got no light so very little grew there, and the atmosphere was so dank that branches which fell soon rotted. Nutrients were in such demand that everything was quickly reassimilated into the forest.

Wide green leaves spread out overhead, the sun straining through them. The sunlight was an almost tangible source of food. I realized that we were walking through pure photosynthesis, the brilliant green leaves lit up like stained-glass windows.

As I followed George's cracking pace I was also surprised by how little we saw. I expected there to be signs of life everywhere. There was nothing. It was also uncannily quiet, but for the occasional deep-throated cooing of a pigeon. The most spectacular trees were the bamboo clumps. These were huge, the size of houses, with the fat trunks ringed with fringes of hair like a cannibal's ankle bracelets.

After a three-hour march we came out into a clearing. By this time we were sweating pure water. George took some bruised mangoes out of his knapsack and we sucked at them, wiping our fingers on the grass. By now I had realized that we were not going to see parrots flapping around the trees at arm's length. I had not even heard the smallest echo of 'Pieces of eight!' George was disappointed. Despite working with the parrots in the aviary, he had never been into the forest before and had never seen parrots in the wild.

'Why haven't you been here? It's not so far,' I asked him.

'I'm very busy. I feed Oswald and Lucy every day. I cannot get away at weekends.'

'But couldn't someone help you out?'

'Well, they could.'

Only later did I realize that George had not come here because he couldn't afford the bus fare around the island. I had taken hiring a jeep for granted but this was George's only chance to see the parrots in the forest.

We carried on further. I was walking slightly slower as the prospect of the long walk back began to haunt me. Then from over our shoulders came a fierce clacking sound, a real nut-cracker noise, and a large shabby bird flew straight overhead, flying as hard and fast as a pheasant, black against the sun. It was a parrot.

'Jacquot!' George shouted and raised his fist to punch mine in celebration.

'They fly like that?' I was astonished.

'Yea, man. They fly damned fast.'

I couldn't believe it. Nothing in the time I had spent researching them or watching them in their aviary had indicated that parrots fly as fast as a top-speed pheasant. It was so incongruous. My perception of parrots was entirely wrong. Although I had admired their spectacular colours, I had never taken them seriously as birds. I had only seen them flap or swoop between branches. They suddenly seemed much more precious because of this power of flight. It is hard to explain why – perhaps it was because they had shabby wings and so rather than being perfectly aerodynamic and soaring around like curlews, or even flying smoothly like ducks, these parrots really had to beat the air to get going. This one was going like the clappers.

Later on, as we climbed up a hill, we disturbed another parrot in the trees below us. It squawked and flew out of a tree, curving around the side of the hill. We looked down and saw the brilliant green of its coat as it turned in the sunlight.

In the flash of a moment it conjured up all the intoxicating excitement of the tropics. Of course there were the associations of pirates and sailing boats and treasure – no Caribbean island is complete without them – but there was also a primeval sense that this was a glimpse of what the islands were like before the invasion of man who brought with him rats and goats and banana plantations. The empty forest, the leaves flat against the sun, the flash of the parrot – everything was so clean. Life was made up of sunlight and water. With my walking boots and sweaty shirt I felt hopelessly clumsy. I was also dying for a cold beer.

Well, we had seen two parrots. Tired, mud-spattered but jubilant we returned to the jeep. We drove out of the forest and into the banana plantations and down to Soufrière. I thought of the parrots up in the hills behind us, their forest being stolen piece by piece. As parrots are highly visible, we had seen them relatively easily. Had we been looking for frogs, we would have had a tougher time. No one knows how many other species in the forest are threatened with extinction. The parrots are like the canaries in the coal mines, a charming, colourful warning sign. When the canaries died, the miners knew they should get out. There are now just 300 parrots, so the signs are quite alarming.

The cricket match at Soufrière was over. Michael Bob, who had scored 43, was nowhere to be found. George and I debated what we should do to celebrate that evening. He dismissed the cinema as a 'stagnant situation'.

'Man, nothing happens. You sit in silence. Me I like for to boogie a little.'

We set off back towards Castries. As we rounded a corner we found three girls thumbing a lift. George, who had scrupulously avoided all other hitch-hikers, advised me to pull over and pick them up.

They crowded into the back of the jeep chattering and gathering together all their baskets. They were going to Les Arches, a

St Lucian Parrot.
"amazona versicolor"

seven-mile walk. They only spoke patois, so I understood nothing of their conversation with George apart from his repeated references to Jacquot. An hour later we arrived at their turning. It was dark. The girls said something to George and he asked them to repeat it.

'Petula wants to invite you to supper. She says she has never been given a lift by a white man before. Would you like to eat with them?'

Our arrival caused great commotion. Petula's parents greeted George and me like royalty and then turned on her and flew into a great argument. The rest of Petula's family crowded around us, some eleven or twelve children. Girls were dispatched in all directions while George and I sat drinking beer. Twenty minutes later, the entire family and some neighbours came in carrying tables and chairs. Within moments a table for twenty was set and a succession of chicken dishes with plantain and rice brought out. With great dignity the family invited me to say Grace. Simon and Garfunkel were put on in my honour.

At the end of dinner chairs were scraped back and the music changed.

'Do you know how to lambada?' George asked me.

'With you?'

'No.' He made way for Petula's mother. 'With her.'

'Of course.'

However, after a few frigid steps it was clear I was out of my depth.

'Relax,' she said and hugged me to her vast bosom.

The evening ended late. We walked out into the banana plantations. Fireflies buzzed here and there. George burped contentedly.

'That Petula. Man, she was one nigger dancer.'

The next morning I was to leave for Jamaica. At breakfast I found Sanjay in a state of abject chaos, pleading into the telephone.

'Operator, please put me through to anyone in the Ministry of Health. Anyone.'

As I poured myself a second coffee he got through.

'Hello, hello? This is Doctor Sanjay Amal here. Where is my transportation?'

He put the phone down and buried his head in his hands.

'What's the matter, Sanjay?'

'I have been waiting for transportation to the hospital since five o'clock,' he gabbled as if still talking to a long distance operator. 'I must operate on a patient.'

I helped myself to some more toast and commiserated with him. He grabbed for the phone again. 'Get me the Health Minister. Yes, this is Doctor . . .'

He was cut off.

'How far is the hospital, Sanjay?'

He looked at me as if I was mad.

'It's a good fifteen minutes' walk.'

'The patient's probably dead by now,' I consoled him, 'I wouldn't worry.'

The next morning I left for Jamaica. George waved me off at the airport. Under his arm was a brown paper bag.

'What's in there?'

'To keep de momentum going.' He shyly showed me the top of a bottle of sparkling wine. 'Also Petula knew nothing about Oswald and Lucy. Nothing, man. I need for to teach her. And you saw all her family? Big family. They all grow bananas. They had never heard of Jacquot. We need to be telling people like them all about him. If they don't know, what's the point?'

I sat in the departure lounge. Soon enough the radio sang out something about Jacquot: 'Parrots of the world unite man!' The disc jockey joined in. 'Yea, that's right. Parrots of the world unite!' It seemed rather a sensible idea. Clearly the Caribbean was beginning to get to me.

I had left St Lucia feeling fairly hopeful about the St Lucian parrot and pretty relaxed myself. As I walked through Kingston to catch a taxi, this genial state of mind was quickly fractured.

'Hey, man! I wanna talk to you.' A tall rangy Jamaican materialized by my side.

'I'm fine, thanks.'

'I'm a friend. Take it easy. You been in Jamaica before? We all take it real easy here.'

'I've just arrived from St Lucia.'

'Listen, brother. I want nothing from you, right? I'm just a buddy.' He loped alongside me with easy strides.

'That's fine by me.' I didn't really want his attention, but didn't like to appear unfriendly.

'What have you got for me?' The tempo changed abruptly.

'Nothing.'

'Give me ten dollars, man.' He towered over me.

'No.'

'Are you a racist?'

'No.'

'Give me ten dollars then.'

'No.' I stood my ground and turned towards him.

'I hate you, white man.' My buddy turned away in disgust. I read the caption on the back of his T-shirt: 'Jamaica – No Problem'.

For a country in which 'no problem' is presented as a way of life, Jamaica is surprisingly violent. The Kingston telephone directory lists over 200 security firms to protect a population of 750,000. Every morning the *Daily Gleaner* records who was shot or mashed up (hacked with machetes) the night before. Everybody has a security guard, yet the sound of reggae on Saturday night is only topped by the blast of congregational singing on Sunday morning.

Rhema Kerr is the head of Hope Zoo in Kingston. She lives in a small cottage by the zoo. Her cottage has been attacked twice, and her security guard killed once. The current replacement is a bent old man who dozes in a corner of the garden with his gun on his knee. The month before I arrived, someone had crept up and stolen it off him.

As it happened security was the first thing Rhema and I talked about. When I reached the zoo I saw a number of dubious men looking rather like my buddy on the street lounging around the entrance.

'Are these men safe?' I asked Rhema. 'Would you like me to ask them to go away?'

'Yea man!' All Rhema's answers started with 'Yea man', laconically pronounced as 'Yemen'. 'These guys are my guards.'

'Guards?' I pointed at them scandalized. 'But they look like thugs. Anyway what do you need protection from?'

'People want to steal our gate money, even though it's only peanuts. And they might cause trouble with the animals. You've seen all the Rastas around? Their symbol is the lion. Last year a crazed Rasta came in here and wanted to commit suicide. He jumped into the lions' cage.'

'Was he successful?'

'Not at first. It wasn't feeding time so the lions were very mellow. They just looked at him. The security guards pulled him out. But he came back at feeding time in the afternoon and jumped in again. That time he was chomped.'

'What else?'

'The crocodiles provoke a lot of people. They hate them. Unfortunately most of our trees in here are mango trees. When the mangoes start dropping, people pelt the crocodiles. We have to have somebody stop that. And the snakes. People really hate the snakes. I've started walking around the zoo with one round my waist just to show they're not dangerous.'

Running a zoo in Jamaica clearly involves problems that would not occur in England.

'Problems!' Rhema theatrically threw her hands up. 'Let me tell you about my problems. I have four big problems here. I'm a woman and the Jamaicans don't take educated women seriously. I'm very black, and there's a lot of racism amongst the blacks as to who's black and who's not so black. People here hate animals and so trying to educate them to conserve them is difficult. And people around here suffer from what we call niggeritis. We all like to have a nice sleepy time, especially in the afternoon. So getting anything done is impossible. And of course we have no money coming through from the government, that's the fifth big prob-

Jamaican
Hutia
(Geocapromys brownii)

lem. You could call it the Fifth Amendment. Whenever it comes to funding anything, the Department pleads the Fifth Amendment!'

That evening Rhema took me to a Kingston bar. It was set in the grounds of Devon House, a large and well-preserved planter's house. She described the shades of racism which she encounters in Jamaica.

'I would never come to a place like this by myself. Look around you – I am the blackest girl here. In the Seventies it was all "Black is Beautiful" and Afro haircuts. Now people aspire towards being American and making money. Everyone straightens their hair and puts on pale make-up. If you went for a job with a high haircut (haircuts in Jamaica are measured by height, high or low) nobody would take you seriously.

'At a party recently I overheard a guy say to his friend, "I want to introduce you to this girl. She's bright and funny and guess what? She's black. She's actually black!" They were talking about me although you probably wouldn't have noticed any difference between us.'

So while the paler mulattos move up into the affluent middle class, the black Jamaicans stay behind. Rhema told me what this meant for her job.

'You see as people are all out to earn money, they don't care about conservation. They'll chop a tree down if there's a cent of profit in it. Also good people don't work in conservation because they don't get paid. So there are no educated people working with me.

'And the black people are left with the menial jobs like being guards or zoo keepers. And they see nobody respecting them so they don't give a damn either. So the government ignores us, business ignores us, the public ignores us. It takes an organization like Jersey to care for us. Nobody else does.'

Jersey's interest in Jamaica started with the hutia, a large brown rodent and an unlikely candidate to star in a conservation programme. Hutias are nocturnal, shy and elusive. 'Save a large brown rodent' is hardly the most enticing call for help, and as soon as people hear that it looks like a guinea pig, they become almost indignant. 'Well, it should learn how to breed like a guinea pig. Then it wouldn't be in such trouble.'

'We have a lot of trouble raising money to conserve the hutia,' Gerry had told me. 'It's because people are only interested in the glamour animals like pandas or rhinos or golden lion tamarins. Hutias can't help being rather doleful and discreetly brown – most nocturnal animals wouldn't get far if they were flaming orange.

'But although people may think it's a boring old fogey of an animal, and I admit I haven't laughed a great deal in its presence, the hutia is absolutely fascinating. Thank God it is shy and retiring. There wouldn't be any of them left if it wasn't. And they live in these spectacular limestone caves in the middle of the forest. They're like Rip van Winkle, they don't know the rest of the world has changed outside.

'They need about fifty different species of plant for their diet, and they distinguish between them all. This is a very useful guideline for botanists because they know that if there's a surviving population of hutias, the forest is healthy.

'And the beauty of hutias is that you won't find them in any tourist guide-book. Nobody is interested in "going to see the hutias" in the way that they go on safaris to see the rhinos. This means that you're working with an obscure animal in a totally unspoilt environment. There aren't tourists poking cameras everywhere and leaving litter and generally changing the landscape. Without these outside pressures, the animal is completely in its natural environment.

'The flip side of this is that if nobody's interested in saving hutias, hutias won't be saved. But you go and see them. You'll understand what I mean. For a start you won't see one, but if you do I bet you won't be able to write more than a line about it.'

In order to be able to write more than a line, I read all about the unnoticed, unloved and thoroughly boring hutia. The most comprehensive article, one of only four ever published about it, was by William Oliver, a research assistant at Jersey who had come over to Jamaica with fifty Jersey-bred hutias to try to reintroduce them into the forest, a project he had worked on with

Rhema. The opening remarks set the tone for the rest of the article:

> The Hutias – *Geocapromys* – comprise a small family of medium- to large-sized hystricomorph rodents, the *Capromyidae*, known only from the Caribbean islands of the Greater Antilles and the Bahamas. Approximately thirty-three nominate species and sub-species of six genera are currently recognised, although over half of these forms are extinct.
>
> In Jamaica, the disappearance of two large heptaxodontid rodents probably pre-dated human settlement; whilst a Rice rat, *Oryzomys antillarum*, and several species of birds and reptiles have been exterminated in recent times through predation and competition pressure by human and commensal animal species; a process latterly exacerbated by the accelerating rate of habitat destruction. As a result the hutia, *Geocapromys brownii*, is now Jamaica's only surviving endemic terrestrial mammal. It has almost certainly managed to survive only by the fortuitous circumstance of predominating surface limestone formations which furnish protection from predation in the form of abundant fissures and solution cavities.

'So what's all this about?' I pushed a copy of the article over to Rhema.

'You read it?' she said, with unbridled astonishment.

'Well, I deduced that the hutia won't go extinct from lack of words.'

'The hutia?' Rhema laughed. 'You mean the coney! We call them "conies" here. And if you really know what you're talking about you call them "cooooony". Trust the English to purse their lips up and say "hutia"! Conies are Jamaica's only natural mammal. And they hide away in the rocks so nobody ever sees them.'

She had admirably summed up the first page. And 'coney' sounded much more appealing than 'hutia', although I quite liked '*Geocapromys brownii*'.

'So what happened with the conies? Jersey took seven from Jamaica, bred over a hundred, gave fifty back to you and you reintroduced them into the wild. Then they disappeared. That much I can understand. But what did you actually do?'

'Boy, it was a long saga! It started back in 1972 when a Jamaican member of Jersey Trust gave Jersey two conies. In 1975 they got five more. I wasn't around then, but they took ten years to breed them all up. And they had given away several satellite populations to other zoos so if they had disease they wouldn't lose them all.

'Then in 1985 we began to talk about reintroduction. We talked and talked, and William Oliver came over here to survey the island for sites. You can't imagine more complicated, intricate, incomprehensible negotiations.'

They sounded like a William Oliver article.

'The government had to agree to the importation of fifty conies, the zoo had to house them and then we had to find a site to release them. But finally everything was agreed. If you haven't realized already, things take a long time to happen here. So the conies were flown over and kept here in Hope Zoo. We found a wonderful landowner who agreed to have the conies put back in his forest, and have us stay at his house for two months. We transported them over the other side of the island to his house, built some coney warrens in the rocks and let them out into enclosures. Then they went out more and more and we gradually stopped feeding them.

'But this makes it sound so easy! Like the details of what we did – we spent two weeks counting every tree in the forest to see whether the conies would have the right things to eat; we had to take cement and water up to the coney warren sites; we had to build release cages. Man, I'm talking about big business here. And ticks everywhere, cattle ticks all up your legs.

'But after two months in the wild the conies were all fine. So we left them for a bit. I had to run the zoo and William had to get back to Jersey. Then three months later we could only find eight, but two had bred so that was good. Then two months on there were none. They had all disappeared. It was a mystery.'

'How did you watch them?'

'Well, that's difficult too. We put a splash of phosphorescent paint on them so we could see them in the dark, and we tagged their ears. But we had no radio transmitters, we couldn't afford them. And the forest is thick and the conies are shy. They just vanished.

'We don't know what went wrong. It was the only reintroduction programme ever done in Jamaica so there were bound to be mistakes. There were no hunters and no dogs there, so we think it was disease. The cattle ticks carry leptospirosis which wild conies will be immune to. But these were Jersey-bred conies so they may not have had that immunity. As we couldn't find any, we don't know. Also there were the worst rains in memory after four months which might have weakened them. They wouldn't have been used to rain at the zoo.

'But we're building up our collection and will try again in a couple of years. And in the meanwhile I'm trying to educate people to stop hunting them.'

Rhema educates people in two ways, by having open days at the zoo and by visiting the coney hunters out in the country who never come to the zoo.

I went to one of the zoo open days. All the Kingston primary schools attended and were shown around displays which pointed out the natural beauty of Jamaica. They were invited to hold various animals – baby rabbits, parrots and the dreaded Jamaican boa which is entirely harmless. The day was concluded with speeches from civil servants. All the speeches were lengthy, but the longest of all was the vote of thanks which went on for twenty minutes. Every politician who might at any time be helpful to the career of the minister proposing the vote of thanks was lengthily eulogized. I pointed this out to Rhema.

'If you don't work through bureaucracy and protocol nothing happens,' she said, 'so you have to. And still nothing happens, but something *might* happen. That's the difference.'

Western conservation organizations have to work through this system. The Jamaicans are very intolerant of foreigners who come in and try to browbeat them. Progress through the apathy and protocol is therefore slow, but at least something might happen rather than nothing.

'Other organizations get into trouble in Jamaica,' Rhema told me. 'They pour money in and then leave when nothing happens. Jersey are different. It started with the conies. Since then they have helped me draft fund-raising proposals, they have financed projects and trained our staff. They even arranged for Princess Anne to come and see Hope Zoo. The local politicians had not thought the zoo a suitable thing for the Princess to see, so they were very impressed. If the zoo can be seen to be important, then more people will support it. Jersey understands the Jamaicans and the politics. It takes a lot of time, Jersey has been at it since 1975, but good things are beginning to happen.'

The other side of Rhema's work leaves protocol far behind. She took me off to visit some notorious coney hunters. We drove west from Kingston up into the mountains. Rhema pointed out tracts of secondary forest.

'Charcoal-burners have logged this. The vine is the first thing to grow back. It suffocates the saplings underneath so they take much longer to establish themselves.'

Seeing the forest through Rhema's eyes made it come alive. She told me that Jamaica has over 3,000 species of flowering plant compared with 360 in Britain. A third of these plants are indigenous. The vine which carpets the forest floor and suffocates the saplings is *Hedychium gardneranium* from the Himalayas. Another foreign plant which attacks the forest is *Pittosporum undulatum* from Australia. Ironically this tree was first planted in Hope Zoo and has now spread all over the island. It gains space by growing thick leaves all the way down its trunk which cast an impregnable shadow and stop any rivals growing near it.

We turned off the road into a sugar-cane plantation. Set out on a grid system the cane was almost twelve feet high. It towered over the car like a giant maze. The only way to keep a sense of direction was to stop and stand on the roof to look around. We navigated across to one corner and found various houses where we asked for Owen Sluie. Most of the people we asked turned out to be his children. More and more people clung to the roof of the jeep to show us the way.

In the lee of a steep limestone outcrop on the edge of the plantation we found a wooden shack. Owen and Mikey Sluie were sitting by a fire smoking ganja. They were astounded that Rhema had found them. They pushed back their woollen beehive hats and repeated her name several times as if trying out all its variations.

'De Rhema. Rheema. Rheeema! How is it?'

Rhema slipped into a much stronger vein of Caribbean than I had heard her use before.

'It's good Owen. What don't kill fat is good.'

'Rheema! Rheeeeema! De Rhema!'

We talked about the sugar and then the conies.

'Now have you been hunting them, Mikey?'

'Rhema!' This time it was said incredulously.

Their language was the richest English I have ever heard. It sounded just as I imagine Shakespearian English would have sounded – full of rhythm and strong emphasis, powerfully intoxicating. Owen and Mikey would talk together, one echoing the other with extraordinary relish. When they eventually conceded that they still hunted conies, they described their last hunt.

'We found de coney in de rock.'

'In de rock, man. De coney was in de rock.'

'And we sent in de dog – Dred's dog. And de Dred's dog he caught de coney and he licked de breath out of him.'

'He licked him.'

'He licked de breath out of de coney.'

'He licked him, man.'

'And de coney cried. He cried like a baby.'

'Like a baabee.'

'But for why you catch de coney?' Rhema asked.

No answer.

'You eat de coney, Owen?'

'No, man. I'm a Rasta, man. I no for eat de coney.'

'But Mikey, Mikey – why for you catch de coney?'

'De coney he eat my crops, man.'

'Your sugar?'

'No, man. De coney eat my ganja.'

I suggested we build a fence around it.

'But ganja is illegal here,' Rhema pointed out.

'Yea, man,' Mikey echoed softly. 'Illeeeeegal.'

'And if the government built a fence around the ganja, it would be protecting it.'

'Well, try stopping people from smoking ganja.'

'Yea, man. Try stopping de Rastas!' Mikey rocked on his heels and poked the fire.

'Well, what do we do?' Rhema appealed to me. 'You have illegal ganja and endangered conies.'

Night had fallen and we huddled closer to the fire.

'You want to see de conies?'

'How for we see de conies?' Rhema asked sharply. 'We hunt de conies?'

'Yea, man, but not with Dred's dog. With Mikey's dog. Mikey's dog not catch de conies.'

By the time we set off on the coney hunt it was black night. Owen and Mikey stocked up on ganja and took cutlasses. Mikey called up his dog and led the way. He carried his cutlass in one hand, a beer bottle with kerosene and a burning rag in the other. We left the flat plantation and climbed up into the limestone forest behind.

It was a magical night. The moon turned the forest black and silver. Fireflies flashed on and off. One crashed into me and buzzed crazily about my shirt like a firework. We walked through this bewitching black and silver forest for hours. Owen and Mikey kept up a lazy talk which I could barely understand. The tracks between the trees and vines were tiny, but their cutlasses kept flashing away and we squeezed through. Toads and bull-frogs croaked against the background roar of cicadas. At one point we came out of the forest and walked through waist-high grass. Limestone outcrops of forest rose around us, the cliffs shining bright white in the moonlight. We plunged back into the forest. After a while it became clear we were lost. Owen and Mikey were so stoned that they had no idea where we were.

Mikey's dog started yelping in the undergrowth. He had finally put up a coney. Mikey and Owen floundered through the undergrowth after him, waving their cutlasses. Rhema screamed at them. The dog came back howling. The coney escaped. I ran madly into the trees trying to get a glimpse of the coney. 'Come here!' I yelled. 'All I want to do is write one line about you.' But just as Gerry had predicted, the coney vanished into the forest.

Owen and Mikey sat down, put their heads between their knees and rocked with laughter.

'De Mikey's dog – noooo good, man. De Dred dog – he would have licked de breath out of him . . .'

'Killed him straight, man.'

'Man, I'm pleased we no have de Dred's dog,' said Rhema sternly. 'Now where are we, Owen?'

We finally found our way back and sat under a coconut tree. Mikey sliced open some coconuts for us with his cutlass. We sat and smoked and talked of conies. Owen remembered his heyday as a coney hunter.

He had been employed by a co-operative to catch the conies which were eating their cola beans. They paid him £3 for each coney he caught. As his daily wage was then only 11s. 6d., it was good money. After he had caught all the conies in the cola plantation, he began catching conies elsewhere and pretending they were from the plantation to claim his £3. Eventually the co-operative grew suspicious. No coney had been seen for some time, yet Owen was still presenting bodies. They called in a vet to find out what was going on. He told Owen that he would conduct autopsies on all the conies he caught. 'Because I'm a Rasta-man he didn't think I knew what an autopsy was.'

Owen began catching live conies, keeping them in cages and feeding them with cola beans. The vet confirmed that Owen was indeed ridding the plantation of cola-eating conies. Owen continued in business for many months.

'But now you don't catch no conies anymore.'

'Dat's right, Rhema.'

'And if I build your fence you won't neither, eh Mikey?'

'Dat's right, Rhema. De ratta know for which sampatta to bite.'

When we returned to Kingston there was a power cut, a 'power outage' as Rhema said. We sat on a sofa and shone torches over our legs looking for ticks. When Rhema found one she would twist it off with a satisfying crack like breaking off a crab's claw.

'What did Owen mean when he said something like "De ratta know for which sampatta to bite"?' I asked her.

'He was saying that rats know who they can bite and get away with it. Sampatta are shoes. He was promising not to hunt any more conies. Do you understand?'

'Yea man,' I said.

'That's good,' Rhema congratulated me with surprise. 'The last Jersey man who came over here could never say "Yemen". He only got as far as "Okay. Yah, man."'

'Good-day, Miss Kerr,' greeted us everywhere as Rhema showed me around the zoo.

'No, no, Molly!' Rhema shouted, running over to a woman sweeping the branches off the lawn. 'Don't just leave them in the flowerbed. They'll blow back across again.' She looked round. 'Sibert! Sibert! Come here and show Molly what to do.'

Sibert came running. He looks after the reptiles, cleaning the cages and trying to encourage them to breed.

'How do you get them to breed?' I asked him.

'I don't know. Get them happy and well fed, that's what Jersey say. Then maybe they breed. But they suffer a little disturbance when boys throw mangoes at them, so I have to stop that as well.'

The other animals are a haphazard collection of macaws from South America, lions from Africa and assorted monkeys.

'What I want here is a collection of West Indian animals. We never had lions, so I'm waiting for them to die. Nobody else wants them. But they do bring in the visitors, if for the wrong reasons.' I remembered the suicidal Rasta. 'And I want to educate everyone about what there is in Jamaica, like the conies and the boa and some of the rare lizards. There's also an iguana which everyone thought was extinct until a hunter brought one in from the Hellshire Hills last year. It just walked back from extinction.

'I'm also encouraging the zoo to be more involved with the

outside world. This is something Jersey taught me. The zoo used to be just a collection of animals which nobody realized lived in Jamaica. But they do! They're crawling all around us. I try to teach people how to live peacefully with them so the zoo has some influence outside these cages and becomes part of everyday life.

'My dream is to have a zoo where people get really involved with the animals, where walkways take you right by them, where boats take you near crocodiles and ski lifts take you up amongst birds in the tops of trees. There is a limestone cliff at the back of the zoo which is perfect for a full coney warren.

'We don't need to keep reptiles and snakes in glass cages, they live in this climate anyway. But we need to design a really good alternative. We're stuck with a whole lot of cages which we've inherited. But this means a lot of money and our government has other priorities. So I'm trying to raise money privately and from outside. In the meantime I try to keep it as clean as possible and improve the animals. What else can you do?'

I left Rhema at Hope Zoo and went across Jamaica to Montego Bay, where I was to stay at the house where the conies had been reintroduced. I decided to go by bus.

'Be careful,' Rhema advised, 'get straight on a bus. Don't listen to anyone. They will all encourage you to get on their buses. Choose the one you want and stay on it. And watch your luggage.'

I have never been given encouragement like the encouragement at the Kingston bus stop. A fleet of buses all bound for Montego Bay slowly patrolled the bus stop. They were armed with men hanging off the running board who grabbed anyone who expressed any interest in Montego Bay and hustled them inside. Vendors ran alongside the buses selling sweets, cold drinks and T-shirts to passengers. I was set upon in a frenzy.

'Mobay? Mobay?' A man shouted at me.

'Montego Bay?' I asked.

'He wants Mobay!' he yelled. My rucksack was pulled off my back and carried at a sprint to a bus. I tried to follow it, but a man built like a Harlem Globetrotter blocked my way.

'Mobay?' he said.

'I want my pack.' I tried to dodge past.

'Here.' He grabbed my arm and led me to another bus, a tiny clapped-out van.

'Get my pack.' I realized he was the man to do it.

My pack and the impromptu porter were manhandled back to me, clearly unwilling to be separated. By now a small crowd had gathered round me chanting 'Mobay! Mobay! Mobay!' until I yelled out, 'Shut up! Which of you is cheapest?'

'All the same price, man,' said one.

'Mobay! Mobay! Mobay!' shouted the others, pressing forward.

I saw a largish and delightfully empty bus to hand.

'I'm going in that one.'

The driver wrestled my pack off the porter.

'The man want my bus.'

'At least it's empty,' I said. 'When does it go?'

'Now, man. The bus goes now.'

An hour and a half after I got on, the bus finally pulled out of the station. Even as we were driving down the road, the driver had his head out of the window and was shouting 'Mobay! Mobay! Mobay!' to anyone who might be tempted on the spur of the moment to take a bus ride to the other side of the country. During the six-hour journey an old crone at the back began to sing praises to the Lord. She was blind and her feet swung under the seat, too short to reach the floor. My sympathy for her turned to irritation at her horribly cracked voice, especially when other people on the bus joined in and said 'Allelulia!' By the end of the journey she had begun to ask for money.

'Give it with love, brothers and sisters.'

Other old women shamed me by digging into their tiny purses. Finally we arrived. The bus emptied and we dispersed. I sat on my rucksack waiting to be picked up. After an hour I saw a familiar figure – it was the old lady striding purposefully along, clutching her purse in one hand, her white stick in the other like a cudgel. She had been miraculously cured of her blindness.

Peter Williams came to pick me up. He had been assiduously polite over the telephone, calling me Mr Whitley every other sentence. His eyes passed over me with the distaste everyone feels for an unshaven traveller sitting on a rucksack. He then realized I was the only person expecting a lift.

'Mr Whitley. . . ?' The question died on his lips.

'You may as well call me Edward. I think we're the same age.'

'I was expecting you to be one of those boring old conservationists. Thank God! Let's have a beer.'

Peter's family came over to Jamaica in the eighteenth century and originally owned sugar plantations. Just before sugar beet replaced sugar cane and the price of sugar slumped, they sold their lowland sugar plantations and bought an estate up in the mountains behind Montego Bay to ranch cattle. Peter runs both his late father's estate and his uncle's estate next door. His uncle lives in England and it was his estate which was used for the coney reintroduction, and where I stayed.

I woke to a shocking pink dawn and walked out on to the veranda to have a look. The valley below me could have been eighteenth-century England, a wide view of grazing pastures with patches of dark green woodland. Cattle stood under the trees. There were no houses or roads to be seen. A peculiar whirr of wings made me look over the balustrade. A humming-bird, dazzling blue with a long quivering tail, shimmered for a moment in front of a red flower. It vanished and reappeared at another flower. I watched it farm its way systematically along the flowerbed, until a small gong rang behind me. Hyacinth was summoning me to breakfast.

I ate in state at the head of a large rosewood dining-table. The house comprised a single storey, spread out low and full of faded rosewood furniture. The prints on the walls showed Kingston and Montego Bay looking impossibly unspoilt. I thumbed along the bookshelves and came across *Birds of the West Indies* by James Bond. I paused: eye-catching name. Forty years earlier in a house in the north of the island, this was exactly how Ian Fleming had chosen the name of his hero in *Casino Royale*.

I wandered into the kitchen to chat with Hyacinth. She was with Merlene the cook.

'De conies!' Merlene exclaimed. 'It was so nice to have de

conies here. We had such a fine time. And Miss Rhema, she worked so hard out all day in the forest, and out all night with the conies. And Mr William, he would go off for food, and come back and say "This is for us; this is for the conies." He split it all down the middle. "Merlene, you cook this, I'll give this to the conies."

'But no more conies. Oh, it's sad, it's very sad. We loved de conies. Will they bring them back?'

I said I hoped they would soon, they were breeding more.

Someone knocked at the door.

'De coney man!' Hyacinth exclaimed.

The coney man was tall and thin. He had a shaved head and a cutlass stuffed down his black school trousers. He wore no socks and ankle-high rubber boots. He explained to Hyacinth, all the time looking earnestly at the floor, that Mr Peter had told him to show me the coney holes.

'But them all mashed up,' said Hyacinth.

'Mr Peter had said,' said the coney man.

'But it's hot,' said Merlene.

'Mr Peter had said,' said the coney man.

As Mr Peter had said, we set off in the morning sun and climbed steeply up the hills behind the house. The track ran between drystone walls. The cattle in the fields were Lincoln Reds, but a few white zebu bulls (with a hump above the shoulder and wide spreading horns) stood serenely amongst them. The zebus are introduced to give the Lincolns strength in the heat. The hump disappears when they breed.

We reached the outcrops of forest and the coney man slipped inside. While he managed to walk without touching the greenery, I got myself horribly snared up. I was scratched and bitten by mosquitoes, and fell on to the limestone which was as sharp as coral. We to-oed and fro-ed a bit before arriving at an outcrop of limestone.

'De coney hole.' The coney man pointed at it.

We looked at the coney hole in silence.

'Him all mashed up,' the coney man finally said.

The coney hole had vanished without trace. The natural limestone outcrop remained, everything else had been swallowed up by undergrowth or had melted away into the forest floor.

We visited the sites of six coney holes and found the same devastation at each. It was hard to imagine the excitement which must have surrounded them as they were built, the conies put into them and then released.

'We used to spend long time watching the conies – maybe all night,' said the coney man. 'Now, no more conies.'

He slashed at the undergrowth with his cutlass and we set off back towards the house. The coney man walked with a straight back, gliding through the forest or the tall grass while I floundered behind. By the time we returned to the house, I was raw from scratches and bites. It needed a Rasta to emphasize how I felt:

'Him was licked, man. De breath just fell out of him. Him was nooo good. Him began to cry – like a baaaaby!'

Peter was waiting for me.

'Are you alright? I thought you'd enjoy seeing the coney holes. Jolly hot though. Best to keep in the shade when it's like this.' He led the way inside. 'You look like those Jersey men. They would stagger back from the wilds with very anxious faces. And covered with ticks. Absolutely covered.' He offered me a freshly squeezed lemon juice clinking with ice. 'Only way to get them off is to douse yourself with kerosene. You'd better look sooner rather than later. You'll find them all over your legs. And heading north.'

Turning on my heel, I headed for the bathroom and engaged in a frantic rearguard action against an army of ticks. Whilst they merely had numbers and recalcitrance on their side, I had speed and kerosene on mine. Smelling like a petrol station, I rejoined Peter and my lemon juice.

'Got 'em all? Good. There was a Jamaican girl with the conies.' Peter started where he had left off. 'She was first-class, a real winner. But the conies didn't last. Very sad. I'm sure rabbits would have done. Probably be all over the island by now. But I suppose that's hardly the point.'

Brown, furry and dull, the coney continues to slide towards

extinction. What will happen when it goes extinct? Probably nothing. Life in Jamaica will go on much as before. Owen and Mikey Sluie will find something else to do apart from going on crazed coney hunts – they might take up motor-bike scrambling or buy a telly and watch American football. In fact they might even take up Peter's idea and import rabbits to hunt. There will just be no conies left. Few people will notice. I cannot imagine even the *Daily Gleaner* giving them a decent epitaph such as 'Last coney mashed up!'

So another species goes extinct. The whole heaving mass of ecological hieroglyphics which makes up one side of the equation which equals 'life', on the other side is changed by the factor of 'coney'. Not much of a factor. A boring brown little mammal, a rodent to boot, what has a coney ever done for us? Well, probably not much. But it is undeniable that without conies, life as lived in the world would change. We assume that we can do without them and it looks a good bet. There aren't many left and there have been no bad side effects so far.

But although the odds look good, the stakes are infinity. Once conies have gone extinct, they don't come back. This is what extinction means. So we disregard the coney and life carries on. But then what about the next animal? Can we live without rhinos? Well, this is a little more telling. For a start the Chinese would not be able to grind down their horns to use as an aphrodisiac, and Yemeni men would not be able to strut around with rhino horn dagger handles. But I imagine that despite the loss of these creature comforts, life would go on much the same as before. So we can survive without the rhinos. Fine, we'll certainly have to – as well as elephants and gorillas and chimpanzees and an obscure starling in Bali and many others.

In fact the experts who specialize in making these sorts of forecasts (ten years ago they were the first people to talk of global warming and holes in the ozone layer) now say that over the next thirty years 25 per cent of the world's animal and plant life will become extinct.

As more and more animals disappear, the world's bio-diversity shrinks, the food chain shortens and the equation becomes simpler. As increasingly less factors make up 'life', so each factor becomes more important, and its loss more significant. Eventually we will reach a point where the stabilizing influence of a broad bio-diversity will disappear because so many species have fallen out of the equation. Life on earth will become horribly volatile. And then we will remember that we too are part of that equation of life, and if the equation doesn't add up then we are going to be affected. We are of course just another animal. Then we might wish that we had never let the rot set in by ignoring the Jamaican coney.

The expression 'bio-diversity' is one of the latest buzz words used by scientists which represents all that is good in the world before man started interfering. On my last day in Jamaica I came across a vivid example of human bio-diversity. I was in Montego Bay. After dodging through a crowd of pink-legged tourists who were heading purposefully for the concrete shopping mall and the soda fountains, I turned down a side street and found myself in a quiet square with a view of the sea. A young Rasta was asleep on a bench.

Rastas are under increasing pressure from other Jamaicans. They are surrounded by a burgeoning evangelical movement in which other Jamaicans follow the God-fearing ideals of low-denomination American churches. They see good and evil in clear relief and are hellbent on doing good. This means getting a decent job, having a low hair cut, and getting on in the world. Wherever 'on' is, the Rastas are not there and the evangelists treat them with contempt, refuse to give them jobs and basically try to squeeze them out of mainstream life.

I approached the Rasta to see what was written on his T-shirt. It was a yellow T-shirt with a green and red collar. The slogan across the front read 'DWAAT – CELTGBA'. He opened an eye and looked at me.

'What does that mean?' I asked.

'Don't worry about a thing, man, 'cos every little thing's gonna be alright.'

'So there's an "M" missing?' I said after I'd re-read it a couple of times.

'What?'

'An "M" for man.'

'No problem, man,' he agreed, and settled down to sleep off the afternoon. 'DWAAT – CELTGBA.' He seemed quite sure of this. I hoped he was right.

Two

Brazil

The *Leontopithecus* conference in Belo Horizonte – The extinction programme – Gooooooola and the tragic samba – Claudio Padua and the BLT – A frog's last lesson in the survival of the fittest – Frozen zoos and robot tamarins – A forest too small to get lost in

Everybody thinks they know about Brazil.

'The rain forest,' they say, making engulfing motions with their arms, 'miles and miles burned down every year, an area the size of Wales, or is it France? Anyway, it's destroying the ozone layer and causing all this global warming. Amazonian tribes are wiped out. The Body Shop does all those authentic rain-forest lotions, meant to be wonderful though I haven't tried them myself . . .'

But I was not going to the rain forest; I was going to Belo Horizonte, an industrial town north of Rio. It was not where I had expected to end up in Brazil, but I was going to attend a conference. Coming fresh from Jamaica, where the mashed-up warrens represent the uphill struggle to put the conies back on the map, I was going to visit one of the best documented conservation programmes in the world, the lion tamarins of Brazil.

The telephone had rung on the day of my return from Jamaica.

'Edward! I'm so pleased I caught you.' It was Jeremy Mallinson, Jersey's zoo director. 'The *Leontopithecus* conference has been brought forward a week. I'm leaving tonight.'

'Where is it?'

'The Meridien Hotel, Belo Horizonte.'

'Will we get to see any leontopotamusses?' I asked.

'*Leontopithecus*? One never knows. Everyone involved with *Leontopithecus* will be there. The conference will last four days. We might cadge a donkey-ride into the forest afterwards. Bring jungle juice just in case.'

In the event I needn't have bothered to bring anything. When I was the last person left standing at the luggage carousel in Rio, it became clear that my pack had vanished. It was 4 a.m. so I sat and waited for the British Airways office to open. British Airways discovered that my pack had gone to Buenos Aires. They would retrieve it and send it to me. I tried to change my travellers cheques, but found that they were of no interest to the exchange bureaux at any price. When the bank finally opened, I was asked to produce proof of their purchase. 'The slip is in my pack which has gone to Buenos Aires,' I shouted through the bullet-proof glass. I produced my passport, credit cards, driving licence, plane ticket and a phone card.

'Não change,' said the man and pushed all my proof of existence to one side.

I caught the first available flight to Belo Horizonte and arrived with no money, no clean clothes and in a foul temper.

'Monkey delegate?' asked the hotel doorman suspiciously.

The conference had just started and the room was full. Sixty people were arranged around a fan of desks. Up on the dais in front of the screen, Jeremy was giving an introductory address. He wore an old tweed jacket, patched at the elbows, a red and white striped shirt, cavalry twills, and the most brightly polished brown brogues I had ever seen. He stands well over six feet tall, and his sheet of soft silver hair hangs down like a Romantic poet's. His nose, an arresting feature even from the back of the conference hall, is described by Gerry as 'Duke of Wellington'. He is feared by the staff at Jersey Zoo where he is an unswerving perfectionist and has been chosen as the 'Expert's Expert' zoo director in the *Observer* magazine. At home, his wife calls him Pongo, and is exuberantly uninterested in animals.

At the sight of me, Jeremy paused and momentarily lost the thread of his speech. The Brazilians were listening through headphones to a simultaneous translation. Jeremy's regimental accent is such that a number of Americans were also listening to the Portuguese translation in the hope of gleaning a little more of what he was saying. Jeremy finished, took his bow and came over to me.

'My dear boy.' He shook my hand with both of his. 'Are you quite alright?'

I told him.

'You'd better borrow one of my shirts,' he said, 'I don't have enough underpants. And then have some coffee. It's frightfully good here – you know, Brazil, where the beans come from.' When Jeremy is amused, he throws back his head, opens one side of his mouth and abruptly howls with laughter. Various monkey delegates turned around in alarm to see what the joke was. I slipped off as he began to explain it.

'Blast!' I heard him say. 'Nuts not beans.'

I took the lift upstairs and let myself into Jeremy's room. I chose a red and white striped shirt from his collection of red and white striped shirts. On reflection I also took a shower. With clean hair, a shaved chin and a red and white striped shirt, I was a different proposition for the doorman.

'Monkey delegate,' he said warmly, and let me through.

Leontopithecus is in fact not a monkey but a tamarin, a lion tamarin, and there are three sub-species – black, golden and golden-headed. They are only found in Brazil where they live in low-lying coastal forest. This forest originally stretched all along the coast from the corner of Brazil near Salvador right through Rio and swept inland south of São Paulo. It is a dry forest, not to be confused with the tropical rain forest in the Amazon basin. The trees are shorter, around fifteen metres high. This forest has been the most devastated of Brazil's forests. Since the turn of the century 98 per cent of it has been cut down, 50 per cent of it in the last thirty years. Rio de Janeiro and São Paulo, which sprawl right across land originally inhabited by lion tamarins, each have a population of ten million. They are the largest cities in the tropics and growing. Even Belo Horizonte, which was a small town in the 1960s, now has one and a half million inhabitants.

The three sub-species of lion tamarins live in three separate pockets of forest, the black lion tamarins (*Leontopithecus chrysopygus*) about 400 miles west of São Paulo; the golden lion tamarins (*Leontopithecus rosalia*) just north of Rio de Janeiro; and the golden-headed lion tamarins (*Leontopithecus chrysomelas*) up in the north-eastern state of Bahia. In the trade the tamarins are called BLT, GLT and GHLT. Each time I heard 'BLT', I thought of a limp British Rail sandwich – bacon, lettuce and tomato.

The Brazilian government's Department of the Environment, IBAMA, has formed committees to supervise each sub-species. The work of the GHLT committee is representative of the sort of work they all do. In 1988 the GHLT committee elected Adelmar Coimbra-Filho, head of the Rio de Janeiro Primate Centre, and Jeremy Mallinson as joint chairmen for a three-year stint. Other members of the committee are a combination of Brazilians and foreigners – Devra Kleiman, previously a researcher for Desmond Morris and now director of research at the Smithsonian; Russell Mittermeier, chairman of the IUCN primate group (IUCN stands for International Union for the Conservation of Nature, a non-governmental Swiss agency); Jordan Wallauer, head of the forestry division of IBAMA; Georgina Mace, from the London Zoological Society; and Faical Simon, chairman of the sister BLT committee and head of the primates at São Paulo Zoo.

Over the last two years, the committee has traced other GHLTs held in captivity in order to include them in the captive breeding programme; it has agreed to allow a further twenty-five zoos to accept GHLTs when surplus stock becomes available and a number of captive GHLTs have been swapped around. There are 285 GHLTs in captivity, compared with 64 BLTs and 541 GLTs, and the committee keeps a stud book to avoid inbreeding.

The committee has also made efforts to save their habitat. There is an official reserve of 11,400 hectares, but IBAMA only owns 5,342 hectares of this forest, the rest being in private hands. The committee has encouraged IBAMA to buy more land and has raised funds to purchase a further 243 hectares. The other major landowner in the region is CEPLAC, the cocoa farmers' co-operative, which the committee lobbies to transfer land to IBAMA.

The four-day conference would review and share all the current information about every aspect of lion tamarin life and then draw up answers to the overriding question: How can the lion tamarins be saved from extinction?

The conference was chaired by Professor Ulysses Seal, head of the IUCN Species Survival Commission. An American from the Deep South, he has the booming rhetoric of an evangelical preacher. He wore a short-sleeved shirt with a line of pens in the top pocket, thick black glasses and a thick white beard. Hugging the microphone close to his chest, he set out the parameters of discussion for the conference. I noted down such phrases as 'strategic goals', 'population viability assessment' and 'key recommendations and implementations'.

'We today form an unrivalled group of expert conservationists,' Ulysses intoned, 'each a specialist in our own field. The outside world will look to us and our publications as a model for a multi-faceted conservation programme which can and should be used for the conservation of the entire world of endangered species.'

The American contingent burst into applause at this unprecedented juxtaposition of clichés. Through my earphones, I faintly heard the Portuguese translator struggling to raise his voice to the same inspirational pitch.

As an impartial observer I could study the meeting rather as a primatologist might study a group of monkeys. I noticed a broad division between those who worked in the field and those who worked on captive breeding. The field researchers, Brazilian or American, spoke Portuguese and wore beards and bushy hair. A number also had bad scars on their faces. ('Leishmaniasis disease,' said the monkey delegate next to me, pointing at one speaker's pitted face. 'A parasite grows out of your face. You get it from certain kinds of mosquito.') These were proudly displayed rather like German duelling scars. Field researchers spoke hastily, stumbling over their words and putting up clumsy hand-drawn slides. Recurrent themes were lack of definite knowledge, inability to find animals, lack of funds, bad living conditions and deforestation.

The university researchers were all clean-shaven and self-assured, albeit with receding hairlines. They gave measured talks with computer-designed graphic slides. They studied captive animals and had a vast amount of statistics supported by comfortable funding and excellent research facilities. They had started out as field researchers themselves but had moved up the academic ladder towards larger grants, mosquito-proof sitting-rooms and powerful computers.

On the second day the conference began to feed numbers into a computer model developed by Jon Ballou, an American mathematician. The model was simply called 'The Extinction Programme'. For the first time I saw the process of extinction explained in numbers which proved how easy and imminent it is. Jon specializes in genetic inheritance. He asked the respective committees to confirm the numbers of lion tamarins and the areas available to them.

Each sub-species of tamarin is now confined to a reserve. The BLTs have a reserve of 36,000 hectares of which 29,000 hectares are suitable habitat but highly fragmented; the GLTs have 5,500 hectares of which 3,300 are forested; and the GHLTs have 11,400 hectares of which only 5,585 are guaranteed to remain as forest. The current estimates for the wild populations are 350 BLTs, 290 GLTs and 565 GHLTs.

Jon put all these figures into his computer. Within seconds the lion tamarins' fate was printed out. Even assuming no natural disasters or diseases and that the forest remains intact, all three lion tamarin populations will be extinct by 2025.

He explained that this would be due to genetic inbreeding. The problem is that with so few animals there is a progressive loss of genes. This is called 'genetic drift'. The loss of genes is an exponential process. It starts very slowly with 1 or 2 per cent in the first four or five generations (lion tamarins are ready to breed after eighteen months so generations clock up very quickly). But once lost, a gene is not replaced. The resulting animals become less able to adapt to changing environments, they breed less (thus compounding the problem), they become more susceptible to disease and they suffer more infant mortality. The vicious circle of a small population which leads to increased inbreeding which leads to decreased reproduction quickly becomes a giddy downward spiral.

Extinction will probably come sooner than 2025. Jon pointed out that his calculations assumed that all the forest was available to the lion tamarins, that there was an even chance of them all interbreeding and that each animal would breed. This does not happen. First, not all animals breed, so the effective population is only a fraction of the actual population. Second, even if the lion tamarins' habitat stayed intact, it is fragmented and the populations are isolated from each other. As a lion tamarin will not walk along the ground, a tarmac road is an effective border. If two adjacent populations are separated by a new road, as in the case of the BLTs, they cannot interbreed. These small pockets of lion tamarins will become extinct much more rapidly than if they had all had access to each other. As the forest is segmented by roads and logging, it dries out and becomes more vulnerable to fire. Thus once the forest is cross-quartered, the trees, the lion tamarins and of course everything else living there begin to disappear progressively faster, a process which Jon described as 'the extinction vortex'.

Jon concluded that in order for the GLTs and the GHLTs to avoid imminent extinction, each group would have to have 25,000 hectares of unbroken forest, five times what they currently inhabit. With the current pressure on the forest growing all the time this is impossible. In the Una Reserve, the only stronghold of the GHLT, there were seven sawmills in 1980. By 1987 there were twenty-three. As word goes round that the government may appropriate their forest as reserve, the farmers burn or cut it down in order to avoid losing their land.

The conference fragmented into different committees as each tried to refine the data which could go into the computer model. Time and again they came up with new possibilities and we crowded around the computer. Jon filled in varying assumptions for heterosis, recessive genes, levels of environmental stochasticity, reproductive rates, binomial variance of mortality rates and the lethal equivalents per diploid genome. He scribbled down for me the calculation for genetic drift, which he said held good whether measured by heterozygosity, additive variance in quantitative traits or the binomial variance in allelic frequencies. I nodded in a noncommital sort of way. The calculation is:

$$Vg(t) = Vg(0) \times \left(1 - \frac{1}{(2Ne)}\right)t$$

where Vg is the genetic variance at generation t (time is measured in generations rather than years), and Ne is the effective breeding population rather than the entire population.

Even with progressively optimistic assumptions, the computer print-out was the same:

'Population did not survive . . . Extinction at year 26.'

'Population did not survive . . . Extinction at year 15.'

'Population did not survive . . . Extinction at year 71.'

But conservationists are optimists. At dinner that night I sat next to Ulysses. I asked him about the computer forecasts of extinction.

'Very bad,' he said, his voice by now slightly croaky after two days of relentless exhortation. 'But hell, in the last six months I've chaired conferences where we've saved the black-footed ferret, the Javan rhinoceros and the Bali starling. And the Arctic wolf. And in each case the computer was forecasting they would be gone.

'We're breeding them fine in captivity. Captive breeding is amazing. We can now do cross-species breeding. Nobody is talking about it yet but if you were to give me a normal spotted leopard, within three generations I could breed you a snow leopard.'

'But I thought a leopard never changed its spots.'

'You thought wrong. You take a six-year-old child from the slums of Cairo and put him in America. Give him a diet of good American food – hamburgers, chips and Cola. By the time he's sixteen, the shape of his cranium will have changed to an American shape. Species change.

'What they're working on right now is the mammoth. You find

a good-condition frozen mammoth in the tundra and fiddle around with the DNA in the surviving tissue. Put that into some elephant sperm, you're going to get pretty close to the original mammoth. What do you think of that then?'

I thought about it. 'Pretty sick really. Where's it going to live?'

'Oh, you're one of the "Extinction with Dignity" brigade are you? Let'em go extinct as long as we remember them fondly as great beasts.'

'Not exactly, I just don't see how a mammoth would get on in the world if it came back.'

'That's no reason not to breed it in the meantime,' Ulysses said. 'Let's get them back first and then think about that. We could always freeze them again.'

The conference moved to its conclusion. Ultimatums and recommendations to save the lion tamarin from extinction were drawn up to be submitted to IBAMA. More money was needed, more land was needed, more government action, more education, more publicity. A meeting with key IBAMA representatives was scheduled for the last day.

But while the conference had been going on, the World Cup had also been in progress. The conference had overlooked the fact that in the outside world every afternoon was punctuated by highly excitable football commentaries. From radios and televisions all over town hysterical screeches could be heard – 'Gooooooooola! Gogogogogoggooooola!' as if someone had slammed his finger in a car door. The hotel waiters had the television going behind the swinging doors, and whenever the door was left open, the lunchtime conversation would politely rise a few notches to shut out this intrusion.

'I took these urine samples back to Washington.'

'Do you need a permit for that? I know I did for semen.'

'Yeah, and blood too.'

'Why not urine?'

'Well, I guess the difference is that they just give you urine. I mean you have to scrabble around for it but if you're patient, you get it. But with blood and semen you have to take it. Hey,

Ilmar, could you pass me the tomato juice?'

The grand meeting between the three committees and IBAMA was scheduled for the last day of the conference. It was also the day when Brazil were to play Argentina. Over breakfast that morning I picked up rumours that the whole conference had been a waste of time. IBAMA were pulling out of the key meeting. Nobody knew why. It was darkly hinted that politics were the cause. Even Ulysses was stumped for words. I asked him what time the meeting had been fixed for.

'Three o'clock,' came the sad answer. 'And they've pulled it. They're just washing their hands of the problem.'

Now I know nothing about the politics of conservation, but I did know that Brazil were playing Argentina at 2 o'clock that afternoon so a 3 o'clock meeting anywhere in Brazil was clearly out of the question. I pointed this out to Ulysses.

'No! Don't be absurd. A game of football? God dammit, it's not even American football! Do you really think so?'

'Just try their reaction if you ask them for 11 o'clock.'

To his delight Ulysses found that 11 o'clock would be perfectly suitable and the vital IBAMA meeting went ahead.

As this meeting was private, I wandered out of the hotel. The city was deserted, but the bars were full. Many women were wearing Brazilian football kit, and bottles of beer and kebabs were piling up on the tables. I went into one bar and room was made for me at a table.

The match started. There was a confident hum of expectation and I began swapping beers with my neighbours. The television picture changed from colour to fuzzy black and white and then space invaders. But we could still hear the excited commentary. During half-time a woman in white shorts, Brazilian football shirt and feather boa began to samba.

When tragedy struck with a goal from Argentina there was shocked disbelief. At the end of the match there was silence. People slumped back on to the streets. The woman with the feather boa sobbed inconsolably. I went back to the conference. The doorman looked suicidal.

In contrast, the meeting with IBAMA had been an unqualified

success. The resolutions had all been agreed and would be put to the government in the hope that some of them would be supported by law. The conference came to an end.

'Excellent.' Jeremy beamed, looking as if he had just emerged from a meeting with his merchant bankers. 'This is the most exciting development for *Leontopithecus*.' He could never bring himself to say 'BLT'. 'IBAMA have agreed to endorse all our proposals. This could really secure the future of *Leontopithecus*.

'And I've organized a trip to the forest. We're going down with Claudio to Morro do Diablo to see his work with *Leontopithecus chrysopygus*. Devra Kleiman is joining us.'

Claudio Padua is a Jersey trainee and his story is an interesting one. After university he joined a large industrial company. His father had been governor of Minas Gerais, so he was well connected and poised to rise to the top of the Brazilian business world. Everything went swimmingly well for him. He lived in Rio and married an interior designer. They had three children and were beginning to look for a larger house in Rio when in 1978 Claudio abruptly decided to go back to university to study biology.

They rented out their house and moved into a small flat. His wife Suzanne supported him with her increasingly successful interior design company. After taking his degree, Claudio worked at the Rio Primate Centre with Coimbra-Filho. In 1983 he went to train at Jersey. The following year he started his thesis on the behavioural patterns of black lion tamarins, which were previously unstudied. In order to do this, he and Suzanne had to move to where the black lion tamarins live, Morro do Diablo, which was our destination.

'We left everything behind in Rio – our house, my career, Suzanne's career and our children's education,' Claudio said. 'Our families and friends thought we were crazy. To study at university had been bad enough. Our friends thought that was just a fad. But to leave Rio! Nobody leaves Rio! And we were not just leaving Rio, we were going to live in a forest. No Brazilians live in a forest, only Indians. And there aren't many Indians left.

'So we decided to live in Morro do Diablo. Suzanne thought she would be the education officer for the reserve, and we could educate our children at the local school. When we arrived, it seemed we had made a big mistake. You'll see when you get there.'

We reached Morro do Diablo after a day's flying. I saw what he meant. The drive from the tin shack that constituted the airport to his local town took two hours across a barren muddy landscape littered with blackened stumps, the charred remains of a recently burned forest. Large crevices cut through the grass and red mud spilled out into the ditches. The town was a small collection of whitewashed houses, its streets muddy and lined with abandoned cars. Chickens ran around the edges.

'Suzanne wasn't too pleased about sending our children to school here. It's not too bad actually, under an hour's drive to our house from here.'

We continued through cleared grazing pasture, mile after mile where nothing happened.

'All this used to be a forest reserve,' Claudio told me. 'In 1942 the governor of São Paulo state, Fernando Costa, established what he called a "Grande Reserva do Pontal", a reserve of some 297,000 hectares. But the Grande Reserva was not supervised that well, and by 1962 only 75 per cent of it was left. That's not bad, 220,000 hectares. If that had remained, it would have been one of the most important forest reserves in the world.

'But in 1966 the then governor, Ademar de Barros, was short of votes. He was not a popular man so he decreed that the reserve could be used for forestry and agriculture. There was a stampede into the reserve like a gold rush, and in about five years most of it was burned down. Today we have just 36,000 hectares left. And only 29,000 of this has any forest, a tenth of the original reserve.'

We reached the entrance to the reserve and entered the forest. The drive to Claudio's house was relatively short.

'This is just one of the patches of forest left. When we first arrived we found a wooden house for us and a few rangers' huts.

Black Lion Tamarin
"Leontopithecus Chrysopygus"

I've since built another house for visiting scientists, an education centre for Suzanne and a research lab and library. We paid for this with money from a hydro-electric project. They dammed the river and flooded another 2,000 hectares of the reserve. They gave us some money as compensation. It was bad but it could have been worse. With this government they could have flooded more and paid us nothing.'

We piled out of the car. With the engine shut off, I realized that after the incessant pressure of four days in a conference, I had barely been outside. This was the first time I had been surrounded by silence rather than the bickering of monkey delegates. We were in the middle of nowhere. Overhead the night sky was pure black, that rich velvet black which comes from having no reflected neon lights, and studded with stars.

Claudio and Suzanne welcomed us into their home. It was a log cabin, comfortable inside with sofas and rugs. There were two bedrooms, a bathroom and a kitchen. The main room had furniture built from the same timber as the walls, so it looked all of one piece.

'Home,' Suzanne indicated the living-room, 'a long way from Rio but home. I hope you like the interior design – the rustic look! Supper's just ready. Have a whisky.'

Full of roast chicken, sweet potato and whisky, we made our way over to the visiting scientists' hut. Jeremy and I slept in bunk beds in one room. 'Just like the army,' was Jeremy's last approving thought on the matter before he fell into a stertorous sleep.

I was on the top bunk near the ceiling and an awesome collection of mosquitoes. My face and arms were smarting from heavy applications of jungle juice.

'Leishmaniasis,' I thought.

'*Oh what a beautiful morning*!' Jeremy bellowed suddenly, apropos of nothing.

'Jesus!'

'*Oh what a beautiful day*!'

'What time is it?'

'Rendez-vous for breakfast at 0400 hours,' Jeremy said and ruthlessly switched on the light.

I blundered in Jeremy's wake over to breakfast. He was wearing First World War army boots which laced up to his knees and creaked like floorboards. His shirt shone red and white in the gloom of the murky dawn.

'Porridge?' Suzanne asked. I couldn't have been more thunderstruck had she offered me caviar. Porridge was followed by bacon and eggs.

We set off into the forest. Claudio was wearing full army jungle kit. An army cap pitched low over his beard completed the similarity with Fidel Castro.

'Tell me about Jersey,' I said as we trudged along. 'How did you end up there?'

'It was a real breakthrough for me. I had studied biology at university which was fine, but I was thirty-five and had no practical experience. I was interested in primates, and the only place you can study them in Brazil is at the Rio Primate Centre with Coimbra-Filho. So I worked there for a while and then Coimbra-Filho suggested I go to Jersey to get all-round experience before choosing a specific subject. He knows Jeremy very well.

'So he wrote to Jeremy and I went to Jersey. They taught me a lot. I could handle all the animals, which I hadn't done before. This is important because now I need to put radio collars on them and weigh them.

'I learned a lot about real animals rather than illustrations. And with so many different animals, I could learn other techniques relevant to the lion tamarins.

'University had taught me about collecting data, but in Jersey where they're actually working with animals, you see what data is relevant. There was a university student at the conference who gave a speech giving an analysis of what lion tamarins eat with percentages going to two decimal points!

'When I returned, things really took off. I applied to study the black lion tamarins here. Nobody had studied them since Coimbra-Filho in the 1970s and he had only found one group. I was accepted by the Rio Primate School and applied to write my thesis for Maryland University. Jersey have given me funds to do the work here and have paid for my staff – there are eight trackers who follow the tamarins. They also pay for equipment such as radio collars and education material which Suzanne uses.'

We came out into a clearing and found a tracker holding a large aerial.

Claudio introduced me to José. They spoke for a moment and José pointed somewhere.

'Okay,' Claudio said, 'the tamarins nested over there somewhere. About half an hour away. We'll have to be quiet.'

It was cool in the forest and, just as I had found in St Lucia, surprisingly quiet. There was no undergrowth so we walked quickly, José in front listening to his aerial through a pair of bakelite headphones. I heard the odd hoot from a bell bird, otherwise there was silence. José began to get excited. We all started moving faster. From a bird's eye perspective we would have looked like a menacing gang of primates slipping through the forest towards the tamarins.

I smelt the tamarins before I heard them. A rich musky smell hung in the air, a smell I had only previously encountered in a zoo. Then I heard a high-pitched tweeting, just like a bird. Some shaking branches caught my attention and something small and black ran overhead. I swung my binoculars in its direction and followed the line of a branch. Suddenly the viewfinder was full of a black lion tamarin staring back at me and chattering its teeth in agitation. It was much smaller than I had imagined, the size of a kitten, but had a large head with a lion's mane arranged in a perfect centre parting. Its fingers were long and artistic and held the branch lightly. It bobbed its head a few times and then spun off through the canopy. It moved so fast it was little more than a blur through the branches.

'Good Heavens!' I heard Jeremy say to himself. 'What an enchanting thing.'

We were introduced to the trackers. They watch the tamarins all day, walking quietly below them, note where they go to bed at dusk and tell the next shift. There were seven tamarins in the group, and we drifted along underneath them as they made their way across the canopy. They began to relax after their first flurry at seeing six strangers. Two tamarins in the group wore radio transmitters in the form of collars with the aerials standing out from their necks. The aerials are springs, so they bend whenever necessary and do not alter the animal's behaviour. I realized that as we walked less, just keeping pace with the tamarins above us, I heard more bird-song.

'Yes,' Claudio agreed when I pointed this out, 'when you walk in a straight line, you hear nothing in the forest. The forest was not designed for straight lines. You only hear things when you have been here a while.

'When I first arrived it took me three months to find a group of tamarins. They can hear you from miles away. I could never get near them.

'Then one day I found droppings at the foot of a tree. There was a hole in the tree where they nest. But they nest in six or seven places, so I had to wait there every day until they came back and nested. Then we climbed up the tree and trapped them and put radio collars on them. 'I've now found fifteen groups of tamarins around the forest.'

'It's micro-manipulating, Claudio,' Devra interrupted. 'Look at that.' She pointed at a tamarin which was ferreting around in a bunch of leaves.

'It's got a frog,' Jeremy hissed.

Sure enough the tamarin had pulled a frog out of the leaves. It held it in its fingers for a moment and then bit between its legs. The frog wriggled, kicking its legs uselessly. The tamarin held it like a Mars bar, twitched its head quizzically and began to eat the frog from the bottom up.

'Why doesn't it bite its head off?' I asked Devra. 'Put the thing out of its misery?'

The frog minus its bottom half was still very much alive. Devra's answer was pre-empted by a skirmish up above. Two other tamarins had spotted this treat and came crashing through the trees. The tamarin dashed off, but dropped the frog in its haste.

With an exultant cry, Claudio dashed over to where the frog lay, picked it up and put it out of its misery by plopping it into a bottle of acid. The tamarins congregated overhead and, standing on tiptoe, chattered angrily at us.

'They're just bluffing,' Claudio said. 'They would never come down to the ground.'

We crowded around him and inspected the evidence. The chewed frog slowly rotated in its acid bath, its eyes staring out of its head giving it a rather surprised look. It had all happened very quickly.

'You're very lucky,' Claudio told me. 'This is only the second time I've seen this happen. Many people would not believe that tamarins eat frogs.'

'Life and death,' Jeremy rubbed his hands together, 'it's a jungle out there.'

The frog, which had received its first and last lesson in the principles of survival of the fittest, was carefully stowed in Claudio's pocket. We continued our observation of the tamarins for the rest of the morning. Nothing exciting happened, the forest went on as normal minus one frog, and the tamarins busied themselves with some berries. Claudio made notes of how much time they spent foraging, feeding or grooming each other. There was a good deal of talk about their vocalizations.

'Have you tried play-back tapes?' Devra asked. 'It's a technique I developed.'

'No, I don't have the right recording equipment.'

'I'll try and get some to you,' she said.

We walked on beneath the tamarins. If we lost sight of them, it was easy to tell where they were because the branches of the trees started shaking. There was no other movement in the forest.

'What are playbacks?' I asked her.

'In 1984 I released sixteen golden lion tamarins into the wild, four of which came from Jersey. We thought they would adapt instinctively, but we found that they had no concept of how to live in the wild. They couldn't recognize any food, they had no sense of direction and they had no sense of predators.

'Then I recorded their vocalizations. When I played them back and analysed the sound waves, I discovered that these zoo-bred tamarins were calling in an entirely different way from wild tamarins – they couldn't even communicate. So basically although they looked like tamarins to us, and we called them "tamarins", they weren't tamarins. They were robots. A tamarin is only a tamarin if it behaves as a tamarin. More to the point, it was clear that they wouldn't survive a week in the wild if they couldn't jump around the branches or eat or avoid predators. Very quickly they really wouldn't be tamarins at all, they'd be dead tamarins.

'This meant that we couldn't count up our captive golden lion tamarins and say we've got 300 tamarins ready to reintroduce into the forest. So this brought into question the whole point of zoos. Now you met Ulysses Seal, he's a genius at captive breeding. He is experimenting with freezing sperm and eggs and keeping them in liquid nitrogen. He wants to keep embryos frozen so he can bring them out at a later date. In a way this is just what Gerry Durrell's doing. Gerry's got real animals on ice, Ulysses has got frozen sperm. Not as much fun visiting Ulysses' zoo, but the end result is the same.

'But I argue that if you bring out an elephant in 200 years' time, it won't be an elephant. It will look like an elephant, it will have the anatomy of an elephant, but it won't know how to behave. Also its environment might have changed. So within a pretty short time it will be killed by something, a predator or a disease which wasn't around when it was frozen, and then it certainly won't be an elephant.'

'So what do we do?'

'Well, although the old tamarins all died out when they were put back into the forest, the young ones adapted. We tried everything to teach the parents to adapt but they could only learn so much. However, if we managed to get the young ones into the company of an old wild tamarin, they learned fast.

'But when you reintroduce an animal you've got to be careful not to introduce diseases, or merely to introduce a captive animal which replaces a wild one which would have been born. You should do it to introduce new genes. When a wild population is isolated for a long time, they can lose genes and these need to be bolstered.

'Basically, the idea of a Noah's Ark is a fallacy. You cannot keep animals out of their habitat and then put them back and expect them to be the same as wild animals. You have to keep interchanging them, you have to keep them in touch with their habitat. It's sad but predictable, but there's no substitute for keeping the forest alive.'

We eventually left the tamarins to the care of the two trackers.

'Just think,' Claudio said to me, 'we'll have been amongst the last few people to see those animals before they go extinct.'

'Sounds like being the witnesses to a murder.'

'Well, I suppose we are.'

We walked back through the forest. It seemed very quiet and no time at all before we reached the jeep.

That afternoon we climbed Morro do Diablo, an anvil-shaped mountain which rises up from the plain. 'Diablo' derives from the Portuguese mercenaries, *bandeirantes*, who invaded the forests in the seventeenth century. They killed the Indians and staked out vast estates which they burned and planted with sugar cane. Jesuit priests tried to help the Indians, but by the end of the century most of them had been killed either by the *bandeirantes*, or by life as slaves on the sugar plantations, or by imported European diseases.

Some *bandeirantes* had reached the mountain and found the corpses of previous *bandeirantes* nailed to trees by the Indians as a warning not to trespass further. As if they had never seen such atrocities before, they piously called it Morro do Diablo, and took their revenge. The Indians were quickly exterminated.

When we reached the summit, the entire 29,000 hectares of the reserve were visible. The forest canopy spread away from us, green and bunched like broccoli spears. It was surrounded on all sides by yellow grazing pasture. A thin road cut through the middle of it. Further away there was another unnaturally straight line which Claudio said was the railway.

'I say!' said Jeremy, squinting down his binoculars, 'Howlers!'

Sitting at the top of a tree which towered over the rest of the canopy was a troupe of howler monkeys. They were reddish brown in colour and sat slumped lethargically on the branches with hunched backs and rounded shoulders, looking like so many plums in a plum tree. They didn't move for the half hour we looked over the forest. As they didn't have binoculars, they couldn't see us. I wondered if they had ever seen man or knew what lay outside the forest.

The next day we went to another part of the forest. This entailed taking a boat up the Parapanema river, which is an Indian name meaning 'River of no fish' or 'Luckless water'. The river formed the reserve boundary and there was no forest on the far side. On our side, a few birds cackled at us and then flew off as we nosed by. We pulled up to the bank and entered the forest. It took us an hour to track down the tamarins until at last we saw the tell-tale shaking of branches and there they were.

I stared up at them and wondered if they had any idea how rare they were. I had no concept of what sort of things they communicate to each other – did they discuss the new road, or the railway, or the shrinking size of their home? They just seemed to be intent on getting on with their daily business of foraging around, grooming each other and generally looking inquisitive. They paid scant attention to the group of anxious primates who stood below and cricked their necks to look up at them.

Claudio spends all day in the forest following tamarins. I asked him if he ever felt bored or lonely.

'No,' he replied. 'You must understand that being in the forest is a cumulative experience. When I first came here I saw nothing. I used to get very lonely and depressed.

'But consider – these are about the rarest primates in the world. They're as rare as the mountain gorillas, both have a population of 300, and they are primates like us. We have a lot in common and we can learn a lot from each other if only we work hard enough. But time is against us. Right now we're standing in the last tract of a forest which used to stretch well past Belo Horizonte and took a day to fly over. Now it's reduced to this. This forest has been like this ever since the beginning of the world. This is how it is meant to be and it's very precious.

'I find that when I'm alone in the forest I can think properly. We weren't meant to work in cities. We used to be able to live in forests, and a few tribes still do, but most people just cut them down. So it is a strange place to be. It is like trying to re-establish our ancient way of life. Now we are in danger of losing the possibility of even being able to study the forests, let alone live that way of life.

'I still can't count every tree, but I can't get lost in the forest and that's very sad. You saw those computer print-outs at the conference. They're very realistic. Where we're standing now could be grass in five years' time.

'I'm forty-two now and I have three children who will go to Rio and wonder why they're not brought up like all their cousins.' He paused and opened his arms in a gesture which embraced the forest standing all around us. 'This is the answer. If I am wrong, then I will have to live with the accusation that I have impoverished my family for no good reason and that I would have been better selling chemicals.'

'Thank God Claudio did decide to stop selling chemicals and do something about his country,' said Gerry when I described the scene to him. 'It may sound a crazy decision to a forty-year-old bureaucrat hellbent on buying his second house with a swimming pool, but in fifty years' time everyone will wonder why they didn't do it too. "What did you do in the conservation war, Daddy?" their children will ask, and "Buy a second house" just won't be a good enough answer.

'The lion tamarin project is still on the edge. We're dealing with such small numbers of animals and tiny pockets of forest that they might be wiped out. But it is an example of how conservation should be done. All the people you met at the conference work together, the zoo directors, the forest officers, the education officers, and if they save the lion tamarin, they will have saved everything else in the forest. It is a textbook example, a pocketbook edition which we can learn from when confronted by larger problems like the Amazon forest.'

THREE

WEST AFRICA

WILDLIFE ON THE MENU IN GAMBIA – ALPHA JALLOW ON £1 A DAY – HARD CURRENCY CONFERENCES – UP COUNTRY TO THE IMMIGRANT CHIMPS – BURNING MAHOGANY TO COOK CORN – SQUITS AND TSETSE FLIES, A SIMULTANEOUS ATTACK – POACHERS' THUMBPRINTS – THE VILLAGE SLIDESHOW – THE HIPPOS' LAST STAND – ERNEST LAMPTEY IN GHANA – NO ANIMALS IN THE ZOO – THE £100 ANNUAL BUDGET – PRESBYTERIAN GIN AND SCHNAPPS AT A FUNERAL – MATTHEW DORE IN NIGERIA – A WEDDING IN LAGOS – HOW THINGS ARE DONE – CROCODILES FOR SALE – THE OBA, PRINCE DORE AND THE NARROW DOOR

For most people conservation in Africa means big game – elephants, rhinos, lions and giraffes. In Kenya, Tanzania, Zaire and Zimbabwe conservation is big business and a constant stream of zebra-striped jeeps take tourists into the game parks. The future of the big game animals hangs in the balance as people try to decide whether they are worth more dead to the farmers and poachers or alive to the tourists.

'I went to Zimbabwe once', Gerry said. 'I wanted to see what was going on there. Everyone was rushing around trying to save the elephants and the rhinos. Each different organization thought that they had the answer, and they were each shouting louder than the other "Save the white rhino!" "Save the black rhino!" "Save a horny friend!" They were like a bunch of Japanese waltzing mice, which go along in a straight line and then turn three circles. If I had had £20 million to spend I wouldn't have known whom to give it to.

'What you need is one person to say "Everyone gather round, I'm going to tell you a fairy story. Now this is how it's going to be done – you're going to do this, and you're going to do that."

'So I haven't funded any projects in East Africa. Jersey simply doesn't have the financial muscle to compete. I prefer doing smaller projects where I can measure their success.'

'What about West Africa?' I asked.

'West Africa? You won't find any of those nice zebra-striped jeeps there. There are no animals and no tourists. The only people going to West Africa are going to do shady oil deals. Animals are pretty low on the list of priorities. High on the menu but low everywhere else. You'll be going where very few conservationists have been before.'

I was intrigued by this. It would be a chance to see a part of Africa where the people have been left to their own devices. I turned to my list of Jersey trainees. There were trainees from Gambia, Ghana, Liberia and Nigeria, each working in a government department.

Jersey's involvement with West Africa has also been minimal.

'I haven't started any projects in West Africa either,' Gerry said. 'I know that our money can be more usefully spent where we have more impact, and West Africa would suck up a lot of money before there would be any results. Compared with Brazilians, West Africans are about twenty years behind in understanding their wildlife and their ecology. Sadly they're also about twenty years in front of them at destroying it.

'Jersey has trained a few wildlife officers, which is a beginning, but I haven't committed any funds on the ground. This is not to say that work isn't desperately needed, it is. It's just that they'll eat an animal as soon as look at it or understand what it signifies for the health of their country.'

Liberia proved an extreme example of this. Six weeks before I left for West Africa, Alexander Peal, a Jersey trainee in 1986 and director of Monrovia Zoo, advised me to delay my visit as there were 'civil disturbances'. These disturbances developed into a brutal civil war. Alexander escaped to Sierra Leone and then to America. The animals he left behind in the zoo were slaughtered and eaten.

I had my first taste of West Africa when I applied for a visa at the Nigerian Embassy. There was a complicated queuing system which involved four queues interwoven into a knot that ensured that nobody actually got anywhere. Queue-barging was easy, and beefy Nigerian men in shiny grey suits took full advantage of this. They carried crocodile-skin briefcases, they wore lizard-skin shoes, they occasionally flipped open snake-skin wallets or pushed their tortoiseshell glasses further up their noses. The more bits of animal they wore, the more effortlessly they queue-barged.

Sadly Itang Isangedighe has left the Nigerian Forestry Division and disappeared to live with his parents up country. It was impossible to contact him, so I never discovered whether he had found the magnetic fish hooks. Liberia was out of the question. I visited Alpha Jallow in Gambia, Ernest Lamptey in Ghana and Matthew Dore in Nigeria. I started off with Gambia.

I was surprised by how easy it was to get there. I ate breakfast at the normal time, caught a 10 o'clock flight from Gatwick and arrived at Banjul at 3 o'clock, with no time difference. Alpha met me and took me back to stay in his parents' compound in Brikama, a muddy town built from rusted corrugated iron six miles out of Banjul. By teatime I was sitting in Alpha's mud compound surrounded by a biblical scene of countless children, goats, chickens and ancient bare-breasted women. Through the gate on to the street outside I caught glimpses of girls going to and from the well. On the way there they swung the buckets lightly in their hands; on the way back they carried them serenely on their heads, the water sloshing up against the rim and trickling down their long straight necks.

Alpha and his wife moved out of their room and left me with a comfortable mahogany bed. The only other furniture in the room was an electric fan whose ungainly head turned stiffly to and fro blowing away the mosquitoes. But it rained every night and the power was cut off.

The compound was three-sided around a square dirt yard which was swept clean every morning. Some of the walls were mud, others plaster, and like all the compounds which sprawled across town they were topped by a rusty corrugated iron roof. Goats and chickens scratched around at the back where the leftovers were thrown and everyone pissed into the mud. A wicker shed housed the deep drop lavatory. By night the hole was jealously guarded by six or seven cockroaches. Fat and glossy, they were strangely impervious to the torch beam and carried on grazing around the edge of the hole, their whiskers flickering and twitching. I preferred to go by day, when a shabby pink-headed vulture sat on the roof and eyed me up through the slats as potential fodder.

Alpha heard of the Jersey training course through a couple from Jersey who came on holiday to Gambia. His application was accepted with the provision that he had to find some sponsors to fund his travelling expenses. The Wildlife Department was unable to do so, and none of the Banjul organizations he approached could help. When Alpha wrote back to tell Jersey this, he was awarded a scholarship.

'I loved my time at Jersey. I had never travelled outside Gambia before, so I experienced all the process of getting a passport and applying for a visa. The British make it very hard for us to get visas.

'I learned all about conservation in other parts of the world. I made friends with people who I have stayed in correspondence with ever since that time. And I wrote a project about the behaviour of the gorillas.'

When Alpha returned from Jersey in 1988, he found that he had been married in his absence.

'I was a bit surprised,' he admitted. 'I was engaged to another girl and we had a daughter. But this girl was my uncle's daughter, and as I had lived with him for a time my father thought that I owed him a favour. Islam teaches you to respect everything your parents do for you.'

He also found that his Jersey training did not particularly help his career.

'I am the most educated person in the Wildlife Department. But I am still paid very little, and my boss always tells me there is no money to do any of the things I learned about. So I do very little. It is difficult because I have to support my brothers who are still at school and my sisters who have not married and my daughter.'

Most of Alpha's sisters had married and left the compound. There were two young girls whose hair was plaited in stubby spikes around their heads so that they looked like sea mines; one was his sister, the other his daughter. They were the same age. Various tall brothers emerged out of the darkness, shook my hand softly and wandered off to lie down somewhere. Alpha's father, a tiny inert man, sold peanuts in the market by day and lay on the veranda by night listening to the prayers broadcast from the nearby mosque. His mother had the exclusive contract to sell sugar ice at her youngest son's school. She was a magnificent broad-shouldered woman who walked around the compound bare-breasted. She made the sugar ice in the evening with her two daughters and set off for school with her son in the morning. He carried his table and chair on his head, she carried a polystyrene box full of tiny bags of sugar ice.

In the morning we were up at 5.30 with the cocks screeching in the compound. We set off to work through the mud streets between the rusty corrugated iron walls, and joined the general movement to the bus station like any commuter. The main road into Banjul was made of bitumen mixed with sea shells which crumbled away leaving large pot-holes.

Gambia is a tiny country, merely a tidal strip of the River Gambia which flows west out of Senegal. It only exists because the British commandeered the estuary and 200 miles of river so that the French who owned Senegal would not control the slave trade. The country looks like a worm in the side of Senegal, which was probably pretty much how the French saw it.

For some bizarre reason it has been promoted as *the* African holiday resort, and more tourists come to Gambia than to any other African country. What they find when they arrive is simply a line of hotels along a three-mile coastal strip. They generally stay on the beach and do not venture much into the rest of the country. But if they make one trip it will be to the Abuko Game Reserve, the only tourist attraction in the country. Alpha is the warden in charge of the Abuko Reserve.

Although the reserve covers only 100 hectares, it is astonishing that it is there at all. Gambia is one of the most densely populated and impoverished countries in Africa. It is almost perfectly flat, and the west side of the country is an unbroken succession of rusty townships. The reserve is a mini forest with a crocodile pool and a sorry animal collection in the middle. The visitors, who are exclusively tourists, pay 9 dalarsi to enter (60p, equivalent to half the average daily wage). They wander around with expensive cameras and take snap shots of the hyenas, South American parrots and lions, which incongruously have been supplied by Longleat.

Alpha took me to the education centre by the crocodile pool. It was a wooden shack with a number of posters. Most of the posters had been supplied by the World Wildlife Fund, and the RSPB, but there were a number of others including 'Save the Cotswold Heritage', 'Save the Whales' and something about owls and partridges in France. Most of the posters were of no relevance to Gambia.

'I want to educate Gambians,' Alpha said, 'but only schoolchildren come here. Otherwise it's all tourists, mainly from Britain and Scandinavia. I get all these posters from the WWF and people also send me newspaper articles.'

I asked him why there was a Save the Whales poster which would have no meaning for a Gambian schoolchild.

'It's all I have. I don't have Gambian posters. The WWF don't send me anything specific to Gambia. And I also like to show the Scandinavians that although they may criticize Gambia, everything is not so good in their own backyard either.'

Just as the Western world uses Africa as a dumping ground for end-of-the-line products, so it sends off surplus conservation material without stopping to think whether it is appropriate, or making the effort to translate it into the three local languages, Mandinka, Wolof or Fulah.

There is also the problem of local apathy which was well illustrated by Alpha's office. His desk was set in the middle of a room piled high with boxes of slides, posters and a projector.

There were no shelves, so everything was scattered across the floor.

'Do you write to any of the organizations which send you this stuff?'

'No.'

'Do you know who it is at the WWF who is sending it?'

'No, it just arrives.'

'Do you ever reply and tell them what you really need?'

'No.'

When I asked Alpha what incentive he had to work in the reserve, he showed me a list of salaries for the Wildlife Department.

'I earn 630 dalarsi a month, that's £42. Now I am the second most senior person here, I'm on Grade 4. A ranger will be on Grade 1 and will earn 297 dalarsi a month. My boss, Dr Camara, he earns 2,066 dalarsi a month.'

'Where is he?'

'He is currently away on a wildlife conference in Tenerife. You see if you go on a conference you are paid £90 a day living expenses.'

I did some quick calculations.

'So Dr Camara only has to attend a five-day conference and he has earned the equivalent of your annual salary?'

'That's right.'

'How many conferences do you go on?'

'Well, not that many. You see Dr Camara goes on them all.'

I had no reason to suppose that Dr Camara had anything other than wildlife on his mind, but nonetheless I could see another attraction of these conferences. I wondered whether their organizers realized that for some people conservation could easily become less of a draw than hard currency.

'I've had a number of ideas, like I want to print a guide to the reserve with pictures of its animals and trees, but Dr Camara always says there is no money. My friends who work with the tourists just guiding them around earn ten times what I earn. I'm thinking of becoming a tour guide myself.

'You see, I would like to take a second wife, the girl I was engaged to before. But on this salary I can hardly support my first one. I save no money. Dr Camara, he saves a lot of money. When you reach the top at Wildlife you can earn a living.'

The reserve attracts 100,000 visitors a year and raises 900,000 dalarsi, £60,000. It is therefore extremely lucrative but there is no budget for improvements. With laborious paperwork, the gate money just disappears into the Ministry for Water Resources, Forestry and Fisheries.

With nothing to do, or rather with no incentive to do anything, Alpha took me to a football match. He is president of the local football team and walked on to the pitch with a clipboard to sort out the teams. From the no-nonsense way he sent players off and bossed the linesmen around to clear the pitch, I realized he had great organizational talents. If these could be harnessed at work, the Wildlife Department would be a different place.

The pitch was brown mud apart from the four corners where luxuriant weeds grew. Both teams wore red football shirts with Nescafé emblazoned across them. The toss not only decided which team kicked off but also who had to remove their shirts. Some players wore football boots, others went barefoot. There seemed no obvious advantage either way. The game was a series of short sprints and high kicks as the ball bounced wildly off the baked mud or stopped dead in the weeds. Scraps of English punctuated the excited commentaries around me, 'Yellow card' and 'Offside', and at one point Alpha muttered to me in the best manner of an English football manager: 'The lads are very unfit.'

Afterwards we found a little bar which advertised 'Food and Drinkables in a Neat and Tidy Atmosphere'. Inside a string of blue light bulbs hung overhead. The neat and tidy atmosphere consisted of loud drumming music. The fridge had packed up, so we drank warm fizzy beer out of brown bottles. Two rounds of drinks cost a day's worth of Alpha's salary. Alpha was flushed with the success of his team's victory and said that we would go up-river the next day to stay at the Gambian Upriver Chimpanzee Project.

The chimpanzee project is privately funded and is run by Stella

Brewer, the daughter of David Brewer, a Welshman who was Dr Camara's predecessor in the Wildlife Department. Stella travelled around Spain and bought up all the chimpanzees which were being pedalled on the beaches. She took them back to Gambia and released them on an unspoilt island 200 miles upstream in the River Gambia. The island was declared a nature reserve by her father, and is now inhabited by forty chimpanzees who have been trained to live in the wild and have formed their own community. Two researchers live in a camp on the bank opposite the island. They are self-sufficient in their work but they cannot enforce the law, so when they are worried about poachers they contact Alpha. They had recently written to him, and he had promised a visit.

The next day we were picked up by Barra, the Wildlife Department's driver, in a huge Toyota pick-up. We left the rusty walls of Brikama and drove out into scrub savannah. The countryside was flat and dotted with enormous spreading baobab trees. The effect of the rolling grassland and towering shady trees was rather like English parkland. Barra stopped to pick up people on the roadside and negotiated ruthlessly over the price. The roads were deserted apart from the occasional minibus or taxi truck. These were grandly painted and carried Christian slogans on their headboards such as 'God Will Save' and 'God is Able' and the enigmatic misspelling 'Except the Lord'. Barra seemed to know everyone in the country and leaned out of his window to slap hands with the drivers of oncoming vehicles as we passed them. This was particularly precarious as the pot-holes tipped us into each other so that we lurched through the landscape with the pitch and roll of a boat in heavy seas.

Apart from the vultures drifting overhead there was little movement in the countryside. Women were bent over in the ricefields; children in school uniform scuffed their shoes on the edge of the road in the middle of nowhere. Any girl over school age carried a baby in a sling on her back. This was detectable from the front as a pair of tiny pink soles sticking out from either side of her hips. Along the roadside were neat bundles of firewood for sale.

'Mahogany,' Alpha told me. 'We find it burns very well. It gives good long-lasting cooking heat.'

After six hours we drove off the road and followed a footpath through the savannah. The villages we passed typically comprised seven or eight round mud huts. The first tsetse fly bounced across the inside of the windscreen. We came down to the river bank and Barra finally turned the engine off. The river was thick, brown and slow-moving. The low-lying shoreline opposite was jungle. I realized the river was flowing the wrong way.

'It's still tidal up here,' Alpha confirmed. 'The whole country is tidal.'

Barra hollered and immediately set off a chain-reaction of screeching and squawking as baboons and chimpanzees went wild – literally apeshit – on the opposite bank. The tsetse flies zoomed in, biting through my shirt. Unlike mosquitoes which drift gently around you, tsetse flies land with a thump and bite hard and viciously before you can knock them off.

Then we heard an outboard motor, and a small tin boat came round a bend in the river. It was steered by Philippe, a tiny Frenchman wearing the sort of egg-shaped wire-framed glasses worn by Schubert. He wore no shirt and his back was a lumpy rash of insect bites, red and white like rice pudding with jam. His French accent was perfect for exclaiming 'Ah! Ze tzetze fly!' as he slapped at his shoulder-blades. We loaded up the boat and set off along the slow brown river for the camp.

The jungle on the other side of the river turned out to be the chimpanzee island. The squawking and howling of disturbed chimps and baboons continued as we slipped downstream.

Philippe cut the engine and the boat swerved into the shore. There was a short pier and we scrambled up the mud bank to the camp. The camp was built three years ago and has four huts. In the middle stood a large cage. Inside it, swinging by her arms, was a female chimpanzee, the latest acquisition from Spain. Philippe was training her to look for food among the trees. We went over to meet her. She looked at us with beseeching brown eyes and pushed one finger out through the mesh.

'Do not give her too much attention,' Philippe warned.

'It is important that she doesn't trust men.'

She looked at us in silence. Her eyes and the shape of her skull were very human. Despite Philippe's warning, I touched her finger with mine. I was surprised to see she had fingernails. Her hand was black and her finger was hard and rubbery, the texture of an old washing-up glove. Here I stood next to man's closest cousin (we are as closely related to chimpanzees as the African elephant is to the Indian elephant) but entirely unable to communicate. So we just stood in silence and stared into each other's eyes like a couple of young lovers or old drunks.

Her cage was also on the way to the lavatory and when I went there, walking rather quickly as I knew something pretty strong was brewing up in my stomach, I discovered that she had good reason to watch me with such sympathy. I went behind the wicker screen, pulled down my trousers and pants, squatted and presented my bottom to the hole. So far so good. Then the tsetse flies zoomed in.

What do you do when faced by a simultaneous attack of the squits and a swarm of tsetse flies? Well, it's not something I ever want to practise again, but I'm sure there are several alternatives. I squirmed around, flailed my arms and slapped myself all over – none of which had any effect. Tsetse flies bit my neck, arms, thighs and bottom. I panicked, lost my footing, crapped down one leg and nearly slipped into the hole. I saved myself by putting one hand on the ground and kicking the loo roll away from me. I hunkered after it, still farting and crapping intermittently, mopped up my leg and thighs and pulled up my trousers. When I staggered back past her in a muck sweat, the chimp pursed her lips and gently hooted at me.

Over supper in the yellow light of the kerosene lamps, with insects crawling and fluttering all over the mosquito nets above us, the talk was of fixing the pump, finding spare parts for the cooker, receiving mail, gossip about researchers who had just left and the difficulty of buying decent bread. Philippe described how the only edible bread available nearby was just over the river in Senegal. To reach the bakery, he had to pass through customs and have his passport stamped. There was now no room on his passport for any further stamps, so the Senegalese customs officers refused to let him through.

Then we talked of the poachers. They had not been on the island, but they had trapped some colubus monkeys just along the river bank. Philippe thought he knew who they were. Alpha's face assumed the same ponderous expression as in his photographs. He was not going to let them off lightly. He produced the photocopied form he intended to serve on them. We flattened it out on the table between the breadcrumbs.

If the poachers could speak English, they would be frightened men. The form read:

SOLEMN PLEDGE OF INTENT

> I, ... do hereby solemnly pledge that I shall from this date and henceforth abandon any attempt to trade in any way in contravention to the Wildlife Conservation Act 1977, which at all times I loyally observe and respect. I am aware of the contents of the Act and will particularly observe Part VI sections 36–43.
>
> As a measure of my integrity when making this pledge I wish the signing to be made in the presence of and witnessed by His Holiness the Imam Banjul.
>
> Finally I fully appreciate that if I should again transgress the above-mentioned law, the full imposition of the law may be expected as a matter of course. I sign this pledge freely and without any coercion in full knowledge of my action.

THUMB-PRINT

Alpha said he would visit the people and get their thumb-prints. How would he know he had got the right people? He would ask around. With supreme logic he concluded that if they were innocent, they would sign with a clear conscience.

The next day Alpha went off along the river to tackle the poachers. Philippe took me upstream to explore the waterways between the jungle. Visitors are not allowed on the island, so we coasted up alongside it. Philippe cut the engine and whooped a few times. Eventually two chimpanzees stepped out on to the shore and stared at us unswervingly. They stood almost upright, leaning forward on the knuckles of their hands. I was struck by how large they were. Despite all Philippe's whooping they remained implacably grave. We drifted downstream away from them. It was like being seen off by primitive tribesmen.

'If there are other monkeys here why have the chimps had such a bad time?' I asked Philippe. 'I thought they were more intelligent than other monkeys. Why should they go extinct in Gambia?'

'There never were chimps in Gambia,' he said. 'We tried putting them back in the top of Senegal where they came from, but they got attacked by the existing wild ones. So we brought them here.'

I digested this information.

'So this is just like a zoo?' I finally said. 'They're marooned on an island in the middle of nowhere. They're not contributing anything to the wild.'

'You could argue that,' Philippe conceded. 'But at least they're almost self-sufficient and they don't expect chopped-up eggs and bread to eat. If the Senegalese population goes, then these can replace them.'

That evening Philippe's assistant, Boirot, was to give a slide show at a nearby village. We packed up the generator and projector and took the boat up to the first jetty. Alpha was in high spirits as he had secured two suspected poachers' thumb-prints. He admitted that he wasn't sure whether they were those of the particular poachers he was after, but Dr Camara would be pleased. I offered to give him another thumb-print if it would secure a bonus, but he refused. Barra drove us through the savannah to the village. The only lights at the village were the red embers of the braziers which were burning mahogany to roast corn.

The slide show was a great occasion. The entire village, some eighty people, came out of the darkness to watch. A sheet was draped over a mud fence beneath a huge baobab tree and the projector aimed at it from the other side of the road. Barra went off to see to some business. The village chief stood over the projector and grunted loud approval at every slide. Rather nervous in the face of this towering interest, Boirot began his talk. He spoke in Fulah. Whenever there was a picture of an animal, everyone squealed with laughter. The moon was high overhead, the mosquitoes settled down on us and the cicadas roared all around.

After well over two hours headlights appeared down the track. The slide show was spectacularly interrupted by Barra who drove straight through the audience, scattering us piecemeal, and parked right in front of the projector. Apparently oblivious to the distorting green slide over his face, he turned the engine off and began chatting to Alpha. The village waited patiently, slapping and fanning at the mosquitoes, until Philippe finally lost patience and indignantly waved him on. Barra revved up, covered us with hot exhaust and moved on a couple of yards. The village reassembled so they could get a view of the screen.

When the show was finally over, Alpha and the chief had a long public argument. When I later asked him what it was about, he told me that it concerned hippopotamus barriers for the paddy-fields. Alpha said that when he last lectured the village about the government's policy to provide free barriers, nobody was interested. Now they wanted them. It turned out that the chief had not been interested because he thought it would involve a lot of hard work. Now the paddy-fields had been repeatedly invaded by hippos and nobody could scare them away.

'I was just giving him some reflection on that,' Alpha concluded, clearly pleased with his efforts.

When I congratulated Boirot on his performance, he told me why it was so difficult to explain conservation here.

'You see their word for wildlife is *suvo* which means meat. So it's like telling them to conserve their meat, or asking them which meat they prefer. They think I'm crazy.'

So the glorious pictures of chimpanzees and monkeys shrouded by jungle foliage had been enjoyed simply as menus. In fact the pictures of the chimps had been particularly irrelevant as there are none in the wild in Gambia.

But the hippos are a real problem. They swim up the river and climb out to graze in paddy-fields. At the moment people do not have the firepower to kill hippos. A home-made shotgun would simply irritate them, so they munch away unscathed. But if people had the weapons, they would kill them as soon as build a barrier to keep them out or divert them on to their neighbours' paddy-fields.

I pointed out to Alpha that he should turn his attention to the hippos. The chimps were fine on their little island, the villagers did not have to learn how to live with them and they would never poach them. But the villagers had to learn to live with the hippos.

'But they hate the hippos,' he said. 'They do not want to see a slide show of their worst enemy. They want to see nice animals like the chimps and giraffes.'

'They're irrelevant,' I said. 'They need to understand how to live with what they've got. In years to come, they will love seeing pictures of hippos. "They used to be such a problem," they'll say, "but aren't they lovely! How sad that there are none left now."'

'They'd think I was mad,' Alpha said. 'Hippos! They never want to see a hippo again.'

'I'm sure they won't have to wait long.'

We returned to Banjul with mixed feelings. I had seen the only chimpanzees in Gambia, about as relevant as seeing the only pandas in South America; Alpha had extracted two thumb-prints to prove to Dr Camara that his conservation efforts were working. Perhaps best pleased was Barra, who had made about 400 dalarsi from giving people lifts and had filled up the back of the pick-up with mahogany firewood.

Three days later I was in Ghana. Gambia does not have a national airline, so I flew on Nigerian Airways. The flight stopped at Bissau, Conakry and Freetown, soared high over Monrovia, then landed at Abijan and finally arrived at Accra. At each stop I looked out of the window and saw swarms of passengers rushing across the tarmac towards the plane. They were generally very large and wore correspondingly monumental clothes – yards of cloth wrapped around into long dresses, headscarves and totally unsuitable high-heeled slippers. The reason for their running became clear when they fought their way up the stairs into the plane and began looking for seats. At each stop the plane was hopelessly overbooked and the last stragglers, the particularly fat or aged, had to get off and return to the airport. I wondered how long they had been waiting for a flight. Some of them looked old enough to have been waiting all their lives.

The in-flight service was also an eye-opener. There was no sign of an air hostess, no ushering to seats or safety demonstrations, until somewhere between Abijan and Accra a girl in a lime-green suit sprinted down the aisle and neatly threw packets of crisps into our laps from a large cardboard box.

I was delighted and surprised to be met at Accra by Ernest. My last telegram had given a date two days earlier and I had not had the chance to send another.

'How did you know when to meet me?' I asked him.

'No problem. Let's go.' Ernest led the way out of the airport as if he had just been there three minutes. I was to discover that 'No problem' and 'Let's go' were his two favourite expressions, both of them particularly un-African. He was short and broad-shouldered, almost square in fact, and neatly dressed in white trousers and a short-sleeved navy blue shirt. I felt rather ragged beside him.

'No, but really,' I insisted, running alongside him, 'how did you know?'

'I waited for your plane which you weren't on. So I worked out that you'd be on a later one.'

I digested the implications of this. I had arrived two days late on a delayed Nigerian Airways flight.

'I just waited until you arrived,' he said matter-of-factly.

I apologized, deeply embarrassed.

'No problem.' He dismissed my concern. 'This is normal. You saw all those men waiting at the airport? They never know when their friends are coming in. Nobody ever does. Flights are late or cancelled all the time. So we all wait.'

Ghana was originally called the Gold Coast, a name which

derived not from real gold, although some was found there, but from the riches the Europeans earned from trading black gold – slaves. The Gold Coast was the major base for exporting African slaves. In the seventeenth and eighteenth centuries England, Holland, Portugal and, bizarrely, Denmark, all competed for space on the Gold Coast. They built forts in which to store the slaves and defend themselves from each other. There are seventy-six forts along the Ghanaian coast, one every six kilometres.

As well as being immensely profitable for the Europeans, the slave trade also enriched the Africans who supplied the slaves. The Ashantis in the north of Ghana were particularly successful. They gathered together poorer Africans from across West Africa and sold them to the coastal traders. It was a cash-and-carry business – they took the cash and the slaves carried themselves down to the coast. But in 1873, after the end of the slave trade, the British decided that these Ashantis had become too powerful. They invaded their territory and occupied their capital, Kumasi. The Ashantis refused to accept Queen Victoria as their sovereign, regrouped and finally attacked the British in 1900. It was a desperately close-run thing. The British were surrounded and besieged inside the fort at Kumasi for two months until reinforcements arrived.

A letter dated 4 August 1900 from Major Carleston described his journey to relieve the troops at Kumasi:

> Every now and again you are blazed at from the forest by unseen enemy. The path is so slippery that the carriers can hardly keep their footing. Now a fearful smelling swamp. In you go to your knees, boots full of liquid mud. So on for half a mile. After 8 to 16 hours rate 1 mile an hour. Camp. I have 1,000 soldiers and 2,000 carriers huddled in close. Fires lit everywhere. Your eyes stream from the smoke. Bed, and up again at 4 a.m. So on, day after day.

We had a much easier journey up to Kumasi, where Ernest lives, by bus. The ground was cleared of forest and swamps and we drove through a land of brown dry mud.

Ernest's sister had died the previous week and he did not want his parents to know that he had returned home.

'The morgue gives free accommodation for twenty-one days,' he explained, 'then they charge rent. This is very expensive, 2,000 cedis a day. But by then we should have arranged the funeral. The problem is that my parents have asked me to provide the gin and schnapps, but I can't afford them. They think that I'm still waiting for you in Accra.

When we reached Kumasi he took me to a friend's guest-house and slept in the next-door room. 'My parents will not bother me at the zoo, but if I went home they would hear about it.'

Ernest is in charge of Kumasi Zoo which is right in the centre of town. All around is the relentless chaos of African traffic. As such it is a valuable site. It is also the only shaded area in the town. And with ten acres of leafy gardens and a picturesque stream running through the middle, people could come and rest here; schoolchildren could come and learn about their national wildlife. In Japan it would be a beautiful spiritual place.

Relaxation and education, this is Ernest's vision for the future.

At the moment this is some way off. The stream running through the middle consists of untreated sewage, although this does not stop men from washing in it. There is a large swamp containing wild crocodiles which have learned not to go downstream into the town because they get stoned. Ernest pointed out one six feet long sunning itself by the hedge.

'Nice that they're not all captive,' I said to him.

'We can't catch them.' He lobbed a stone and the crocodile slid into the purple-grey water. 'My men are too frightened.'

I had rather preferred it out on the bank where I could see it.

The zoo cages are made of concrete and thick iron bars. Many of them are empty, their occupants having died. The remaining animals – tortoises, two chimps, a baby elephant, dwarf crocodiles and birds of prey – are fed on bananas or day-old chicks depending on whether they are vegetarian or not.

'We need more animals,' Ernest told me. 'The big ones like the elephants, the lions, the leopard and several chimps have died. I am expecting delivery of two lions from a Dutch dealer.'

'Why do you want these big animals?' I asked. 'Why not have smaller animals which you can really look after?'

'You're right. I do not want to have lions. But people in Ghana want to see the big animals. They will only come into the zoo if there are big animals. That is how they measure a zoo. Where are the elephants, the lions, the chimps? I need these animals and then I can start educating people about what they should be thinking. But I cannot educate people if nobody comes in.'

The zoo falls under the Wildlife Department and Ernest is a government employee.

'I have a budget of 1.2 million cedis a year, that's £800. It's October now and guess what I've received? 150,000 cedis! £100! What can you do with £100?'

Ernest could have done nothing. Nobody in Kumasi or in the Wildlife Department would have blamed him if he had sat around lamenting his fate. But in the absence of any government support, he has founded a private zoo committee which obtains funds independently. The private committee had raised £300 which they used to build a wall around the zoo. This protects the animals from being stolen for the cooking pot, and from the exhaust of the traffic outside.

'We also took advantage of the wall to steal some extra land.' Ernest chuckled apologetically. 'We built over some other government land and won ourselves another five acres. There was a great uproar from the government, but one of the members of my committee is well connected in the town and he managed to smooth things over.'

After his return from Jersey, Ernest established an intensive care centre for orphaned animals which are brought to the zoo, he made a deal with the local chicken battery that they would give him the reject day-old chicks and he has the cages cleaned twice a week.

The zoo has no transport so it relies on people to bring it animals. Although he does not like it, Ernest sometimes accepts animals from poachers.

'Sometimes I confiscate them, other times I have to buy them. If I don't take them, they get taken across to the Ivory Coast. The

Ivory Coast has no regard for CITES (the international convention on the trade in endangered species). They ship them over to France. France has no regard for CITES either.

'I bought two porcupines recently. They cost 30,000 cedis each. But they had been badly injured when they were caught and they died after two weeks from internal bleeding. I bought a red duiker in very bad condition. The dealers do not feed them because it is a waste of money. He cost 18,000 cedis and he died too.'

'Couldn't you do it a different way?' I asked.

'Yes.' Ernest looked canny. 'Now I don't pay for two months to see if the animal survives.'

'No, what I meant is to exchange animals with other zoos without paying money to poachers.'

'We have no transport. No other zoo will transport an animal all the way to Ghana and then up to Kumasi. And I cannot contact them. Road works outside the zoo have rendered the telephone ineffective. It has been ineffective for two years now. And zoos give us the wrong sort of animal. There was an American zoo which wanted to give me a grizzly bear. What would a bear do in Ghana? It would boil to death! Let's go!'

Ghanaian men walk hand in hand, and I found it oddly touching to have Ernest grab my fingers between his as he showed me around the zoo. When they shake hands they hold them for a long time and only reluctantly let go with a vigorous snap of each other's fingers.

Ernest led me to the zoo café where we ordered Maltina, a foaming black drink which is made by and looks like Guinness. It comes in a stout brown bottle but is non-alcoholic. The first sip tastes like a Malteser, delicious. The rest of the glass tastes of Bovril and bran flakes, not so delicious but certainly memorable.

'What about catching animals in the wild?' I asked Ernest. 'There must be endangered Ghanaian animals which you could breed here.'

'I'm not so good at breeding yet,' Ernest confessed. 'The zoo is mainly to show off animals and then they die. But some monkeys had a baby once.

'I went on an animal-collecting expedition last year.' He took a deep swig of Maltina. 'Never again. These bloody animals. We had no transportation so we caught buses. We were going after porcupines so we were loaded down with nets and boxes. We arrived at this place. It was so hot. God, it was hot. We walked in the heat of the sun all day. But we found nothing.'

'Aren't porcupines nocturnal?' I asked.

'Exactly. Bloody nocturnal. So we found a burrow and we dug a big hole. Nothing. We had no food and the village charged us 2,000 cedis for a meal, that's a day's wage. We gave up after three days. Let's go!'

There is easy tolerance of all religions in Ghana. Ernest himself professed to be Presbyterian, 'A moderate Presbyterian I would say.' One of the curators at the zoo was Muslim. Ernest enjoyed teasing him about this: 'You Mohammedans never do any work. You spend all day praying with your heads on the ground. Like a lot of chickens! Like fowls!'

The men in Kumasi wear bright-coloured togas, but today as we walked around the streets I noticed they were wearing black ones. The women wore black or red and black long dresses which gave them an exciting flamenco look.

'Saturday is funeral day,' Ernest explained. 'Everyone is wearing black because they will be going to a funeral somewhere.'

It is an indication of the size of the average family that each one has a death practically every week. Ernest's family tree which he had drawn for me the previous evening had spread to sixty first cousins. At the sight of all these mourners, Ernest became slightly edgy. He had only a week left in which to produce the gin and the schnapps.

To show me what happened, he took me to a funeral celebration held on a football pitch on the edge of town. The entire pitch was crowded with mourners. All the men wore black or indigo togas. They also wore black lacquered flip-flops with bright orange pom-poms over the big toe. It was raining slightly, and the sight of so much black, red and indigo cloth set against wet black skin was sinister and seductive.

A chief walked through the crowd. A carved stool was carried

Porcupine
"hystrix cristata"

in front of him, and an umbrella held over him from behind. He carried a gold staff and wore an embroidered toga of black and indigo which hung around him in folds which were dark, rich and clinging as bats' wings. Two men beside him carried bottles of gin and schnapps. Ernest explained what happened.

'When you leave your house to collect the body from the morgue, the family elders pour gin and schnapps on the ground and there are prayers. You repeat this at the morgue and then again at the cemetery. Everyone comes to say goodbye at the grave and throws money on the body. Then they retire and the family gather the money from the body and pour gin into the coffin. Then they bury it.'

'And this is a Presbyterian ceremony?'

'No, but it has Presbyterian elements.'

'Where does the tradition of the gin and schnapps come from? You can't have had those before the British came.'

'No, exactly. Those are the Presbyterian traditions. You should know that,' he said accusingly.

Amongst the swarm of black I spotted dashes of colour. Some people were wearing bright patterned head-dresses with clusters of what looked like eggs hanging off them.

'They are eggshells,' Ernest confirmed. 'Those are family of the deceased. They wear eggs to show how brittle life is – it can be crushed just like an egg.'

'Yes, we have a similar saying: You can't make an omelette without breaking eggs.'

'Is that Presbyterian?'

Although I denied it, I could see from Ernest's gratified smile that it might well be slipped into his sister's funeral service as an authentic Presbyterian prayer.

We went to a restaurant that night. As we sat eating chicken with plantain and palm oil, Ernest outlined his plans for the zoo.

'You see a government zoo is difficult,' he explained between mouthfuls. 'My staff just see it as a job. There is no money and there is no motivation. I met Gerald Durrell and I looked around his zoo in Jersey. Usually when a man is that successful, everyone just wants to eat off his plate. But his staff are all trying to achieve things for themselves. That is very unusual.

'I would like to build up a team like that. But my staff do not care. They just want to earn their money and go home. Visitors to the zoo do not care. They just want to see the big animals and go home.

'But I will change this. You come back in two years. I will have an education centre in the zoo, and everyone will see what I am doing. At the moment nobody understands what is going on.'

On my last day with Ernest he took me to the Ashanti war museum. It was predominantly a collection of guns which the British had used to kill the Ashantis in 1900, and then, looking pretty much the same, guns which the Ashantis had used in the Second World War when they had been called up to fight. They had fought against the Italians in Abyssinia and against the Japanese in Burma. Pictures of the Ashanti troops showed unsmiling soldiers wearing heavy coats, puttees around their shins and bare feet splayed out.

'The English thought the Ashantis would be good at fighting in the jungle. This is why they chose us to fight in Burma. Look at this drum.' Ernest picked up what looked like a bent chicken bone and scraped it across the skin of a drum. It made a deep-throated rumbling roar like a lion.

'A lion. We would stand in the edge of the forest and do this. The English all got very scared. It frightened the Japanese in Burma too. They thought it was a tiger.'

Ernest kept on scraping away at the skin. The roar echoed around the museum until I couldn't tell what direction it was coming from. I understood why it scared soldiers.

'But now it's useless,' he said.

'Why? Because soldiers have better guns?'

'No. Because there are no more lions here. And because there is no more forest for them. There is not even an edge of the forest for us to stand in to hide.'

On the way to the airport the next day I asked if we could stop at an alcohol shop. Ernest chose a bottle of gin called Akpeteshi and a bottle of WF Schnapps. 'Make it a Special Occasion!'

exhorted the label in bold red capitals.

'Make sure your sister is out of the morgue before you drink this stuff,' I said.

'Don't go to Nigeria. Come to her funeral.' Ernest shook the bottles encouragingly in my face. 'I can now go back to my parents. Next Saturday we will bury my sister. It will be a good day for her. Come back and visit me soon. You will see many changes.'

The immigration officer at Lagos picked up my passport and shook it in my face with the same gesture as Ernest had shaken his bottle of schnapps.

'What do you have for me?' he asked.

'What do you mean?'

'I've stamped your passport. I needn't have done. Give me some money.'

'But I've got a visa.' I remembered the queue at the Nigerian Embassy. 'Anyway, isn't stamping passports your job?'

The queue behind me was growing impatient. He waved me through, an awkward customer.

I was due to visit Matthew Dore in Benin City, but I only had a PO box number for his address. There is no such thing as directory enquiries in Nigeria, and I had no idea whether he was expecting me. Unable to get any sense out of the telephone operator, unable to catch a connecting flight to Benin City, and unable to bear the men swarming assiduously around me any longer, I caught a taxi for a smidgen over four times the normal fare and threw myself on to the hospitality of my only contact in Lagos, Judge Lardner.

The taxi stopped at a house which I assumed was a restaurant, for crates of Fanta and beer were being stacked up outside.

'No, no, no,' the beaming judge assured me, 'it is my daughter Bola's wedding tomorrow. You have arrived just in time. Are you Anglican? Excellent, it will be an Anglican service.'

In the event the wedding was about as Anglican as Ernest's sister's funeral was going to be Presbyterian. It was held in the Church of Christ the Redeemer. The congregation looked spectacular. The men wore voluminous white agbadas topped with little embroidered fezes. The women wore high-shouldered dresses of shimmering pinks and yellows, their matching headscarves towering square and monumental above them. The overall impression was of heaps of Christmas presents piled around me. Halfway through the service a rainstorm broke overhead and all the windows crashed shut. We had only sung seven of the eleven hymns when Bola and her new husband Ayo abruptly walked out.

As the wedding party sheltered from the rain in the porch, a number of beggars began crawling between us. They wore flip-flops on their hands and pulled their twisted knobbled legs behind them. Taxi-drivers stopped and began pulling at the arms of guests to drag them into their taxis. My taxi had apparently been firebombed recently – the inside was burned black, wires hung from the roof and my seat was no longer attached to the floor.

The first reception was at a hotel. There were two Masters of Ceremony who gave an alternating series of deeply sycophantic speeches about the Chairman of Ceremony, a government minister. Bola and Ayo received scant attention.

By the afternoon we were back at Judge Lardner's house. We ate lunch under tents on the road outside. Water dripped over the tables and the downpour had caused the sewers along the edge of the road to overflow. The beggars caught up with us and crawled under the tables. A band of nomadic Yoruba drummers arrived and stood drumming frantically at each table until they were paid to go away.

By the end of the afternoon the lavatory was blocked, bottles were strewn across the carpet, plates overturned and someone had been sick in the basin. Ayo and his friends left to set up their own party. Judge Lardner buttonholed me and asked where I was going to stay in Benin City.

'Mr Dore?'

I nodded.

'I do not know him. It is dangerous to visit someone you do not know and who is not expecting you. I will ring up my friend Judge Akpovi in Benin City. He will look after you.'

Just before midnight Ayo returned, resplendent in a bright yellow agbada and a silver fez, and led Bola out of her parents' house. We piled into decrepit cars and tore across Lagos after them. We heard the drumming from the house long before we could find our way in. Inside, people on the dance floor were plastering each other with money. If you liked the look of someone, you slapped banknotes on their forehead. Bola and Ayo were covered with money all night. We ate roast mutton and dried fish, and drank warm beer and sweet cognac. I left around four in the morning. Judge Lardner was still dancing.

Five hours later I caught the plane to Benin City. I was one of three people on the Fokker and was surprised when someone stepped forward to greet me at the deserted airport. It was Judge Akpovi.

'Judge Lardner telephoned me this morning. I have checked up on Matthew Dore and he is perfectly alright. You will stay at his house and he will look after you.

'Actually, I had to send his uncle to prison several times but he can tell you all about that. Also his grandfather was a local prince around here when the British invaded. I daresay he can tell you about that too. We can call him up when you've rested.'

When I expressed my surprise about the whirligig last two days, he patted my arm gently. 'This is how things are done in Nigeria.'

'Yes, my uncle was a very wild man,' Matthew agreed when he arrived at Judge Akpovi's house. 'He was always in trouble.'

'He was very handsome,' the judge said. 'I liked him a lot. He just had to go to jail a couple of times to calm down.'

'He died a couple of years back,' Matthew told him.

'I'm sorry to hear that.'

'Yes, someone threw acid all over him, gave him an acid bath.'

The judge shook his head.

'Well, I hope that man went to prison, although I don't remember such a case.'

'No, he ran away and was never caught.'

Matthew took me back to his house. It was a large bungalow built on colonial lines. The rooms were spacious and cool. In the front room four sofas faced each other and a fan stood to one side, its face turning back and forth like a sunflower. A stereo system occupied pride of place. Matthew saw me looking at it.

'I bought that in America,'

I wondered whether the Gambian £90 a day living allowance was in force in Nigeria, but Matthew put me right.

'I studied for a year in America. I worked by night as a researcher. The biology lab was experimenting with the effects of radiation on rats. I used to take the rats out of the radiation chamber and weigh them. Nobody else wanted to do that job, but I didn't mind. It was the sort of money I could never earn anywhere else, $90 a day. I bought this stereo with the proceeds, and also an encyclopaedia for my children. I shipped home five crates of books as you cannot get books here. So I didn't mind exchanging a little dose of radiation for all these books.'

Matthew joined the Department of Forestry within the Ministry of Agriculture and Natural Resources after studying biology at Benin City University, one of the best in West Africa. Initially he was a forestry officer but he moved to the Wildlife Division in 1980.

'You must understand that wildlife is a new thing for Nigeria. I am the first generation of wildlife officers. The rest of the department is only interested in timber. They do not really see the link between wildlife and forestry.

'When I want to prosecute a man who has been poaching, they say "What has this man done? He has killed some animals to eat them? Why, he is just trying to feed his family. Let the poor man be." And I find it hard to disagree with this.

'Around Benin City, the villagers and indeed some of the town people rely on wildlife for their food. I have worked out from wildlife available in the market that people take 25 per cent of their meat requirements from wildlife. And of course when the economy gets worse, which it has, they rely even more on poaching wildlife. Lots of people go out into the forest, and they're not going to look at the trees!'

Matthew has a staff of seven in the Wildlife Department. He sits in an office with crocodile skins around the walls and an electric bell hanging down on a wire over his head. He pressed this to call his secretary and he asked her to retrieve the file on his crocodile reserve and farm project.

'Look through this. It is a good example of why nothing gets done here.'

The file was a series of letters concerning a proposal by Matthew to build a crocodile reserve. It is illegal to trade in any form of wild crocodile products, so Matthew was proposing a scheme whereby people farmed them. This would be in the form of a reserve which would also release crocodiles back into the mangrove swamps at the delta of the River Niger. The villagers would have a stake in the reserve and share the profits from selling the farmed skins. They would be taught that there was a value in sustaining the crocodile population rather than in killing all the young ones.

Matthew had gathered together impressively detailed quotes for building the reserve and had meticulously filed all the correspondence with those concerned – the chief of the local village, the builders, the suppliers of raw materials, other crocodile-farming experts and food suppliers. But the file was topped by one brief letter from the head of the Forestry Department which dismissed the idea. The file stopped there. A perfectly good scheme to increase the numbers of highly endangered crocodiles was now filed away.

'This man knows nothing about wildlife,' Matthew said. 'He just wants to cut down as many trees as possible. For him wildlife is a new idea and not one that he understands. So I cannot proceed.'

But Matthew is still trying.

'One of the things Jersey taught me is never to take no for an answer. They said that everyone will always tell you that something is impossible, but it never is. In the meantime I have set up a small crocodile farm in the grounds here. Let me show you.'

Sure enough there was a small enclosure with seven or eight crocodiles basking alongside a square pool. At the sight of Matthew in his white kaftan and black velvet fez, they slithered into the water.

'Crocodiles eat animal protein. I have found out that the cheapest source of animal protein is snails. So I farm snails here to feed the crocodiles.'

'Where did these crocodiles come from?' I asked.

'They were on sale in the market. It is illegal but what can you do?'

Matthew took me to the market where we found five crocodiles for sale. Their feet and mouths were bound up with vines, so they lay there looking horribly vulnerable. One had blood trickling from its mouth.

'They catch them on hooks baited with rotten meat.'

'Can't you put a stop to this? Can't you arrest them or fine them?'

'No. You see they would just sell them somewhere else. And to arrest them I need a permit from the head of the department. And as I said, he is not interested in wildlife, he is just interested in forestry.

'What I want to do is approach it a different way. If I can set up a reserve, I will show them that they can make more money from farming crocodiles than from catching them wild. Look how small these wretched creatures are. Nobody in Nigeria thinks about animals as a charity like they do in England. They purely want to make the most profit out of them. So if you want to save crocodiles, then you have to choose the way which makes money. No other way will do.'

The Ministry of Agriculture and Natural Resources is too unwieldy to convey effectively to people the idea of conservation. But there is one mechanism which Matthew feels may be more appropriate to communicate with large numbers of people, the royal family of Benin City. There is a large palace in the middle of the city where the Oba and his court still live.

The Oba is the king, but his function is now purely ceremonial as the military government has taken all executive power in the country. However, he still owns a good deal of land in Bendel State, and a number of people, particularly the elderly, see him as their ruler. If the Oba can be persuaded to convey some of the reasons for conservation, then the idea may stick. Military dictatorships come and go, and nowhere more quickly than in Nigeria which has seen eight military coups since Independence in 1961, but the Oba remains a constant figure.

We went to the Oba's palace to investigate. We were shown into a side office where a charming old man rose from behind his desk to welcome us. He was Prince Eweka, an uncle of the current Oba.

'What did you say your name was? Dore?'

'Yes, sir.'

'Are you related to Prince Dore Numa?'

'Yes, sir, he was my grandfather.'

'Was he indeed?' Prince Eweka looked severe. 'He did us a great deal of damage. He was bought off by the British when they invaded Benin in 1900.'

He and Matthew then embarked on a fierce argument about Prince Dore Numa. Matthew reckoned that he had led a faction off to the River Niger delta to found his own principality where he had made a treaty with the British. Prince Eweka countered with the accusation that he had merely fled because the Oba had not forgiven him for siding with the British. The Prince skipped over to his bookshelf and pulled out a history of Benin City.

'This is the man.'

The picture showed a vast man wearing what looked like a maternity dress.

'Yes,' Matthew agreed proudly, 'he was unable to get through many doors on account of his size.'

The Prince and Matthew agreed to differ over Dore Numa's *realpolitik*, and after a while we took our leave. Matthew was highly excited by the discussion.

'I didn't mention my idea about wildlife because it would have been premature. We needed to have that conversation first. Also it is good to keep him guessing. He knows that I want something but he is not sure what. He will look forward to my next visit.'

I realized how wrong my first impressions of the country had been. Among African countries Nigeria has an unrivalled reputation for aggression and corruption. The most aggressive and obviously corrupt person I met was the immigration officer at the airport. Once I had penetrated the surface of the country, I had been looked after with far-reaching generosity. I wondered if I would have invited a scruffy Nigerian with a rucksack in off the street if my daughter was being married the next day.

When I left, Matthew was still thinking about the Oba.

'If we can resolve the question of Prince Numa that's good. But I wonder whether they will have heard of my uncle? That would not be so good.'

'Perhaps Judge Akpovi could put in a good word?'

'Yes, that's an excellent idea. Judge Akpovi. I bet he believes in wildlife.'

I could see the *realpolitik* of conservation was taking a turn for the better in Nigeria.

On the plane home I sat next to a large Nigerian. He put his crocodile-skin briefcase in the locker overhead, eased off his tight lizard-skin shoes and opened the in-flight magazine. He was not wearing tortoiseshell glasses, but his watch had a crocodile-skin strap. We talked about the politics of Nigeria and then my trip to Benin City. I asked what he thought of wildlife.

'I love it. I like crocodiles and all those things.'

'Why do you wear crocodile skin then? Isn't it illegal?'

'No,' he said indignantly, stroking his watch-strap. 'Crocodiles aren't illegal. I wear it because I like crocodiles.'

FOUR

THE DURRELLS IN MADAGASCAR

FROGS' LEGS AND OYSTERS IN ANTANANARIVO – THE BEARDED MEN AT WWF – AMBATONDRAZAKA AND THE HUNT FOR GENTLE LEMURS – MIHANTA AND THE THOROUGHLY EATEN ZEBU – LEMUR PISS AND ROTTEN BANANAS, THE TRAIN JOURNEY BACK – THE STOLEN WHEELCHAIR AT MORONDAVA – FLIES, SWEAT BEES AND HOT BEER – MY RELUCTANT HUNT FOR GIANT JUMPING RATS – SCREECHING AT THE FOREST, THE WORLD'S MOST FUTILE EXERCISE – GERMAIN RAKOTOBEARISON'S GIANT TORTOISES – HIBERNATION, BUGGERY AND THE PRICE OF RICE – TORTOISE PHILOSOPHY – THE USELESS LANDSCAPE – A BOWL OF FLIES AT THE AMBASSADOR'S PARTY

'It's rather like eating baby Margot Fonteyns,' Gerry said apologetically. He held up a pair of frogs' legs, twirled them about in a pirouette and bit into the meat of one thigh. 'Madagascar is the only place a good conservationist can eat frogs' legs. They've been introduced here from India and are gobbling up all the native Malagasy frogs so it's ecologically essential to eat as many as possible. How are your oysters?'

We had at last met for lunch in the Hotel Colbert. Inside the restaurant it was hard to believe that we were in Madagascar. Waiters in maroon bum freezers and black bow-ties shook open our heavy napkins, handed out impressively embossed menus and stood back a pace as Gerry tasted the local wine.

'I could happily live in Madagascar.' Gerry picked up another pair of frogs' legs. 'It has all the good things of France without the

French – croissants and baguette for breakfast, patisseries and coffee, oysters and frogs' legs, even steak tartar and creme brulée. They make their own wine which is entirely unpronounceable but perfectly drinkable, and excellent whisky. They speak atrocious French which suits me fine, the people are charming and graceful, and of course there are the most extraordinary animals and plants a naturalist could wish for.

'Does anyone want any of these frogs' legs? I can't possibly finish them all.' He looked across at my plate. 'I'll swap two for an oyster.'

We had a table in the corner window. Outside, the red rooftops of Antananarivo tumbled in a ramshackle way down the hillside below us. Antananarivo, 'Tana', is the capital of Madagascar. It is set on a plateau in the middle of the long range of mountains which forms the spiny backbone of the island. The houses in Tana are built of shabby red brick and are tall and thin with steep gables and crooked pillars which support improbable balconies. The city is set around an outcrop of rocks, and cobbled hairpin bends and flights of steps link the different levels so that it seems less like an African city than like a Tuscan hill town. Down on the plain, green paddy-fields invade the edges of the city and the irrigation canals are choked with water hyacinths.

Just as the Nigerian Embassy had given me a glimpse of Nigeria, the Malagasy Consulate gave me a sneak preview of Madagascar, the most remote country I would visit armed only with a fixed date for lunch with Gerry, and my wife Araminta who had improbably chosen to take her annual holiday on this trip. Madagascar's formal name is the Repoblika Demokratika Malagasy which has chilling Stalinist overtones. I imagined a faceless concrete consulate stuffed with closed-circuit cameras and listening bugs. The address is 12 Pennard Road, London W12. W12? What sort of consulate is found in a small street of terraced red-brick houses around the back of Shepherd's Bush? A green, red and white pennant denoted that it really was a consulate otherwise I would have assumed that it was a normal house. I waited in a normal sitting-room and was then invited into a normal dining-room where a pretty, slim Malagasy lady shyly motioned me to a seat. She had wavy black hair and honey-gold skin which was typical Malagasy; many of them are Polynesians rather than Africans.

'Are you prepared for your journey?' she asked. 'It is a big country.'

'Yes, the fourth largest island in the world.' I gaily recited the only statistic I knew about Madagascar.

'It's as big as France, Belgium and Luxembourg combined,' she said proudly.

She jotted down our names and stamped a colossal inky black visa which stained through two pages in our passports.

When we arrived at Tana, I found this same apparently fearsome bureaucracy which evaporated at the touch of human contact. We filled out imposing forms declaring our state of health, the amount of currency we had and the purpose of our visit, all of which were absent-mindedly collected by a smiling customs man who looked genuinely pleased to see us. The drive into Tana was dramatic. Perhaps because the city is built up on granite rocks it attracts extraordinary thunderstorms. The sky darkened to a bruised purple and blue, and lightning began bouncing between the clouds. The warm sepia brick houses were transformed to stark monochrome as the lightning flashed on and off. Throughout West Africa I had not seen any brick buildings, and certainly none above a single storey high with balconies and balustrades. We were emphatically not in Africa. 'It's like Kathmandu,' Araminta said. And the people were emphatically not African either. The men wore straw hats, shirts like checked table-cloths, baggy trousers and flip-flops. The women wore an odd collection of Oxfam clothes and lambas, which are cotton shawls worn as shawls, skirts, or to carry babies or fruit. Like the lady in the Malagasy Consulate, they were tiny and slim with fine, cat-like faces.

Tana was established as the country's capital by King Andrianampoinimerina in 1795. If that name seems long, take a deep breath. It is a shortened version of his full name – Andrianampoinimerinandriantsimitoviaminandrianpanjaka. The

Malagasy have the extraordinary habit of using several words where one will do, in fact several words as long as your arm where one will do.

At the airport I had bought a *Malagasy-Englisy Diksionera,* printed by the Lutheran Press in 1969. Flicking through it I realized I was never going to speak Malagasy. A simple word like 'zoo' is '*saha misy bibidia hojeren ny mpitsangantsangana*'. I painstakingly looked up each word in the Malagasy section and cobbled together a translation: 'a field where animals can be looked at by walking people'. A word like X-ray is '*taratra ateraky ny herimbaratra ka tsy hita maso nefa tanteraka hatrany anaty*' which is something about a beam of light invisible to the human eye which must be withstood with great courage.

That written Malagasy is so preposterous can partly be blamed on an Irish sergeant, James Hastie, who came from Mauritius in 1822 to tutor two Malagasy princes. The London Missionary Society was in the process of writing down the language, which is essentially Polynesian, in the Latin alphabet. Sergeant Hastie helped them. At the time, the king, Radama I, was being tutored by a Frenchman, Monsieur Robin. It would have been too rude to exclude the Frenchman from the project, so his advice was also solicited. Predictably Sergeant Hastie and Monsieur Robin disagreed over pronounciation. There was stalemate until (so the story goes) the king decreed an inspired compromise that the consonants should be pronounced as in English, the vowels as in French. Thus a truly unique written language evolved which had nothing to do with the spoken language. Written Malagasy phonetically reproduces a Polynesian-based dialect in the Latin alphabet and then puts it through a mangle of French vowels and Irish consonants. This sounds plausible, if crazy, until you try to pronounce any word with English (or, even funnier, Irish) consonants and French vowels. Try even a simple name, 'Radama', then move on to a full-blown Malagasy word such as 'Antananarivo'.

All of which proves that extraordinary things happen in Madagascar. And this is true of the Malagasy animals. Eighty million years ago, when dinosaurs were in their prime, the great land mass of Gondwanaland split up into Africa, South America, Asia and Australia. A splinter separated from the African coast – Madagascar. After the dinosaurs disappeared, mammals emerged across the world and evolved into all shapes and sizes, including the primate. An early primate model was the lemur. But across the world a stronger, more aggressive cousin of the lemur developed, the monkey. Monkeys competed for the same space as the lemurs and drove them to extinction apart from some nocturnal types. However, for some reason monkeys never emerged in Madagascar, which left all the lemurs happily intact.

Madagascar bypassed all the evolutionary changes which then transformed the rest of the world. There were no monkeys, and without monkeys there were none of the monkey's other cousins, chimpanzees and gorillas, and so none of their particularly aggressive cousins – *Homo sapiens*. For 80 million years Madagascar lived in a time warp with animals and plants which were obsolete everywhere else in the world.

The first modern primates – Polynesian settlers – only arrived in Madagascar around AD 900. Since then they have inflicted their customary damage and 80 million years' worth of unique evolution has been brought up to date – 90 per cent of the Malagasy forest has been chopped down and half of the forty original species of lemur have been destroyed. Despite this abrupt introduction to the modern world, Madagascar is still the home of animals which elsewhere are only found as fossils.

The most obvious of these extraordinary animals are the twenty surviving species of lemur. But of these, several species are now perilously close to extinction – which is why Gerry was there and why we were sitting down to eat frogs' legs at the Hotel Colbert.

Gerry and Lee had just returned to Tana after six weeks in a camp in the north-east of the island where they had been hunting the aye-aye, probably the most endangered lemur of all. As aye-ayes are shy and nocturnal, it is difficult to know how many are left. Gerry and Lee, a team of assistants and a camera crew had spent five weeks searching for them. There are so few aye-ayes that none were found for five weeks. In the fifth week the cameraman had been airlifted to an army hospital with cerebral malaria, blood poisoning and hepatitis. The film budget ran out and the rest of the film crew flew home. But the next week two aye-ayes were brought in by villagers and five were caught by Gerry's assistants. The world's captive population of aye-ayes had been doubled at a stroke, the first step towards securing their future.

The day we arrived, Gerry and Lee had just packed off the aye-ayes at the airport and were recovering from prolonged negotiations with Malagasy bureaucracy over export licences. Araminta and I were to join them on a trip to Lake Aloatra to look for the almost equally endangered gentle lemurs. Araminta would then go home leaving me to help the Durrells trap giant jumping rats in the south-west.

We began to talk about the giant jumping rats, and Gerry pointed out to Araminta what fun she would be missing.

'They're huge.' He made enveloping gestures with his arms. 'They'll leap up and whip out your throat as soon as look at you.'

'Why do you want them in your zoo?' Araminta asked.

'Because they're rare, almost extinct.'

Araminta looked as if she believed they should be left to get on with their extinction.

'What about the lemurs?' I fingered my throat gingerly.

'The gentle lemurs . . .' Gerry began.

'Let me answer this one,' Lee interrupted. Lee studied lemurs for two years in a remote forest in the south of Madagascar. We leaned forward to hear her opinion.

'They're so cute,' she said. 'You'll just love them.'

As an economy drive or simply through negligence, the Soviet Union cut off funds to Madagascar in the late 1980s. Western foreign aid has gleefully moved in instead. Since it is still very difficult to travel around the country, most overseas aid reps are happy to stay in Tana and discuss the country's problems in the comfort of the Hotel Colbert where there is cold beer, hot water and week-old newspapers. To see who is in town, you just have to sit in the front bar. Seven o'clock is the witching hour when everyone meets for drinks. Lee took us along to introduce us to the world in general.

Gerry refused to appear in the front bar as he dislikes conservationists so much.

'They talk about conservation all day, until the yaks come home. *Yak, yak, yak*. But most of the time they're just talking about each other. It's like an English village – they're all watching one another, twitching back the net curtains. They never get out anywhere and actually do anything.'

So he shuffled off to his bedroom.

The three of us sat in the bar. We smoked Good Look Malagasy cigarettes, drank Three Horses beer and watched the bar fill up. It was rather like being in a bird hide. Lee pointed out the various specimens. They were talking either to soft-spoken and inscrutable Malagasy or to other sunburned foreigners, *vazaha*.

'That's when they want to find out what's really going on,' Lee said. 'The one with the thick straight moustache is from PNUD. He's talking to the American rep from ODA. The one drinking strawberry juice is from the World Bank. He's talking to someone from the Ministry of Agriculture. There's FAO and USAID over there. And I think that's Conservation International and Coopération Suisse. These are just the conservation people.'

'How do they know they're not all funding the same project?'

'Well, they don't. A lot of time is spent trying to work out what everyone else is up to.'

I wondered what sense the Malagasy made of this jungle of acronyms.

The WWF is also active in Madagascar and as luck would have it the entire team was sitting in one corner of the bar. Lee introduced us around the table – Paul Siegel, heavy beard; Martin Nichol, medium beard; Ira Amstadter, monumental beard; John Hough, light beard; and Françoise (the only Malagasy) no beard. Sorting out their business cards I realized that seniority paralleled beard size. They all wore Panda emblems on their collars. Ira's was depicted in gold, Paul's was black and gold and worn as an earring, the others were black and white, natural panda colours.

I asked Paul a vague introductory question along the lines of how things were going. Thin, bespectacled and hyperactive, he pounced on my casual remark.

'I'm pleased you asked me that, an excellent question. There are just', he counted on his fingers, 'seven points I would like to make on that one.'

I ducked my head in my beer and lit a cigarette. Paul talked without drawing breath for the length of a cigarette. I was just going to pitch in with another question and take another cigarette, when Ira held up an interjectory hand like a Red Indian greeting.

'Let's eat.'

At this point Lee went off to look after Gerry, and Araminta and I joined the WWF team for dinner.

We went outside to a huge white WWF jeep. From the shadows all manner of people converged on us. We brushed off the first wave of street vendors offering newspapers, toys and embroidered table-cloths. There was one man encased in leather trunks, another with a set of bookshelves towering on his head. I wondered whoever made a spontaneous purchase of bookshelves on their way to dinner – clearly enough to keep him in business. The beggars were more persistent. They had the most to lose.

'Anyone here got a 100?' Paul fumbled for the car keys. 'John, got a 100? Give it to that one. No, not her. The one with the gooey eye.'

This discrimination caused even more outrage than if we had flatly refused the lot of them. A hopelessly crippled girl with a baby pressed herself against the window.

'Monsieur,' she wailed, *'je suis malade.'*

'Je suis aussi malade.' Paul revved up.

'La vie est difficile.'

'Bien sur, pour moi aussi.'

'Vous n'est pas très gentil . . .' was the last we heard as her face slid away down the window.

Paul hunched over the wheel, swerving fast around the cobbled corners. At one point he almost knocked over a boy crossing the street.

'You know what?' he yelled over his shoulder. 'These kids

ome people are real envious. "Man! Why should that George Antoine go to Jersey? All he does feed parrots all day. That's a child's job." But it shows that what I do is important. None of ese builders on St Lucia gets to fly off to Britain to study how to build. And their houses will robably blow down in the next hurricane!'

ıema Kerr, the head of Hope Zoo in Kingston, Jamaica, where a Rasta committed suicide by mping into the lions' cage, boys pelt the crocodiles with mangoes, and everyone hates the akes. Rhema has studied the Jamaican coney, an elusive nocturnal rodent which Gerry bet I uldn't write more than a line on.

Jeremy Mallinson outside the Brazilian forest. On seeing a frog receive its first and last lesson i
the basics of evolution he commented: 'It's a jungle out there.'

José follows the black lion tamarins all day by radio tracking. There are less than 350 black lio
tamarins left in the forest.

Ernest Lamptey runs his zoo in Ghana on an annual budget of £100. The telephone has not worked in living memory.

Crocodiles for sale in a Nigerian market. There are no more big ones left.

Gerry finds a lemur in a Malagasy village by Lake Alaotra: 'She's a skinny old thing, ribs like a zebu cow. But beggars can't be choosers – look at me and you.'

A Malagasy tomb. In many parts of Madagascar families celebrate *famadihana*, in which they open the tombs, bring out the bones and dance with them. The ancestors are then expected to exert their influence over the weather, the crops and the health of the ubiquitous zebu cows.

Гhere are eight kinds of baobab tree in Madagascar compared with one throughout Africa. In :imes of drought the villagers cut them down so that their cattle can munch the bark, which ıolds water, to quench their thirst.

n a rare fly-free moment Gerry and Lee show off tortoises which they trapped by speed of foot.

Harry Andrews holds up a young mugger crocodile. Its snout is tied up because a few minutes earlier it had bitten him.

Some of the 3,000 crocodiles Harry has bred. There is nowhere in India to put them back.

Paramananda Lahan – 'Paramananda' means 'very much cheerful'. Not so very much cheerfully, he believes that the Indian elephant and rhino will be extinct within twenty-five years.

Paramananda and I go on an anti-poaching patrol armed with two shotguns and eight cartridges. Luckily, we didn't find any poachers.

Marlynn Mendoza taking me to her office in the Department of Environment and Natural Resources. She works in an intricate eco-system of bureaucracy which supervises a colossal amount of self-perpetuating paper.

My eyeball-to-eyeball encounter with a monkey-eating eagle – one of the largest eagles in the world. This one mates with a human. I had a headache.

jump under your wheels to claim the insurance off you. Desperate.' He looked accusingly at the boy who had just scampered out of the way. 'That kid's worth two hectares of rain forest.'

We crowded into the restaurant. All the diners were white apart from Françoise.

'Hey! Will you look at these prices!' Everyone looked at the menu with self-congratulation. Paul carried on where he had left off and described how the WWF was moving away from merely saving animals to looking at the problems of grasslands and urbanization.

'Ninety per cent of Madagascar is now grassland. If that can be better utilized with higher yielding crops and alternative trees, there will be less pressure on the remaining forest. People don't cut down trees because they hate trees. We cannot just defend a patch of forest against all comers; if we did, we'd be left with a few reserves protected by chainmail fences.

'You must remember that the Malagasy do not look at things like we do. They keep zebu cows, the ones with the hump, and they worship their ancestors. To pay tribute to their ancestors they decorate the tombs with zebu horns, the more the merrier. So they don't care how thin their cows are or how much milk or beef they yield. They prefer to have ten skeletal cows rather than five fat ones as long as they've got the horns. Which means they get through an obscene amount of grazing.'

'You cannot make the same assumptions as them,' John added. 'Take population control. We expect our parents to look after us when we're children, give us pocket money and pay for our schooling. In the Third World the money goes the other way, the children are the earners. The biggest family has the best chance of having a tin roof in a village of thatched roofs. You cannot tell them to have less children any more than you can tell a banker to try to earn less money.'

'The most pressing argument', Ira said, forking a lump of zebu steak into the middle of his beard, 'is that two out of three children in the world are hungry. Now I have a child and I'm not happy with that. Have I shown you her pictures?'

By the time the bill came, Paul was talking about his previous trip to Zaire. 'I took a Harley Davidson and my guitar. I'm telling you – those pygmies had never seen anything like that bike. I used to play them Bob Dylan songs. It got me into trouble at the Ugandan border. I was singing "Don't Think Twice" and there's a line "You just wasted my precious time." The border guard was insulted. "So you think we've wasted your time, do you? Well, we'll just have to waste it some more." I was holed up in that dump for another ten hours.'

As we left the restaurant, Ira suggested that we accompany him to the north of the island to see a WWF reserve run by John and Françoise. We made arrangements with Gerry and Lee to meet them at Lake Aloatra. The beauty of travel arrangements in Madagascar is that there are so few options. There are only three train lines in Madagascar, one of which ends at Lake Aloatra. As the lines are single track, there is just one train there and back each day. Gerry and Lee agreed to meet us off the Thursday train. The next day we flew off to Antsiranana on the northern tip of the island.

By the time we returned to Tana two days later, Gerry and Lee had left for Lake Alaotra. There was a hastily scrawled note telling us to get off the train at Ambatondrazaka where they were staying.

Our train departed at 9 a.m. Like most other forms of life in Madagascar, the business of queuing has evolved into a unique system. Instead of all jostling for position or even waiting patiently in line, the Malagasy delegate the tedium of queuing to their baggage. A long line of leather trunks and squawking and heaving wicker baskets marked the queue for the train. We put our packs at the end and wandered off to have a coffee. It never occurred to us that someone would steal our bags. And they didn't.

When the train was announced, everyone returned to their bags and filed past the ticket-collector. The train slipped away whilst people were still loading their luggage on board. As it rarely got above the speed of a zebu cart, there was ample time even for the oldest ladies to clamber aboard. We inched our way along the single track, the driver honking his horn around every corner as if he expected something to come the other way.

We passed paddy-fields which stretch right into the suburbs of Tana. Knife-like flashes of sun glinted off the narrow strips of water. People walked along the narrow banks carrying huge loads on their heads; one man had a vast load of plastic bottles wrapped up in sheeting and a girl carried a Singer sewing-machine on her head, a bundle of clothes in her arms – a supreme display of confidence along the precarious footpaths.

The paddy-fields themselves were a hive of life. Not only was there a good deal of planting and ploughing, but at several paddy-fields women were washing their clothes in the muddy water and laying them out to dry on the banks. Some men sat fishing in one, hunched over their long rods. Gangs of boys swam in another. As the train went past one of the boys, gleaming naked, ran and dived headlong into the water.

At each station women with trays on their heads walked along the train offering lychees and fried bananas. The station-master, generally in khaki uniform and grubby gym shoes, would trot along to the driver's cab carrying a cleft stick which he held up to the window. This contained the permit to proceed to the next station. There was also a blackboard with the train's estimated arrival and departure times, a list so constantly amended that it looked like a bridge score-card.

For train buffs this is one of the great journeys in the world. The railway passes from the central plateau down through layers of dry and then wet rain forest until it reaches the coast. Built by Chinese slave labour in 1913, its tracks are precariously perched over viaducts, wedged between cuttings and taken through tunnels. As we crept along the cliff faces, views gave the same sense of vertigo as those from an aeroplane. We stood at the open door and watched the ground disappear from beneath our feet.

After six hours we pulled up at Moromanga where most of the passengers disembarked. The train performed a bewildering series of shunts and shuffles around the station for an hour. The passengers then re-embarked and off we went. They had eaten lunch on the station platform. The afternoon wore on. It grew dark and we began to wonder when our stop was. The train was stopping for less than thirty seconds at each stop, certainly for less time than it took to say 'Is this Ambatondrazaka?' At one stop a grey-bearded Malagasy came into our compartment. He chatted for a while to someone else, then turned to us with a cigarette in his hand.

'Do you have a light?'

Before either of us could have said 'Ambatondrazaka', he had established that we were English, that we were interested in lemurs and that we were going to the very town where he himself lived. A school exercise-book was produced and carefully laid across my knees. I deduced that Jean Michel, the subject of much congratulation in the book, was a guide who consistently formed the glittering highlight of any stay in Madagascar. The train stopped at a deserted line of track.

'Quick,' said Jean Michel, 'get out here.'

Although there did not appear to be a station, we clambered out of the train. I saw something white moving in the gloom and with it I heard: 'My beamish boy! Is that you?'

It was Gerry. He and Lee came forward. They had with them a laughing Malagasy.

'This is Mihanta. He is our guide and guiding angel.'

I turned to introduce Jean Michel, but he had vanished.

Lee led the way to the waiting taxi, a Renault 4. For a while we stood and stared at it as if it might grow.

'Plenty of room,' said Lee briskly. 'For the Malagasy.'

The four of us squeezed in the back, with Gerry and his stick and our luggage in the front.

'We've got our first lemur,' Gerry said. 'Today. He's sitting in our room complaining about room service like a Frenchman. I keep pointing out that if it wasn't for us he would be sitting in a casserole bubbling around with onions and carrots. Ungrateful sod. We're at this wonderful hotel, well you can judge that. And we've found Mihanta who is related to everyone, and Lee reckons there's hot water in the shower. I think she's hallucinating.'

The Hotel Voahirana was on the corner of the one and only street in Ambatondrazaka. No other foreigners had got as far as here. In my *Malagasy-Englisy Diksionera* 'Voahirana' had two definitions – a water-lily or (passive verb) to be closed, generally of the eyes of the dead. The proprietor promised that it meant a water-lily. He argued convincingly that it couldn't mean 'to be closed' because he was open. A room cost 9,500 Malagasy francs a night. We promptly ordered five whiskies which would have bought us two nights' rest.

Gerry and Lee had a room on the first floor from which there was already a rich damp smell of rotting bananas, wet sawdust and lemur pee. This gradually seeped through the entire hotel. We were the next floor up. A circular mosquito net hung over our bed, greying and ragged. It reminded me of Miss Havisham's wedding dress.

We met downstairs for supper.

'What's your room like? Does the loo have a seat?' asked Gerry. 'I might try to get up there.'

'No seat. But some interesting grafitti and lots of gurgling.'

'I'm beginning to feel like a Malagasy loo myself,' Gerry said morosely.

'It's so exciting to be here on our own.' Gerry lifted his glass. 'Usually we have John or Quentin with us who organize everything so I never see anything. I just get trotted out to congratulate people. I might as well stay in my room and write fiction. But here we are having our own little adventure.'

'Beware of a guide called Jean Michel,' said Lee.

'Jean Michel?!' I told them about meeting him on the train. It transpired that he had come into the hotel the previous day and had offered his services. He found out that they were after lemurs and promised to help. He thought he could buy some for 20,000 francs.

'And Mihanta says the going rate in the village markets is 2,000 francs.'

'They sell them in the markets?'

'Yes. They eat them. You know, that's what they do with all endangered animals.'

The next morning we were to set off on a lemur-gathering

expedition. Gerry and Lee had been kept up all night by a collection of cats which had gathered outside their window and tried to woo the lemur away. Gerry had listened to this from the lavatory, a gratifying distraction to the horrors which were taking place below him. He ordered four fried eggs and a beer for breakfast.

'Best recipe in the world,' he said as we winced at the sight of them. 'Give my stomach something to think about.'

Neither Gerry nor Lee had much by way of animal-collecting kit with them. For the world's greatest animal-collector, someone who had once proffered his toe as bait for a vampire bat, I was expecting at least some nets and snares.

'No,' he said, when I pointed this out, 'much more subtle than that. We're going to hunt them like they hunted the snark:

> They sought it with thimbles, they sought it with care;
> They pursued it with forks and hope;
> They threatened its life with a railway share;
> They charmed it with smiles and soap.

Now there was an animal collector! The Bellman! Although of course they got the wrong animal – the snark was a boojum you know. Very easy to do. I've done it myself.'

Mihanta and his cousin Romulus arrived with the taxi brousse, and our lemur hunt was underway.

The gentle lemur we were hunting is locally called 'bandro'. It only lives around Lake Alaotra, one of the largest lakes in Madagascar. The bandro's problem is that Lake Alaotra is rapidly silting up. The mountains above have been cleared of trees and the rains pour off the hillsides bringing a flood of silt with them. As well as the lake shrinking, the reedbeds are being attacked. As the mud silts up the paddy-fields on the hillside, as a preview of the lake itself drying up, the farmers burn off the reed-beds around the lake to make new paddy-fields. Caught between the shrinking lake and vanishing reed-beds, the bandros take the only way out – extinction.

Two other inhabitants of the lake went extinct last year. The Alaotran pochard and grebe, also both found only on the lake, were declared extinct after an exhaustive search of the diminishing water failed to find any. Neither of them will be as famous as the dodo, but they have both gone the same way. The lake is a slightly quieter place, but nobody apart from a few bird fanatics has heard about them. There has never been an education programme to explain to the villagers that if the birds go extinct, it is a warning sign that life on the lake is dying out. And if all life on the lake dies out, the water will go stagnant.

Gerry's tactics were to drive around the lakeside villages to see whether there were any bandros kept as pets or pending the cooking pot. He would then pay a nominal price for them and explain that they were being taken to breed because they were so rare.

Off we set. We pulled up at each village centre. From what appeared to be a deserted collection of huts would then materialize a substantial crowd. Mihanta ascertained who was the chief and a lengthy conversation ensued in which he eventually mentioned 'bandro'. Then there would be a quick huddle followed by a sad denial ('They've been eaten'). On we went.

Then at one village the conflab suddenly spun us off to a hut where an old woman and a wicker basket were produced. Inside the basket sat a bandro. Gerry and Lee held it up and squinted at it. I caught a glimpse of brown fur and a foxy triangular face with huge glassy eyes, the sort a taxidermist might use. It had that uniquely lemurish way of looking at you in wide-eyed wonder, with not a trace of malice or fear. It just stared back at us with the tranquillity of a teddy bear.

After swift negotiation the old woman sold it to us for 2,000 Malagasy francs. Mihanta explained to her that we were not going to eat it, but send it to Britain where it would be kept in a *saha misy bibidia hojeren ny mpitsangantsangana* and its young would eventually return to Madagascar. I'm not sure how much the old crone understood all this. She just stood there clutching her 2,000-franc note. She may have wondered that if it was worth sending her bandro all the way to Britain, she was underselling herself. But she had never been in a Boeing 747 and had never paid 60,000 francs, two months' wages, for a half-hour taxi ride into London. She just looked at her bandro as we would a rabbit and wondered what she would cook that evening.

At another village there were two baby bandros and at another an old female. Whilst Lee examined her, Gerry stood by the end of the vehicle. A large semi-circle of children formed around him.

'Look at them all. All in this tiny village. What are they going to eat? The Malagasy are the nicest people in the world so I hate seeing them going down the tubes. But these people will leave the remains of forests like a few thumb-prints across the country. They're destroying themselves.

'I hate the lot of you!' he thundered at them.

They giggled.

'How can you hate people as lovely as this?' He turned to Lee. 'Come on, honey. She's a skinny old thing. Ribs like a zebu cow. But beggars can't be choosers, look at me and you.'

We packed the bandro up in a basket and drove up a hill for a view of the lake. It was the dry season so the lake was at its smallest. It had become so shallow that large tracts were only navigable in a pirogue. We could see areas of marshland which were being drained by channels. The Malagasy eat more rice per person than anyone else in the world. I don't know who conjures up these statistics, but I suppose the Chinese are the nearest competitors. Given that the Malagasy eat rice for breakfast, lunch and supper, five kilos per person per day, I don't see how that can be bettered.

By way of example, for our lunch at a village stall we were given a washing-up bowl's worth of rice to accompany a saucer of rotting fish-heads. Looking at these fish with their angry glaring eyes, the prospect of rice seemed very appealing. And with the table teeming with flies, the attraction of rice was that you could dig into the bottom of the mound and persuade yourself that it had not been crawled over by flies. So we methodically chomped our way through twenty minutes' worth of pure rice.

'Don't you ever get bored with rice?' I asked Mihanta. 'I mean one mouthful is much the same as any other, isn't it?'

'No,' he replied indignantly, his cheek bulging with rice. 'It's very good. We sometimes vary it with sauce.'

'What sort of sauce?'

'Sometimes fish sauce like now. Sometimes we pour the water in which we cook it as sauce. Sometimes we salt it. There are many possibilities.'

Not only do the Malagasy have a wide variety of names for rice, rather like the Eskimos do for snow, they also measure distances by the time it would take to cook different amounts of rice. As I methodically processed mouthfuls down my throat, I realized how easy it would be to measure time by eating rice although, as in the Theory of Relativity, the longer the time lasted the slower it would go.

While none of this explains why the Malagasy eat so much rice, it does explain why the bandro is going extinct. And for the Malagasy to eat bandro as an accompaniment to rice adds insult to injury.

We took our four bandros back to the hotel, and I began to see the Durrell magic with animals at work. Lee booked the room next to theirs which became a mini zoo. The bandros were decanted from their wicker baskets into wooden cages. Whilst Gerry and Araminta fussed over them, Lee and I went into the market to buy more supplies. The market was a sprawling affair, much of it laid out on the road. We chose some tomatoes, bananas, lychees, carrots and greens. We returned with our arms full to find Gerry and Araminta staring intently into the cages. Gerry had been watching the three young ones with growing concern. Two of them were bullying the smallest. Eventually he decided to put the smallest in with the large female. He thought this might alert her maternal instinct. The risk was that if she didn't like him she might well kill him.

He caught the baby and put it into the female's cage, keeping his hands around it as long as possible whilst they sniffed each other, then gradually withdrawing them. In an instant, the baby was seized by the female and slung up on to her back.

'Look at them!' Gerry cried.

Inside the cage the baby crouched on the female's back, his

Gental Lemur (Bandro)
"Griseus alaotris"

ludicrously big eyes staring out through her fur.

'He's not exactly Lester Piggott, but I think he'll stay on. I'm calling them Araminta and Edward,' Gerry said. 'I'm afraid that Araminta is a raddled old female and Edward is a neurotic baby, but you can't have everything. They're made for each other. Like the Pilgrim Fathers, they are the founding stock of a great race, if you can say that about the Americans.'

Worse ignominy was to come. When the bandros reached Jersey a month later, Edward was found to be a girl.

Gerry cuddled both bandros in his arms and gave my namesake a syringeful of condensed milk.

'My animals like the most unexpected food.' He squirted condensed milk accurately into the bandro's eye. 'All the experts say "But you can't feed them on condensed milk! Or fruit cake! They never get it in the wild, it'll kill them." But it's like Englishmen and octopus. Once you've introduced them, they gorge themselves. That is to say the English eat the octopus rather than the other way round. Pity, but there it is.'

Over dinner, in the absence of any octopus and to lament the absence of oysters, Gerry gave an impromptu recital of 'The Walrus and the Carpenter'. He played all the parts but particularly revelled in that of the Walrus. I suspect he sympathized with its elderly gourmet inclinations. His beard bristled with pride as he concluded 'For they had eaten every one'. He looked the epitomy of the grandfather figure he has become to several generations of children.

The trouble with being a grandfather figure is that Gerry has to leave a good deal of his language out of his books.

'I love doggerel and dirty limericks. But I can't put them in my books as my readers wouldn't understand. "What's this nice man Gerald Durrell doing writing a whole lot of obscenity?" they'd say. "I won't buy this for little Willie." So I leave it to Larry. Now he's dead, I don't know what to do. So I just send dirty limericks to my friends who I know won't publish them, and threaten to unleash my solicitors on them if they do.'

The next morning Gerry stayed in bed with a high fever. Lee, Araminta and I went off with Mihanta around another corner of the lake. I noticed that we attracted a good many stares as we drove around. The first stares were just ones of incredulity at seeing such an empty taxi brousse – the average Malagasy load is over thirty people in the back. Then they realized we were *vazaha* which really merited an open-mouthed stare and then a frantic wave.

On the outskirts of the villages, generally set on the shoulders of hills, stood large tombs. These were solid brick buildings, much more substantial than the houses and painted white. Although missionaries built many churches in Madagascar, often two to a town as Catholics followed Protestants, the Malagasy remain largely untouched by either form of Christianity. They continue to practise their own more deeply rooted form of religion which revolves around worship of their ancestors.

The Malagasy bury their dead in family tombs. Every seven years they dig up the remains and conduct a bone-turning ceremony. They dress the bones in new clothes, parade them around, the *ombiasa* (wise man) interprets any messages and they return them to their tomb. Bone-turning is such an acceptable part of life that there is a government tax on it, 20,000 francs per body. Amongst the many *fady* or taboos which govern the country, it is *fady* for a foreigner to go near a tomb. If one does, the village will probably enact a series of sacrifices and ceremonies to appease the ancestors.

Mihanta told us that he thought the Western tradition of ignoring the dead was sad. He said that tombs are built to the east of a village and corpses get shuffled around between different family tombs, for example a woman will alternate between her own family tomb and that of her husband. The role of the dead brings the living family together. And as proof of the Malagasy ability to reflect a happy blend of all cultures, the tombs are generally topped with a large cross, although whether Catholic or Protestant they don't specify.

At one village the conflab took us to a man who kept a bandro. In an untypically aggressive way, he demanded 20,000 francs for it. Mihanta shook his head and after some very fast talking expressed surprise.

'He's been told that some *vazaha* are going around the villages buying up bandros for 20,000 francs. Jean Michel told him this. If he sells he is obliged to give some money to Jean Michel.'

When the man wouldn't budge, we left.

By the next day the seven bandros which we had collected were in good shape. They had settled down to a luxurious diet and were happy in each other's company. This could not be said of their next-door neighbours. Both Gerry and Lee were now in bed with a fever and stomach upsets. Araminta had the same fever, so I passed various potions and homemade Get Well cards between them. On one card Gerry was moved to poetry – he obviously wasn't *that* ill – and took up a previous challenge that he couldn't find a rhyme for 'Araminta'.

Of all the places I have bin ta
I have seen some luscious dames.
Blonde, beguiling redheads yummy,
Chocolate skins with jewel in tummy,
Skins like sexy yellow silk,
Skins like roses, skins like milk.
Bosom, buttock, legs a-twinkle,
Girls who have not got a wrinkle.
Girls beguiling, smiles so winning,
Girls who like a bit of sinning.
But in all the places that I've bin ta
None compare with Araminta.

I'm not able to begin ta
Praise the wondrous Araminta.
I would like to say with flourish
What kind thoughts of her I nourish.
A tangle, though, my thoughts get inta
Describing love of Araminta.
It would, I think, be quite a sin ta
Unfaithful be to Araminta.
So my muscles I will flex
And quite eschew the other sex.

Down with girls so long an' luscious,
Buxom girls who slush an' mush us,
Girls who, without hesitation
Tend to give you night starvation.
But, *please*, someone, just give a hint a
Of my love to *Araminta*.

Mihanta arrived with Romulus to take me off on the last bandro expedition. We needed three more bandros to fill our quota of ten. As we had to leave the next day, this was our last chance.

We drove right around the lake, an eight-hour drive. As we drove anti-clockwise, we passed all the bandros left alive on the left-hand side of the car. There were no bandros in the villages around the north of the lake.

'Oh yes,' they would say, 'we get about two a week, but we eat them all. Not as many as there used to be, but they taste delicious. Almost as good as cat.'

In one village Romulus drove straight through without stopping.

'What's wrong with this one?'

'It's *fady* to eat bandro here.'

'Why?'

'Because once a fisherman capsized his boat and, so they say, a bandro reached out and pulled him into the shore. The *ombiasa* declared it *fady* for his village to eat them.'

'Couldn't we get together with other *ombiasa* and ask them to declare it *fady* to eat any bandro?'

'No, the *ombiasa* have their own rules. If you try to persuade them, they may say the opposite.'

'But what if they see the sense of it?'

'They never see the sense of anything.'

We stopped at Mihanta's parents for lunch. His father had fluffy grey hair, his mother two long black plaits like a Red Indian squaw. Lunch was exclusively zebu – zebu kidneys and liver, zebu steak and then zebu brains. BSE couldn't have reached Madagascar, I thought, as I politely ladled them out and slurped them down with ostentatious enthusiasm. Could it?

After this thoroughly eaten zebu, we got going again. At one village we were told of a bandro, but the man who had it was taking part in a circumcision ceremony – not as a participant but as an observer. The ceremony began to make itself heard, a brass-band sound of drums and trumpets coming down the street. There is a strong tradition of English brass-band music. It derives from the taste for it King Radama I acquired in Mauritius. The boys to be circumcised walked in front, one of them rather touchingly cupping a hand over his groin. We waited until our man was pointed out to us and pulled him out of the crowd. He was wearing a smart straw hat and was very drunk. Most of the men had been drinking *toakagasy*, the privately distilled alcohol which occasionally makes them go blind. He agreed to sell us one of his two bandros for 4,000 francs. I assured Mihanta that I would square the extra 2,000 francs with Lee.

At the end of the day we managed to track down a doctor who also kept two bandros. When we told him about the project to breed them in captivity and return them to Madagascar, he was delighted and gave us both of them. We had filled our quota of ten bandros, five of each sex. Or so we thought until Edward turned out to be Edwina. The only bandros in captivity, apart from those held in villages around the lake pending the cooking pot, were now booked on their way back to Jersey to start a breeding colony.

The first leg of that journey was to be with me by train. Gerry, Lee and Araminta were too sick to spend eight hours on a train so they took the half-hour flight back to Tana. Mihanta and I prepared to catch the train the next day. It was to leave at four in the morning.

The train journey back to Tana gave me a clear idea of how Gerry would have transported animals in his earlier animal-collecting days. I was up at 3 a.m., too tired to wonder why Malagasy travel over relatively short distances involves such a trial of endurance. Though it was pitch black outside, the street market was already being set up. The station was busy and it was easy to attract the attention of a crowd of boys who carried the cages on to the train.

We roped them to the luggage rack and watched a lacklustre dawn emerge. I lay in a stupor and recognized the zoo smell all around me, bananas and piss. It was a smell Gerry would have relished.

Later that morning after countless stops the train broke down. We were at a tiny village and there was a run on the lychees, the only thing for sale. Mihanta met three friends, all of them medics, who shared our bench. Beer and rum were produced. The beer was hot and fizzy, the rum hot and sweet with a kick like a zebu. I began to feel much better. After a while someone produced a tin of sardines. They were passed around and eaten with fingers. Mihanta looked for somewhere to wipe his fingers which were dripping with sardine oil. He found nowhere so rubbed them thoroughly through his hair. One by one they fell asleep, each with a beatific expression. Mihanta's head was horribly cricked against the window, but when the train started jolting along three hours later he barely stirred.

The bandros had the most comfortable journey. Whenever I looked in their cages, they stared serenely out at me as if they made this journey every week.

After an uphill struggle for thirteen hours, the train finally pulled into Tana. Lee and Araminta were waiting for us. A night at the Hotel Colbert with hot showers and steaks had put them right. It put me right too.

It was time to confront the giant jumping rats.

Araminta flew to Mauritius for a two-day stint on the beach before returning to the English winter and left Gerry, Lee and me to catch a much smaller plane to Morondava on the south-west coast. John and Quentin had driven on ahead to set up camp. According to Lee's meticulous scheduling, John was due to come out of the forest to meet our plane. Fat chance, we thought.

The plane stopped half a mile short of the terminal. When we got out we realized we had to walk. To our welcome astonishment there was a wheelchair sitting ready with an attendant by the bottom of the steps. With a sigh of relief, Gerry sank into it and stowed his stick across his lap. We made a dash across the tarmac to get out of the heat. Sure enough John was waiting for us, towering a clear three feet above his other competitors at the barrier. He looked bemused to see the wheelchair.

'Where did you wangle that from?'

'What – didn't you?'

Too late we realized our mistake. A commotion broke out back at the plane.

'Vite! Vite!' As if scalded, Gerry leaped to his feet and shooed the horrified attendant back towards the plane with the wheelchair. He ran across the tarmac as if he had seen a ghost.

'What's the camp like?'

'You'll see.' John was tight-lipped. 'I'm taking you to a dream restaurant.' He seemed anxious to change the subject. 'It's right on the beach. You can see the sea . . . lots of water.'

Lee and I looked at each other. Was he addled?

'Well, what *is* the camp like?' We persisted, once we had sat down and John had knocked off a couple of cold beers.

'Flies,' he said succinctly.

'What do you mean? Large, small?'

'No, many. Many flies. None of you has a phobia about flies, do you? I mean being covered in flies, that sort of thing? Buzz, buzz.' He giggled hysterically.

We joined in and laughed. Out here with the sun on the beach it seemed absurd. The sea was pale blue, the sort of thirst-quenching blue found on maps. Fishermen walked past carrying their nets. Their wives walked behind them with the fish. These were individually draped over their heads like outrageous Ascot hats. A number of women walked past wearing tuna. Another wore a five-foot hammerhead shark.

John showed no inclination to leave.

'This is the first cold beer I've had in a week.'

'Come on,' Lee said, 'let's get to camp.'

'You'll regret it.'

On the way out of town we passed a Land Rover which stopped and reversed. A Malagasy bureaucrat leaped out and ran over to greet us.

'My old friends!'

'Aha!' Gerry exclaimed, 'It's you, is it?'

They fell on each other's necks, blessing and thanking each other for all the help each had been. After we had finally pulled away, Gerry turned round and said with vehemence, 'That's that miserable bugger who's fucked us up all along the line.'

'But you looked so pleased to see him,' I objected.

'Well, you have to.'

'But if you always treat him like that, he probably has no idea he's fucking you up. He probably thinks you love him. I certainly would.'

'Oh God!' Gerry looked very Greek all of a sudden, a look he must have learned in Corfu, 'It's too bloody hot.'

The track out to the forest was lined by baobab trees. There are eight different kinds of baobabs in Madagascar compared with just one throughout Africa. The ones around Morondava had vast, plump, cigar-shaped trunks with just a few twigs bristling at the top. If there had been a front door set into the bottom, they would have been perfect houses for Winnie the Pooh.

The forestry reserve at Morondava has been leased to a Swiss charity called Coopération Suisse. The Swiss are trying to establish whether they can log hardwood on a sustainable yet self-financing basis. The tree they are logging, the *Arofy commiphora*, takes 200 years to grow. Sadly the Swiss have found that they cannot make the timber economically viable. If the forest cannot be made self-sustaining under the guidance of a Swiss charity, there can be scant hope for its prospects when attacked by commercial logging interests.

The forest was dusty brown and dry as kindling wood. Without leaves, it reminded me of an English wood in winter – on an exceptionally fine day. It was the end of the dry season and there was no water anywhere.

'The first rains came last week. If you look closely you can see some buds. Otherwise it's parched.'

There were tracks cut at 100-metre intervals.

'This makes it very easy to walk around the forest. And there's someone here doing bird surveys so he finds it easy to count the birds within the grid.'

'Any *Hypogeomys* yet?' Lee said, breaking into fluent Latin.

'None so far. I left before Quentin had returned from the traps this morning.'

'What about *Pyxis planicauda*?'

'Five so far, and a couple of *Ophrus anvieri*.'

'Hang on, you two,' I interrupted. 'You're going to have to give me a Latin glossary to keep up with you.'

'Don't worry,' Gerry said, 'it's all bluff. Actually they don't know their *Arseus* from their *Elbowus*.'

After a series of turns, the track reached a clearing. We had arrived at the camp. There were a couple of huts, an eating area with a thatched roof and our tents set back in the trees.

The flies formed a black shimmering carpet across the table. We drank hot fizzy beer and heard the news. Quentin had caught two *Hypogeomys*, giant jumping rats, in his traps overnight. As they are nocturnal, they were now asleep. Quentin had adapted perfectly to nocturnal life and looked as if he too would prefer to be asleep. We drank to his success. I reached for my bottle and waved away a tight cluster of flies around the top. Quentin and John, someway down the evolutionary path of learning to live with these flies, had already balanced books over their beer to keep them out.

There was a second form of fly, the sweat bee. This was a tiny black bee with a long snout which crawled over you and sucked off any sweat. As we were sweating a good deal, they began to congregate. At first I simply brushed them off. They did not sting and I could just feel a slight tickle when more than ten or twenty gathered together. But gradually the tickling feeling became overwhelming. My skin began to crawl with flies gently sucking off my sweat. I started rubbing them off all together. My finger-nails turned black with their slaughter.

'Flies,' John pointed out unnecessarily, 'you didn't believe me.'

I looked down at the table. There was a tin bowl with some fly-killer in it. It was full to the brim with dead and dying flies. A fly landed on the brim of Gerry's cup just as he was taking a sip. He blew at it to buzz off. It keeled over and fell into his beer.

'Any self-respecting fly would have flown off and buzzed around someone's face to irritate them.' He fished it out with a great finger of froth. 'This bloody thing just plopped in.'

Supper in the form of three live chickens was produced for our approval. We looked away. The cook stroked their glossy necks, stepped back a pace to a log and butchered them. The squawking was reduced by a third, then two-thirds, then it abruptly stopped. The last frantic drumming of wings petered out. We made polite conversation. Some feathers floated past. The flies perked up.

'Look at these legs.' Gerry held up a chicken leg over supper. 'Trust Malagasy chickens – an evolutionary throwback. They're like the chickens we had in Britain 200 years ago. All strong muscular legs, no breast at all. These are what chickens should be like.'

'Practically inedible.' Lee put down a bone.

'Chickens weren't supposed to be eaten. They're natural scavengers, good fighting birds.'

After supper we kitted ourselves up with miners' lamps and set off to look for nocturnal lemurs.

Lee was one of the first field-workers in Madagascar in the 1970s. She wrote her thesis on the communication calls between Malagasy animals, particularly lemurs, so she is the ideal person to accompany on a walk in the Malagasy forest. At night the forest comes alive. The burnt dry smell of dust changes into a rich collection of scents as plants bloom in the cooler air. Baobab trees sprawled above the canopy, superbly individual amongst the tangle of trees. The night sky stretched over the forest canopy. Lee pointed out the Seven Sisters with Mars shining yellow beside them. On one side of the track the leaves glittered silver, and in due course the moon slid up through the forest canopy, huge and round.

Nocturnal lemurs are much slower than their daytime cousins.

They live alone rather than in a troupe, they do not need the safety of lots of pairs of ears and eyes, and they slowly munch their way along the branches. You see them by the reflection of their eyes in the torch beam. But the torch has to be held close to your eyes in order that the reflection shines back. Their size is judged by how far apart their eyes are.

For a while we walked in silence.

'There's one,' Lee said. In the beam of my torch I saw a pair of red eyes staring out of a tree. They moved through the blackness like gems, turned away and then reappeared lower down, travelling slowly. It was twenty yards back into the forest and we could get no closer. Lee made kissing noises and the disembodied red eyes kept staring into our torches.

'A mouse lemur.'

We went on. Lee saw all the lemurs. My torch just played over the forest turning the trees black and silver. We had counted fifteen lemurs, both mouse lemurs and lepilemurs, when Lee remarked that we might even see a *Hypogeomys*.

'You mean a giant jumping rat?' I tried to keep the yelp of panic out of my voice.

'Yes,' she said airily.

'What do we do if we see one?' I didn't want to sound too unprofessional but I was wondering how best to defend my throat against a leaping rodent.

'Watch it. And keep quiet,' she whispered.

We walked on. I kept pace a fraction behind Lee.

'What's that?' Lee levelled her torch on to the track.

'What?' I whispered.

'Don't shout,' she hissed.

'What's what?'

'That.'

Too late I saw a shadow on the ground. It took off.

'Jesus Christ!' I ducked. It flew over my head.

'Wow!' Lee cried. 'Will you look at that!'

'Are you mad?' I was bent double. 'Where's it gone?'

'It's a nightjar.'

And so it was. It flew around us, every now and then visible as it crossed the moon's face, otherwise flitting around like a bat.

We walked on. Lee's torch beam wavered around the forest as she kept remembering my reaction. I heard her chortle.

'It's not that funny,' I insisted. 'It could have had my eye out.'

'It was terribly funny.'

I heard another chortling noise as she spoke.

'Lee, what's that noise?'

'What noise?'

It came again – a sniffing, spluttering chortle.

'That noise.'

We swivelled our torches and there on the track not fifteen yards away from us stood a giant jumping rat.

'*Hypogeomys*,' Lee said.

'Jeepers!' I think I said. 'Is it meant to look like that?'

Hypogeomys, the giant jumping rat, stood up on its hind quarters and sniffed the air. It had a long pink bald nose and a healthy collection of whiskers. Its ears were large and floppy like a rabbit's. The rest of its body was rat-like, albeit on a huge scale. It stood two and a bit feet tall. When it started to move it simply bounced up and down on its back legs like a kangaroo. Boing, boing, boing off it leaped down the track.

'Quick!' Lee said. And we dashed after it.

'What if it turns on us?'

Lee was in no mood to answer. Here was a naturalist set on her prey. Crouching low we ran after it. It stopped. So did we. On it went. So did we. Any lemurs looking our way would have seen two people bent double running after a huge bouncing rat. I didn't hear anything falling out of its tree with laughter, so they must have carried on munching. Our chase came to an end when the rat fell forwards on to its front legs and scuttled, now like a normal rat rather than a turbo-charged pogo-stick, into the undergrowth.

Back at camp Quentin and John were dressing Julian's wounds. Julian was the animal-catcher.

'Mad man,' Quentin said, safe in the knowledge that Julian only spoke French. 'Saw this snake, next moment he's hurtling through the undergrowth after it. Ran straight into a tree and skewered himself on these pencil-sized thorns.'

We went to sleep, or at least the others may have done. I lay in my tent sweating and listening to the forest noises and wondering about large crawling insects. It was too hot to zip up the doors, and too hot to wear any clothes. I had seen earlier the discarded shells of giant snails. Lying naked in my pool of sweat, I felt supremely vulnerable. I didn't fancy any insects and the thought of waking up to find a giant snail grazing over my chest kept me awake for some considerable time. The noises of the night could have been anything – frogs, birds, animals. A great croaking, honking, roaring mass. I only recognized one element of it, by no means the loudest though a worthy competitor, the sound of snoring from Gerry and Lee's tent. Insects, giant rats or giant snails, Gerry was triumphantly asleep against all comers.

It was light at five and getting hotter all the time. Quentin was the first to discover the disaster. There was consternation around the breakfast table.

'Both of them?' Gerry was saying.

The two giant jumping rats caught the night before last had escaped.

'I don't understand it.' Quentin held out his hands in despair. 'They both got out through a hole this big.' He crooked his index finger to describe a clearly impossible hole. No one dared contradict him.

'We'd better get out and check the traps. It's getting late.'

So at 5.30 a.m. we piled into the jeeps and went off to check the traps. Quentin went with Julian to the distant traps whilst the elderly and amateur naturalists went to the more accessible ones. We walked in single file to a trap which had been set by a known rat-hole, a large burrow with a mound of earth thrown up around it. Inside the trap, sniffing at the corners experimentally, was a giant jumping rat. We squatted down to have a closer look. He was smaller and greyer than the one we had seen the previous night. His tail was the most rat-like thing about him, thick and loosely haired. Otherwise with his pink nose, flopsy ears and huge back legs, he was as charming as any *Hypogeomys* could be.

John took off his shirt and wrapped it around the trap. We brushed over the sand so we could spot any other footprints and carried our rat back to the jeep. We all met up in camp at around 6.15. Quentin had picked up two rats. We sat down and felt the heat rise implacably against us.

'So it's 6.30,' I announced. 'What do we do with the rest of the day?'

'Sleep it off,' Gerry said decisively. 'We should be nocturnal. That's what anything with any sense is around here.'

We arranged ourselves around the table in the shade. The heat soared. By 8 o'clock the temperature in the shade was 47°C. It was too hot to sleep. It was too hot to do anything other than wave off the sweat bees. By lunchtime we had fetched water, had hot showers, fidgeted with the cages and started several books. Lunch arrived in the form of a mountain of rice.

'It's too hot to eat.' Lee pushed away her plate. It was immediately covered by flies. The rest of us carried on eating, one hand forking in rice, the other fanning flies away from the plate.

We swapped stories until the heat finally sapped our imagination.

'It's too hot for stories.'

I produced my secret weapon, Scrabble. Gerry had never played before.

'What's this? A spelling game? I won't be able to play as I can't spell. I was never taught.'

In the end he did play, and the flow of words proved either that authors can't spell, or that our brains were addled. My opening word, the longest anyone could produce, was JEW. Gerry continued by adding R and Y to form JEWRY. John opened the board up with TEAR and I added ROAR. Gerry tried ROMULY, an implement he claimed was used to stitch saddles. We pointed out that Scrabble was not 'What's My Line' and squashed him. John wrote THREE and I came up with AT for RAT. Gerry then came out with EVERT.

'As in Chris Evert?' I challenged.

'No.' He looked smug. 'One of the main things you ought to know about snakes before you go charging off into the undergrowth after them is that their penises evert. Very horrible it is too. Turn inside out.'

From then on we hardly got a four-letter word apart from FUNGUS which might have been preying on our minds. Gerry almost won with a succession of key two- and three-letter words such as OI and BY, and a good line in drinks – RUM, GIN and a failed attempt to persuade us that the Russians drink 'Ka'.

'It's too cold in Russia to stand around and say "Vodka", so they say "Ka" – "*Neytachetzchen ilya ka* . . ." Oh, alright. You're so bloody strict.'

John snatched victory when he helped Gerry with a word which left the treble nicely exposed. JETS won him fifty-six points.

My next weapon was draughts.

'Oh God!' Gerry clutched his forehead. 'It's like a bloody Butlins holiday camp. Why don't you leave us to get on with this misery in peace?'

John and I decided to have a quiet game. Gerry professed an urge to read *The Decline and Fall of the Roman Empire*. John had never played draughts, so I taught him. Gerry began to watch. In spite of himself he began to offer John quiet words of advice.

'Now think about that, old boy . . . That's right.'

Soon Gibbon was forgotten in the heat of the game. The advice grew more passionate.

'Now come on, John! Storm down there, get a king and beat the pants off him!'

Gerry scowled over the board, his hair and beard drenched with sweat, like a malignant Neptune. Our game became an out-and-out battle.

'Watch out! He's a cad and a bounder. He'll get out and come and take you – take the piss out of you. Too late!'

By the end, when the table was strewn with decapitated kings, it was cool enough to go out and set the traps. As we drove around the forest, we picked up two more tortoises off the track and saw a troupe of sifaka.

Sifaka, *Propithecus verrauxi*, is a large white lemur. It is not eaten by the Malagasy because it looks so human. We first saw some by

Giant Jumping Rat

the edge of the track. A troupe was lounging around the trees taking it easy. One sifaka sat upright on a branch by the track. It had a black face and hands, a white coat and an expression of great knowledge. We clambered out of the jeep. The sifaka looked down at us, standing its ground like a sentry. Then with astonishing agility it abruptly bounced off through the trees back to the troupe and set them all off. They moved through the forest just as I would love to – keeping upright and bouncing from tree to tree as if spring-loaded, a blur of long outstretched arms and legs, their tails flying in streamers behind them.

The main difference between the sifaka and us was their energy level. As they galvanized themselves and crashed off through the trees, we slunk back to camp exhausted. It took several litres of hot fizzy beer to restore energy levels to the stage where we felt capable of tackling another mound of rice and a camp sing-song. A small ring of foresters' children emerged from their huts to watch. When Lee finished a heart-rending recital of 'Stewball', our moist sniffling was drowned out by loud clapping. John and I then attempted a duet of 'The Runaway Train Went Down the Track', but after the first verse it was decided that we would all go for another walk in the forest before all *Hypogeomys* were frightened back into their burrows.

This time I walked with Quentin and Julian. Quentin quietly recited the names of the local animals we might see. As they were all in Latin, he sounded like a Catholic priest rehearsing his litany. His droning was spectacularly interrupted by Julian.

'*Voilà!*' he yelled and in an instant was sprinting down the track tearing off his T-shirt.

'What the hell . . .?'

We saw a giant jumping rat jump for its life. Julian was gaining on it, until it darted into the forest. Julian crashed in after it. We ran rather lamely after him. We found Julian lying on the ground, his T-shirt spread out over a hole.

'*Il est dedans,*' he gabbled, pummelling the ground with his fist.

The rat had realized his game was up and had bolted down a hole. Julian was on the point of scrabbling after it, when Western sophistication prevailed.

'We'll get a trap,' Quentin said. 'He'll be in it by morning.'

We dug in the trap so the rat had no alternative but to enrol for Jersey's captive breeding programme, and went to bed. When I tried to pull off my T-shirt, my fingers went straight through the cotton and came away with the collar. It had rotted on my back.

The good news in the morning was that we had two more *Hypogeomys*. Julian's rat had duly emerged and was safely trapped. After this tonic, the rest of the day passed in a mirage. We sheltered from the heat and, as Gerry pointed out, bored each other rigid with stories of our grandmother's ingrowing toenails. Lunch was interrupted by a small boy bringing a present for the rats, a cluster of hissing cockroaches. They had been threaded through the shell and their legs dangled down. Like all food in Madagascar, they were still very alive and resentful of their circumstances. Quentin hung them up on a peg.

We also discussed what had brought Gerry and me together in the first place, the ghost of my great-great-uncle Herbert. Herbert Whitley owned Primley House at Paignton where between 1915 and his death in 1955 he established a large collection of rare animals which he kept and bred in his garden. After his death, his house was turned into an old people's home, and his gardens were transformed into Paignton Zoo.

Herbert started off breeding rare farm breeds such as Jacob's sheep and Large Black pigs. In 1926 he bought Tatton Shire Dray, a colossal shire stallion, for 3,700 guineas (equivalent to £1 million today), which a crowd of 3,000 watched arrive by train. He also bred greyhounds and Great Danes. Primley Sceptre, a greyhound, was the first winner of the Best of All Breeds gold cup at Crufts in 1928.

From the 1930s he began to collect and breed exotic animals. This started off with a herd of zebu cows which he used to plough, and progressed to cockatoos and chimpanzees. His pet chimpanzee, Mary, was dressed as a milkmaid and trained to go off to the village every morning to pick up the milk. Herbert's collection continued with fish, reptiles, birds, leopards and bears and finally his first elephant.

By the time of Gerry's first animal-collecting expedition to Cameroon in 1950, Herbert had established Paignton as Britain's second most important animal collection after London Zoo. When Gerry and his hunting partner, Kenneth Smith, steamed into Liverpool on SS *Tetela* with a cargo of 500 animals, they were sold to London Zoo and Herbert. *The Bafut Beagles*, Gerry's first best-seller, is an account of the six-month trip in Cameroon. It is dedicated to Ken Smith who became Herbert's curator at Paignton.

'Your great-uncle was one of Britain's last true eccentrics,' Gerry said. 'I very much approved of this as I had been brought up on eccentricity. But the rest of the world never knew what to make of him. He dressed like a gardener and lived like an anchorite surrounded by all these animals.

'I used to take animals round to him and he would force me to play billiards all night. He never slept in a bed, always in a chair. But he was brilliant. He was at the forefront of captive breeding. He tried to breed an all-black and an all-yellow salamander for a while. He had these long lines of aquariums with increasingly blacker and increasingly yellower salamanders in them.

'He was so shy he had special locks put on all the doors which you had to jiggle with your fingers. If anyone came to see him, he would run through the house shutting all these doors behind him. If they made it to his study, he had built a lift which would hoist him up to the top of the house.

'He had the sort of library I always dreamed of, vast shelves of books. And he knew every reference. "Just reach up there will you, Durrell, you'll find it on page 37." And there it was, on page 37.

'He had a particular obsession for breeding blue things. Part of this was to confound experts. He bred blue pigeons, blue Great Danes, blue ducks.

'I once had a similar obsession, I wanted to have a pygmy zoo with pygmy crocodiles, pygmy hippos, pygmy hogs. They're all out there waiting for it.'

'Yes,' I added, the idea catching on, 'you could have it staffed by pygmy zoo keepers.'

Our quiet reminiscence was shattered by Quentin who returned from his trap setting and announced that he had lost Julian. This was news.

'Lost him?' we said.

'Yes. In the forest. He saw some animal, chased after it and never came back.'

We digested the implications of this.

'Do you think he was eaten?' Gerry eventually articulated what we had all been thinking.

'Don't be absurd. I've been looking for him for two hours, shouting my head off and hooting the horn. He's just buggered off somewhere.'

It was getting dark. We set off to find him.

Out in the forest I realized how easy it is to get lost. The forest muffles and distorts noise. We hooted the horn, but even when I was only fifty yards away from it, I could not tell where it was coming from. We drove up and down until dark and then returned to the camp, ate a quick supper and went out again. This was turning into an emergency.

John and I drove slowly down one track, Quentin and a forester down another. I stood on the roof and when John stopped and turned off the engine, I bellowed at the top of my voice. Shouting at the forest is a strangely futile exercise. As the moon had not yet risen, it was very dark. The forest was silent, but my roars set off a chain reaction of enraged squawking and screeching. I heard the noise gather momentum and ricochet around the black forest, each echo setting off another. As they subsided I would shout again and they would all start up once more.

After an hour John said, 'It's hopeless.'

'So it seems.'

'No, I mean I know it's hopeless. I've just realized. Whenever Julian shouts, he makes the noise of an animal. It's impossible to find him in the forest.'

I looked around the forest and listened to the bloodcurdling yowling I had provoked. Julian could be yowling and whooping for all he was worth, but we would just assume he was part of the background noise. We finally drove back.

'The only thing in his favour', I said to console John, 'is that if Julian can roar like that he can frighten off anything else.'

Julian had still not appeared by the next morning. The emergency was turning into a disaster. Quentin and John had already been out but returned exhausted by 6 o'clock. The heat was rising all the time. Julian had had no water for fifteen hours. Gerry gave him another six hours before he keeled over.

We tried to assemble a rescue team from the Malagasy foresters. To our surprise none of them were interested. They shrugged their shoulders. After close cross-examination, we established that they could not do anything without permission from the head ranger.

'Where is he?'

'Morondava.'

When we pointed out that he need never know that they took three hours out of their day (which was generally spent sitting aimlessly around their huts) to save someone else's life, they were unmoved.

'Ce n'est pas possible.'

When the incentive of some extra cash failed to change their minds, we realized that we were up against the most dangerous legacy of the Soviet Union's influence on Madagascar, unswerving commitment to bureaucracy.

In five minutes we had packed our bags and were driving into Morondava to obtain the necessary authorization for the search party.

Two hours later we were embroiled in the jungle of Malagasy bureaucracy. Lee was speaking beautiful, unhurried French and explaining that one of our party was lost and close to death. The Malagasy was expressing his most polite condolences. Everyone seemed very touched at our concern; it was beyond the call of duty and such a very long drive.

The sun blazed vertically overhead.

Lee hinted that a paper giving authority for a search party might be helpful. The Malagasy spread his hands. Surely such a thing would inconvenience Madame? No, no, Lee assured him, it was all she desired. Would not Madame prefer anything else, a meeting to discuss it? No, no, Madame promised him, such a piece of paper would make her day. Well, if Madame was absolutely sure . . . but a piece of paper needed so many signatures. A brief but fierce coughing fit from Gerry encouraged the official to scribble something on a piece of paper. He signed it with a flourish and dispatched a man to accompany John back to camp. A split second later John had roared off leaving us choking in the dust. Monsieur seemed to be in a hurry? Lee shrugged her shoulders, disowning John's eccentric behaviour. We all parted well pleased.

'The restaurant,' Gerry said, tottering on his stick, 'cold beer.'

That night word came back through the Malagasy that Julian had been found. His sense of direction had led him diametrically away from the camp through the only uncharted area of the forest. He had spent the night up a tree. In the morning some villagers who were scouting for stray zebu had picked him up on the fringe of the forest.

When we finally arrived back in Tana, I realized why so many conservationists prefer to work from the Hotel Colbert. Room service produced cool beer in chilled glasses, the shower produced a thick jet of transparent cold water and there were frogs' legs on the menu.

But the three of us were due to depart the next day for Mahajunga. And from Mahajunga, we were to drive for four hours to the Ampijoroa Reserve.

The next morning Gerry had a fever. He was too knocked up to come with us. Lee and I left him in the capable hands of room service.

'I'm so sorry not to join you,' he croaked.

I caught a gleam in his eye.

'Give a kiss to any sweat bees you find.' He raised his glass of beer and waved us off back to the implacable heat of the west coast to look at tortoises.

As the tortoise walks, Ampijoroa Reserve is about eighty miles from Mahajunga. Given the state of the road, it is not much faster as the taxi brousse drives.

Ampijoroa is where Jersey has set up a project with the Department of Eaux et Forêts to breed the *Geochelone yniphora*, or as the Malagasy call it the angonoka, the world's rarest tortoise. The angonoka is distinguished by a hook which grows out from its shell under its neck. The Malagasy call this an *ampondo* and cut it off as they believe it prevents the tortoise from eating. Westerners have observed that the males use it to topple their opponents when fighting, and to grapple their females when mating. They call the angonoka the 'ploughshare' tortoise.

After all the conservation talk in Tana, it was good to see a project which is a proven success. Jersey has a staff of two at Ampijoroa, Don Reid, an Englishman who has been out there since 1987, and Germain Rakotobearison, a Malagasy who trained in Jersey in 1989. Angonokas are not just rare, they are also difficult to breed. There had been no successful breeding of them until Don and Germain hatched two eggs in 1987. They have subsequently hatched around nine eggs a year and have twenty-seven surviving youngsters.

Ampijoroa is a reserve of 1,000 hectares. The village is a typical collection of miscellaneous families, foresters, game wardens, guides, the essential hangers-on who just stare at everything and the odd overseas scientist, in this case Don. The village is shaded by a teak plantation and although there is no running water or electricity, there are also no flies. Across the road is a lake where the crocodiles tend to keep to one end, and nobody has caught bilharzia. We trusted to the law of averages and had a swim. I had never swum where I could see crocodiles on the bank just fifty yards away, their jaws gaping open.

'It's fine.' Don floated on his back, his eyes shut and his hands behind his head. 'They're frightened of you.'

'The feeling's mutual,' I said.

Don didn't even flinch when I grabbed hold of his ankle.

Germain lives in a house by the tortoise enclosures. It is a wonky sort of wooden house with bits falling off it. As we sat and chatted, I could practically hear the termites eating their heads off. A life spent looking after tortoises might be seen as rather easy. After all, tortoises in Madagascar hibernate from June to September, and even when they're awake they don't need much exercise – you scarcely have to run after them.

Germain put me right. He is a tiny man, with the matchstick arms and legs of a twelve-year-old, but with three children and a fourth on its way. Gerry had described his face to me as the sort you would get if you sculpted one from bronze, leather and chicken bones.

'There are three things you must get right to breed tortoises,' Germain told me, 'the shade, the soil temperature and the humidity. Every day I measure the soil temperature three times. I draw this up into a graph, Jersey taught me how to do this. Then we discuss whether to water the nests or not.'

The angonokas lay their eggs just before they go into hibernation in June. They dig a hole two feet deep, drop in the eggs, urinate into it and fill it up. Both the tortoises and their eggs then spend the dry season comatose. The tortoises come out in September when the males fight each other. Mating takes place in November, and to complete the cycle the eggs from the previous year's mating hatch with the first rains in December.

If there is not enough rain, the ground is too hard for the babies to dig themselves out so they suffocate underground. If there is too much rain, the eggs rot. One of Germain's key responsibilities around November is to decide whether to water the nests.

'You must make mistakes to learn,' Germain said. 'Sometimes I water, sometimes I don't. We work it out. There are other things we learn – the male tortoises always fight and then mate with each other. We tried to stop this. When we stopped them, they refused to mate with the females. Now we let them. They all mate together! And they produce babies!'

'Yes,' Don confirmed when I confronted him with this, wondering whether I had misunderstood Germain. 'They all bugger each other first. It seems part of the foreplay. Probably essential, although I doubt if you would find many scientific papers on the subject. I used to stop them because I was worried about their sperm count. When there were only a handful of these tortoises left, I didn't want them wasting a drop. But I was wrong.'

'We want to show more Malagasy what is going on,' Germain said. 'Now we have a good number of tortoises, we have saved them from extinction. People can see our success. And there are many interesting beliefs about the angonoka which we need to understand.

'Many people believe it stops their chickens from getting disease. We need to examine this. It might be true. Many people like to have them as pets because they are very friendly, they make the family happy. If there are enough angonokas, then this is fine. Let everyone enjoy them. But at the moment there are too few.'

We walked into the enclosure and squatted down by a friendly old giant. He stretched out his neck. I shook it as one would shake a hand. Marvelling at his age and slowness was indeed very therapeutic. He seemed to pull all our madcap rushing around the country into perspective. He would just take his time and do his own thing. If that meant hibernating for four months and then buggering all his friends, fine. Time is what you make of it, and he had all the time in the world. He stretched his neck out a little further, inviting a scratch under the chin. His black eyes shut. I felt rather envious of his supreme sangfroid.

It was a couple of days later when I caught Germain unawares that I really began to understand more of his life in this remote village. He was sitting on the steps of his house, chatting to some rangers and scratching some figures in the dust with a stick. I sat down beside him.

'The price of rice.' He pointed to the sums in the dust. 'It is 400 francs a kilo in the next-door village. But if we go to the one beyond it is only 300 francs. But the taxi brousse fare is 200.'

'That's a free market for you,' I said. 'What are these sums?' I pointed to some more complicated calculations.

'If we buy in bulk, we can buy cheaper – 350 francs in the near village, 250 francs in the far one. I was working out how much we would all buy.'

Ploughshare Tortoise

'This is much cheaper, why don't you do this?'

'Well, it is difficult. It means working with these people.' Germain nodded his head at one of the houses opposite.

'Why can't you do that? They're your neighbours.'

'They are bad people. They are not from here. They are hired by the GPF. They come from Mahajunga and they stay just a year. They do not like the reserve, it is just a job for them. They are all single men and they don't like working. They drink all night. When they get paid, they play music and drink more. This is not good for the angonoka. They are bad men.'

Germain shook his head and viciously scratched out the sums. They would not add up. It seemed absurd that people thrown together in the middle of nowhere could not get on, if only for the sake of mutually cheaper rice.

'And they do not like me,' Germain continued. 'Since I go to Jersey, they do not like me. I try to bring up my family to be educated. I see a lot of *vazaha*, like you, but also I work with Don. So I see the modern way of doing things. It is better.'

'What about *ombiasa*?' Even thoroughly modern Malagasy believed in the power of these wise men.

'They pretend to be clever and tell you what to do,' Germain answered. 'But they cannot be that clever. If they are so clever, why have I never seen a rich one? They are all poor.'

'Perhaps they are not interested in money,' I suggested. 'Perhaps they look at spiritual things.'

'No,' Germain dismissed the idea, 'they try to cure disease and look into the future, but they need money like we all do. I have never seen one with a motorbike, let alone a car.'

'What about when you die?' I asked. 'Will you be buried in your family tomb?'

'No, I will build my own tomb.' Germain provided a modern tax-efficient alternative to the Malagasy tradition. 'If I was to be buried in my family tomb, all the other bones would have to be turned when I joined them. This will be expensive as you pay taxes on the ceremony. So I have my own tomb.' His face fell. 'But I cannot stop my family. They will come into my tomb and turn my bones when I am dead. It is the tradition. They think it is good for me. And they will turn all the other bones too.'

I consoled him along the lines of the best-laid plans of men and mice. Here was a man caught in the hinges between two worlds. As we chatted on his porch, a further example of how Germain is caught between two worlds hobbled past. It was a cat with a broken leg.

'He is mine,' Germain said. 'Those men broke his leg when they tried to catch him.'

'Why did they want to catch him?'

'People eat a lot of cats around here. But he is a pet of my wife's. He is a male, and we castrated him so he would be more tame as a pet. When people eat cats, they castrate them some time beforehand so the meat does not taste so strong. So when they saw he was castrated, they thought he was ready to eat and they hit him with a spade. I had to stop them. Now he has a broken leg.'

When Germain and his family lined up to wave us off, I caught sight of the ruined tom-cat skulking around the corner of his house – one animal that was really living dangerously.

On the drive back Lee told me that Germain had had a great idea.

'Lambas,' she said. 'Everyone wears them and they all have motifs on them. I want to get some printed with the angonoka on them. There are some wonderful local sayings about the angonoka.'

She showed me a list she had jotted down: '*Sokatra tsy matahotra havandrahiraraha*' – the tortoise is not afraid of the hail, and '*Ny sokatra no ela velona mahai-pery*' – the tortoise has a long life because he is stoical.

The landscape we were driving through would test all the stoical powers of the tortoise. It was cleared of forest and covered with coarse scrubby grass, the result of being burned off too many times. Eventually a form of grass takes over which even the zebu do not like. The land then just bakes in the sun and erodes in the rain.

There were a number of pick-up trucks parked in the small gullies caused by landslides.

'They are picking up earth to find fossils,' the driver explained. 'Very big business. Many fossils come from here.'

A bulldozer scraped away handfuls of red earth. Fossils which had been underground for millions of years tumbled out into the light of day. The driver would not hear a word of criticism.

'After all,' he asked reasonably, 'what else is this countryside good for?'

We looked around the parched desert. There was not a thing in sight, not an animal, not a bird in the sky, not even a zebu. We had left the Ampijoroa Reserve far behind.

He had a point.

'The time has come,' Gerry squeezed lemon over his oysters, 'to talk of many kings. Of shoes and ships and sealing wax, and when we must pack our things.'

It was time to leave Tana. John and Quentin had returned from Morondava with their quota of animals nearly full: six giant jumping rats, six tortoises, six lizards. The only ones missing were chameleons, which had not come out because the rains had not arrived. We were having our last meal in the Hotel Colbert. In the bar outside, the talk was of who was going to the Durrells' farewell party. Invitations had been sent with the heavy gold crest of the British ambassador who was to host it on their behalf.

In the event Gerry and Lee had invited everyone who had helped them with the trip and the room was full of an extraordinarily wide range of people who would never otherwise have met each other. There were Malagasy officials from three ministries, Eaux et Forêts, Education and Science, who had processed all the paperwork involved with exporting the animals. They were wearing smart charcoal suits and their wives were laden with jewellery. There were staff from Tsimbazaze Zoo, the keepers wearing jeans and T-shirts. There were the animal trackers such as Julian and Mihanta, likewise in jeans and T-shirts. The other conservationists were there, all bearded, and smarter or scruffier depending on how recently they had returned from the bush.

An undersecretary from the British Embassy fell upon me, a large G and T to hand.

'You don't look like a conservationist. You haven't got the beard for it.'

I admitted as much.

'Ghastly occasions these,' he went on conspiratorially. 'One has to drink so much to get through them.'

We raised our glasses.

'I've just come back from hospital.'

'Really?'

'Yes.' He took another drink. 'Stabbing attack.'

'Good God! What happened?'

'My own stupid fault. We were rehearsing the Embassy play, *Macbeth*. I was playing Banquo. Three of our cooks were playing an assortment of roles like the witches, the messengers, and the assassins. We had this stage knife with a collapsing blade. But at one rehearsal when we went through the attack, you know, "Flee Fleance flee! Aaaargh! For I am dead", one of the cooks stabbed me. But the blade didn't go back into the handle, it went straight through me. Ruptured my kidney and God knows what. An RAF plane flew me out to Réunion to the emergency casualty ward. I bloody nearly died.'

He took an aggrieved swig at the memory.

'It transpired that the cook had forgotten to bring the collapsing knife with him. He'd used his kitchen knife instead. Seems he'd thought it would do just as well.'

'Want another drink?' I suggested.

'I'll have a bite to eat.' He steered me towards the buffet table. 'Thank God we don't have formal Malagasy food tonight. Too many Brits. There's this thing called 100-Year Beef. They take a lump of zebu and cook it until it falls apart. They then unthread all the strands of fibre and bury it. A year later they dig it up and cook it again. It's a great delicacy. Absolutely disgusting. Looks just like pubic hair.'

He spooned in some rice.

'Tastes like it too,' he added thoughtfully.

My contribution to the evening was a handful of black plastic flies which I had bought in the market. I had been wondering where to put them. In a moment of recklessness, I sprinkled them into the vast bowl of rice.

For a while nobody followed us to the buffet. I had time to sit down out of the way. The next people to drift up to the table were a group of Malagasy diplomats. I saw the first one reach into the rice. He started and looked around. Nobody had noticed. With a supreme display of spontaneous diplomacy, he then spooned the rice around in the bowl and covered up the flies. The group passed down the table without further incident. With a great to-do, the ambassador then ushered Lee up to the table. He gallantly procured her a plate, and Lee dug deep into the rice.

'Yuk! What's this?' She recoiled in horror.

The ambassador leaped forward. Commotion broke out. Lee may have screamed. The ambassador turned round, wildly summoning assistance. Before anyone could recognize the flies as plastic, a white-jacketed flunkey dashed to the table and whipped the bowl out of sight. The ambassador apologized profusely. Lee came and sat next to me.

'What was all that about?'

'Oh, nothing.' She was noncommital as the ambassador was still hovering in sight, wringing his hands.

'It was just a souvenir of Morondava.' I showed her a fly in the palm of my hand.

Her fork stopped in mid-air.

'For God's sake, don't show Gerry,' she said. 'He'd die.'

'Too late. There's one in his glass.'

She spun round. But the ambassador had beaten her to it.

'My dear Gerald,' he said urbanely, pouncing on Gerry's glass in which a black plastic fly was floating alongside an ice cube, 'let me top you up.' Before Gerry could point out that his glass was full, the ambassador had whisked it away and was bearing it imperiously to the kitchen. He was probably looking for the cook's knife.

Gerry caught Lee's eye and winked.

'Diplomacy,' he hissed, 'such a tricky business.'

We said our goodbyes to the ambassador. He looked a chastened man. Early the next morning, pre-empting any form of revenge, I left the hotel, caught a taxi and was at the airport in good time for my flight to Mauritius.

The Jersey juggernaut, Gerry, Lee, John, Quentin and the animals, would follow me a few days later.

FIVE

MAURITIUS

THE ABSURD DODO – CARL JONES' HANDFUL OF KESTRELS – THIRTEEN PINK PIGEONS – YOUSEFF MUNGROO'S NATTY TROUSERS – CARL'S RUBBER-BRIMMED BOWLER HAT, ANTHROPOMORPHISM WITH A PASSION – CATCH A FALLING MOUSE – GERRY'S VIRTUAL ARREST – LOADING UP THE ANIMALS, THE THIRD PLANE ON THE RIGHT

The dodo was unique to Mauritius. It looked a silly bird, the sort a child might draw and be awarded 'Tick – Good Effort' by the teacher with an indulgent smile. It had a fat wobbly bottom, a ridiculous sprig of tail feathers, useless fluffy wings and a comic baroque beak. It might have been a turkey in fancy dress.

The dodo was not killed because it tasted good, its meat was tough and bitter. No, the dodo was clubbed to death just for fun. Sailors who came ashore found these silly birds which couldn't fly and didn't run away, so they clubbed them to death simply for the hell of it. Who wouldn't? They must have been irresistible. The dodo was given a crash course in the survival of the fittest. It failed. When a Dutch sailor clubbed the last one in 1680, the happy survivor of millions of years of evolution became the first man-made extinction.

It only belatedly dawned on people that as only dodos could breed dodos there would be no more of them. This is what extinction means.

But extinction on Mauritius didn't stop there. By 1900, the giant tortoises were as dead as dodos (an expression which has a satisfyingly flippant ring to it) as well as various parrots, an owl, a bat and a blue pigeon. After two centuries in which all the ebony trees have been logged and the rest of the island burned off for sugar plantations, the damage can now be easily quantified.

In 1976 an estimated 2.5 per cent of the native habitat was left. Some of the birds could be counted on fingers and toes, some on fingers, and one on the fingers of one hand alone. There were a dozen echo parakeets, a dozen pink pigeons and four Mauritius kestrels.

The beauty of Mauritius for statisticians is that it is small and barren so the wildlife is relatively visible. When you count the birds and find only seven, you know there are roughly seven. A flock will not suddenly fly over from the neighbouring countryside and wreck all your research, particularly irksome if you are just about to publish it.

Mauritius found itself at the top of the Red Data book, host to the world's rarest kestrel, pigeon and parrot. But amid the perfect man-made paradise of rum cocktails, water-skiing and mini-mokes, there is still the odd quirky bird flying around. There is also a tall loud-mouthed Welshman. He clearly doesn't fit in. He is a spanner in the smooth-running machinery of evolution and brainless holidays. What's he doing here?

Gerry had warned me about Carl Jones with an enigmatic combination of mutually exclusive descriptions:

'He's a madman. You'll never get any sense out of him. He's just obsessed with saving birds. But he's absolutely brilliant, shit-hot. He doesn't suffer fools gladly.' Gerry coughed discreetly and waggled a hand in warning. 'I don't know how you two will get on.'

'It was good of you to come and meet me,' I said to Carl at the airport.

'It was, wasn't it?'

'Yes, that's what I said.'

'Bloody good, in fact.'

'Well, goodish.'

Carl is very tall and he unscrupulously used this to his advantage. He towered over me.

'I think we're going to get on very well,' he threatened.

'I don't see why.'

Carl arrived in Mauritius in 1979. He was realizing a lifelong ambition to breed falcons. As a boy he had done nothing except collect animals in his parents' backyard.

'As this was a small Welsh cottage, you can imagine it was pretty squalid,' Carl told me. 'My father despaired of me. I was a complete failure as a schoolboy. I didn't want to do anything apart from poke around under hedges. I had a collection of polecats and magpies, and then got on to falcons. I bred kestrels and hawks at a time when hardly anyone else could. I had read all Gerry's books, so perhaps he was to blame.

'But I finally passed some exams and went to college. In 1978 I went to a lecture by Professor Tom Cade who was the world expert on falcons. This changed my life. He said something about the rarest falcon in the world, the Mauritius kestrel, which might be saved by captive breeding. I thought "Christ, this is meant for me. At last I can actually do something. I'm good at captive breeding and I can save a whole species!" I couldn't sleep for weeks.

'So I applied to ICPB, the International Council for the Protection of Birds, which was running the Mauritius kestrel project. They said how pleased they would be to send me to Mauritius because they wanted someone to close the project down. They didn't want to throw good money after bad. There was one pair in captivity which weren't breeding and two pairs in the wild. They wanted to shut their book on it.

'But when I arrived in Mauritius, I realized that they had given me enough money for a year, if I didn't spend any. And if I didn't answer the telephone, which didn't work, and didn't reply to any letters, I could just get on with it.'

Carl built some cages, took a clutch of eggs from the wild pair and began breeding. This makes it sound absurdly easy. It took five years of Carl 'just getting on with it' before he returned his first kestrel to the wild, five years during which he was working with a tiny number of birds. To show how vulnerable the process is, Carl lost all his captive birds in 1981.

'They all died in one week. All the aviaries. Some bugger had sprayed DDT overhead and that was that. Back to the beginning.

'The only good thing about the decline of the Mauritius kestrel is that it happened so fast during the 1970s that although there were only four birds left, they had a considerable number of genes between them. If there had been four birds breeding for a long time, the genes would have been lost.'

By 1984, the ICPB realized that they were still funding a mad Welshman in Mauritius and checked what he had been doing. They counted up the birds he had released, by that time only five, and reminded Carl that he should have closed the project down when he first arrived; they had forgotten about him. So Carl had a handful of kestrels and no money.

This is where Gerry came in. He had heard about the battle between Carl and the extinction of the kestrel, and threw his weight behind him. He offered Carl a job and a budget.

Carl's subsequent success reads like the rising profits of one of the go-go companies of the 1980s: 1 bird released in 1984, 4 in 1985, 9 in 1986, 21 in 1987, 26 in 1988, 57 in 1989, and 55 in 1990. Carl reckons that 50 a year is about right. He has diversified into the pink pigeon and the echo parakeet. There are also plans to look at marine life such as dolphins, turtles and whales. He has a team of nine researchers divided between the projects and he has set up the Mauritius Wildlife Appeal Fund to raise money from local businesses. The successful captive breeding and reintroduction of the Mauritius kestrel is now a case study at a number of colleges. 'All the sort of colleges I could never have got into,' Carl said smugly.

'The point is', Gerry explained, 'that if you do something well, people will listen to you. Carl can breed kestrels so the Mauritians listen to him. God help them, but they've had no disasters so far. If Carl had been unable to breed a kestrel, none of the politicians would now be listening to his advice about the national park.'

Gerry first came out to Mauritius in 1976. That trip resulted in his book *Pink Pigeons and Golden Bats* and the recruitment of a young man from the Forestry Department, Youseff Mungroo, as the first student of the Training Centre.

Youseff arrived in Jersey in the winter of 1977. He had never left Mauritius before, and had certainly never seen snow. He stayed for eight months. When he returned to Mauritius, he joined forces with Carl at the kestrel aviaries where they worked together for eight years. In 1986 he was promoted to Conservation Officer.

So the legacy of the dodo in Mauritius is Carl Jones, Youseff Mungroo and a team of nine researchers, six of whom are funded by Jersey. In twelve years the infrastructure has grown from two cages to a breeding centre with fifty kestrels, thirty pink pigeons, four echo parakeets and countless mice, plus four jeeps, three motor bikes, a campsite up in the forest and a rented house where everyone lives.

'You'll stay with me,' Carl announced after some thought. 'Most visitors stay at the house, but it's a pit. You'll be better off with me.'

We drove over the middle of the island through Curepipe, the upland village where the French colonialists would come to escape outbreaks of malaria.

'If I had a daughter', Carl speculated, 'I'd call her Malaria. I've always thought it would be a lovely name for a girl. Cholera is quite nice too.'

'Yes,' I wasn't sure how serious Carl was, 'I've always fancied Hepatitis.'

'No.' He was disgusted. 'You couldn't even call a dog Hepatitis. Malaria is a truly pretty name. Your wife's called something like that, isn't she? Gerry told me about her.'

'She's called Araminta.'

'Is that a tropical disease?' Carl said hopefully.

'No.'

'Sounds like it.'

'She'd put you right if she was here.'

Most of Carl's furniture consisted of packing-cases. Piles of books lined the walls, decorated with assorted bones. The fridge contained twelve bottles of beer, two tubs of yoghurt and some UHT milk.

'Help yourself.' He waved a hand at the fridge. 'I've stocked it up for you. I've also cleaned it out. I had two mongooses in there. I pick them up off the road and analyse their stomachs. Useful barometer of what's around. I once found some kestrel remains in one of them. Have some muesli.'

I wondered whether this was a veiled insult, but Carl helped himself to a bowl and took some milk off a shelf. We sat and ate muesli on the veranda. I produced a bottle of whisky. Muesli and whisky went together surprisingly well.

'We're at an incredibly exciting stage of conservation.' Carl loosened up after a couple of glasses. 'We're right at the beginning. Last century people were sending out hunters to shoot animals so they had a sample for their collection before they went extinct. Then this century animal collectors wanted animals in their homes just like other people collected stamps, the rarer the better. Now there are people trying to breed them. And there's people like me who manage a population in the wild. It's changing all the time.

'Everyone knows the answer to conservation,' he said belligerently. 'Everyone. You ask anyone what their views are, just like you asked me, and you'll get a first-class answer. A bloody brilliant answer. There are so many people walking around with doctorates who know the answer that it isn't true. And of course they're right. If you could put their opinions into practice the world would be a better place. No doubt.'

'So what's the snag?'

'The snag is that nobody listens to them. Not even other people who agree with them. Nobody listens. It takes a genius to get anyone to listen to what you say. That's why people have heard of Gerry Durrell. Peter Scott's another one.

'I went to see Peter Scott once. He was painting in his room. "Where do you think this would look best?" he asked me and held a cut-out of a swan up to the painting. I was bowled over. This man was using cut-outs!' Carl collapsed back in his chair at the memory. 'And then he said "I've got lots of other ones if you don't think swans go." And he pulled open this drawer which had wooden cut-outs of ducks, geese, teal, wigeon and everything. You see that's the genius of the man. No other painter would admit to that!'

'What about Gerry?'

'Gerry's the same. He just wanted to have a zoo. It was as simple as that. Peter Scott just wanted more birds around, that was the start of the WWF. Just the same with Jersey. Gerry had this simple idea: I want a zoo to save animals from extinction. So he got his zoo, and he's got everything which followed on from that. He makes people listen to him and bingo! The bugger's halfway down the road before any of your American experts can say "Where's his doctorate?"

'Gerry has an instinctive feel for animals. It's like having green fingers for gardening. I feel it myself with kestrels, I can communicate with them. You have to use your subconscious to communicate with them, there is no other level. And Gerry is great at anthropomorphism. Most people think this is childish because there's nothing scientific about it. But actually there's a lot of sense in it. If you think about it, animals look at each other in the same way as we look at them. That's why camouflage works for both of us. It proves that we're not colour-blind to them, and that is important in recognizing their feelings on different levels. You can get too scientific about animals. They weren't designed to fit into computer programmes. The important thing is to breed them if they're in trouble and live with them if they're not.

'If you want to see what's really happening here, you'd better go up and stay the night in camp up on the mountain. Kirsty will take you up. She does the pink pigeons. You won't see an echo parakeet, there's only a handful of them, but you'll see what's left of Macabe forest.

'Gerry can't do that sort of thing now. He can only write about it, better than you will, but at least you'll have seen it. Then come back down and I'll take you around the captive breeding centre and show you some kestrels. You can have a chat with Youseff. Then you'll have done the lot.

'God, I hate writers!' Carl shouted. 'They come in for three days, four at the most, and reckon they can write about what I do. I've lived here for twelve years, and nobody is at all interested in what I have to say about it.

'I had a writer here last year. I said to him "So you're a writer, are you? And what do you write about?''

''Science fiction'', he said.

''So it's all very clever-clever is it?'' I said. ''Have you written anything I'd have heard of?''

'And he said some hitch-hiking book. I'd never heard of it. Anyway the others were *desperate* to change the subject. It turns out he was Douglas Adams and very famous. Odd sort of bloke; kept very quiet after that. How was I meant to know? I've been in Mauritius for twelve years. Anyway, he reckoned he could write about everything here after a couple of days. Good luck to him, I say. Are you like that?'

I reassured Carl that I wasn't, more's the pity.

Although the English took control of Mauritius during the Napoleonic Wars, the island remains stubbornly French. French families own vast tracts of land here. Eight or nine French families control the sugar plantations and they have retained French habits including hunting, La Chasse. On the drive up to the camp, I noticed the high-wire fences of deer farms and squat wooden watch-towers along the cleared hillsides.

'La Chasse,' Kirsty explained. 'The Francos breed thousands of deer all over the island. They have driven deer shooting.'

'Driven?'

'Yes, they don't bother to stalk them, too many I suppose. They stand up on those towers and blast them as they charge past. They shoot thousands of deer. Look at it.' She waved her hand dismissively at the countryside. 'It's a disaster. They eat anything which grows. You must meet Wendy. She's a WWF botanist who works in Macabe forest.'

We drove higher up into the hills. Down below stretched the sugar-cane plantations, dotted with massive mounds of lava rocks which have been gathered together so the land can be ploughed. From this height the mounds look like molehills, or the droppings of some monstrous animal which might come nosing around the side of the hill. The surrounding sea was divided in two. Close to shore was the pale blue lagoon. A white line of surf broke over the reef, dark blue water spread away beyond it.

The campsite is a motley collection of five or six heavy canvas tents, Boy Scout-style, pitched in a clearing in the forest. The pink pigeon release cage is to one side. There were several pigeons inside, and two sitting on top of the cage eating grain and looking rather perky. Two exhausted researchers came out to greet us, Colin and Kevin, who study pigeons and parakeets respectively. They had been on a dawn watch – three pigeons, no parakeets – and were building a rat-proof food store. They wore army trousers, T-shirts and three-day stubble. We agreed to go to Pigeon Wood for an afternoon watch, and Kirsty took me off to find Wendy.

We found her in the tract of forest which she has fenced off.

'Come on in,' she welcomed us. 'Look out where you tread.'

It was like going into the rarified atmosphere of an art gallery. In the hushed silence we made our way between the trees, treading as carefully as if we'd been walking through a flowerbed. Wendy is slim, pretty, blonde and blue-eyed – almost the last thing I expected to find in the middle of the forest. She also has a formidable knowledge of the plants around her.

'The two main problems here are guava and privet.'

'Privet?' I associated privet with neatly trimmed gardens.

'Yes. It runs riot here. Each privet plant produces bushy branches which monopolize the sunlight. Other plants get squeezed out. An ebony sapling which might grow six inches a year has no chance. And guava. Let me show you.'

Wendy led us to the fence and pointed into the forest beyond. It was a thicket of pale thin trunks. They were so straight and regular, six inches apart, that they looked like the bars of a cage.

'They're like storm-troopers,' she said. 'They grow so dense that they march through the forest killing off everything. People in Mauritius love their fruit. It's a battle to keep them out.

'This plot of forest has great historical interest. It was analysed in 1926 by Dr Vaughan – the first major ecological study done in the tropics. He marked out a patch of 1,000 square metres and measured every tree over 50 centimetres tall. His findings were published in the *Journal of Ecology* in 1941. When I first arrived here he was eighty-seven years old and he became my mentor. I would take him plants from the forest and he would identify them. He gave me his field notes and gradually I learned all about the forest. When he did his field study there was no privet and only two guavas in the plot.

'Dr Vaughan decided to weed the plot and take out any introduced plants. There was a shrubby weed called *Ardisia* as well as the couple of guavas. The Forestry Service weeded it until 1952 when for some reason they stopped. Dr Vaughan was very old then, but he finally managed to persuade them to weed it again in 1972.

'When I arrived here in 1982 I reopened the entire plot and found all Dr Vaughan's markers underneath the guava which had taken over. In 1926 Dr Vaughan had measured 1,785 individual trees comprising 69 species. In 1983 I found 1,072 individuals comprising 60 species. I also measured out a plot of forest which had never been weeded and found only 339 individuals comprising 42 species. So you see extinction is happening amongst plants as well as animals.'

I was interested to see that ebony, even a sixty-year-old tree, is thin and spindly.

'What do you expect?' Wendy asked. 'A Douglas Fir? It has to get up to the light, so it puts energy into growing upwards. But it also doesn't want to rot, so it packs itself tight. You never see a rotten piece of ebony. It can lie on the ground for years and not get eaten by termites. Or it can be chopped down in a flash and made into an indestructible ashtray.

'This patch of the forest is also important because it has plants which have not been found anywhere else in the world. One is *Tambourissa pedicellata*. Dr Vaughan found eighteen, but I couldn't find any until three years ago when I found one which seemed to have grafted itself on to another species of *Tambourissa*. I've taken cuttings and reared some seedlings which I will plant here.'

We left Wendy moving around in the quiet shadows of the forest, squatting down and carefully spreading out the leaves of tiny shoots, knowing that she would never live to see them grow even to her waist.

Back at camp Colin had prepared lunch of baps and sardines, a field-worker's favourite. We collected together notebooks, mosquito repellent and cagoules and set off to Pigeon Wood.

'Pigeon Wood is the only place where there are wild pink pigeons,' Kirsty explained. 'After everyone thought they had gone extinct Gerry came here in the 1970s and captured some to start his breeding programme.'

'How many wild ones are there?'

'Thirteen.'

'Unlucky number.'

'Lucky to be around at all. I'm adding to it with captive-bred birds. I've released nineteen so far, twelve of which are still alive. There were some released in the Botanical Gardens by my predecessor but they all died out.'

'Why?'

'Catapults.'

'Catapults?'

'Little boys came and shot them all. The pigeons are big and pink and nice targets. Straight into the casserole.'

'At least they ate them. That was something.'

'What do you mean?' Kirsty looked offended.

'They didn't eat the dodo.'

'Well, I wish they wouldn't eat my pigeons. I'm going to release more this year, possibly up to ten.

'People used to think pink pigeons were stupid. They couldn't make nests and didn't breed. But in the early days Jersey was trying to get as many eggs as possible from as wide a gene pool as possible. They kept swapping pairs around, taking eggs to make them lay again. There was no incentive for the birds to breed, they never saw their young, and so I think they just lost interest.

'My research shows that pink pigeons pretty much mate for life, so I'm keeping my pairs together for much longer. I'm getting less eggs, but better adjusted birds.'

We climbed up a tall teak tree and sat on a platform built in its highest branches. Through binoculars we watched over the tops of the trees. I say trees rather than wood because Pigeon Wood only measures 200 by 400 yards. Pink pigeons spend most of their

Mauritius Pink Pigeon
(Nesoenas mayeri)

time sitting on a branch doing nothing, so anyone who watches them must do pretty much the same. If you studied frogs, you would spend most of your time lying around getting wet and muddy. I was grateful that we were studying pigeons, high up in this tree-house with a view of the island and the sea and the clean white surf. Colin and Kirsty quickly located three pink pigeons.

One flapped out of its branch and flopped down to another closer to our perch.

'Blue-grey,' said Colin.

'Blue-green,' Kirsty corrected.

I looked at it closely. It just looked pink to me. Pink with chocolate wings. Hesitantly, I said so.

'No, it has two coloured rings. The combination is how we distinguish them.'

We sat and stared at the pigeon. Colin had noted the exact time in his log-book, 15.38: Blue-green.

'Is this what you do all day?'

'Most of it. Usually there's nothing to see. And generally it's freezing cold and misty. You've got the best weather I've had in ages.'

In three hours we saw five birds, 38 per cent of the wild population. They hardly looked like birds each of whose welfare obsesses the entire ornithological world. They didn't even coo. They looked as if they deserved to be knocked off their branches. I began to develop some sympathy for the boys who shot them with catapults.

'Watch out!' Kirsty brought me out of my spiteful reverie. She pointed and at the same time I heard a cry, 'kark kark kark!' True to form the noise echoed around the forest canopy. A lime-green echo parakeet with a longish tail flew straight and true overhead. We all held our breath. It swooped down to a far corner of the wood and vanished.

'Wow!' I said.

'Best sighting I've ever had,' Kirsty said.

'15.48: Echo parakeet,' Colin wrote. He shut his log-book with a snap and said with emotion, 'Worth seeing that, the rarest bird in the world.'

'That's why I sit up here all day,' he went on, in answer to an earlier question. 'I wouldn't do any other job in the world. I earn £4,000 a year here. Frankly I'd do it for nothing. There are people out there earning ten times what I earn, but they'll never have a moment like that.'

'How much would someone pay to see a dodo now?'

It was an unanswerable question.

'Twitchers,' Carl said with relish when I told him of the sighting and Colin's speech. 'Just a bleeding twitcher. They're mad. But they're the people who are saving these birds. You have to be obsessed to work in conservation. We all are. Look at Gerry: you might think he's a nice bloke. He's witty and charming, and given a couple of seconds he would have your grandmother eating out of his hand. But believe me, the man's a nutter. He's obsessed with saving animals. If you were in a firing line alongside a lemur, and he had to choose between you and the lemur, you'd get it straight between the eyes.

'Do you know that in Mauritius, population one million, there are only two twitchers, two people who care about birds enough to go out and look at them?'

When I met Youseff Mungroo I asked why there were no Mauritians involved in the conservation of their country.

'It is a matter of security,' he said. 'A Mauritian coming out of university will not want to enter a cul-de-sac. They are looking for a career, they do not want to waste time with wildlife. There is no money in it, no chance of promotion. They want to get on in life so they can make money.'

'But these foreigners, people like Colin and Kirsty, even Carl for that matter, don't do it for money,' I pointed out. 'They are very poor by Western standards.'

'But they have jeeps to drive.' With a deft shake of his head, Youseff contradicted me. 'They look very rich in this country. And we Mauritians cannot work as hard as they do. Our observation would not be as good. We cannot get up at dawn to watch the birds, and again watch them in the evening, we have families to look after. Only foreigners can afford to study birds.'

'What about you? You're doing conservation.'

'Well, I am the only one. The government will not offer jobs for more people in conservation. I have asked for assistants every year, but they always say there are no funds. Also it took me eight years to get my job. Eight years when I was just working here at the breeding centre cleaning out cages and being a field-worker. My wife didn't like it.

'But now I have a desk job.' He looked well-satisfied.

From his clean soft hands, natty brown slacks and fresh white shirt, it was clear that Youseff had not been out in the field for some time.

We had a moment of glorious misunderstanding when I asked Youseff to draw the hierarchy of command in the Forestry Division. He wrote down the structure which comprised seven grades, each grade having an assistant grade.

'You see, look at the chances of promotion here,' he pointed out.

'Yes, terrible,' I commiserated with him, 'all that waiting for dead men's shoes. Apathy all down the line.'

'No,' he corrected me, his eyes gleaming with the possibilities of it all. 'There are so many chances, you can be promoted every year.'

'But it would still take forever to get to the top.'

'That is not the point. The point is that you would feel promoted. Your wife would feel you had been promoted. Your family would be happy. You would be doing well.'

'But what about getting something done about the habitat?'

Youseff looked at me reprovingly. I had much to learn.

He took me back to the breeding centre.

'Don't mind my car,' he apologized. 'It is a typical field-worker's car.'

We got into a neat Renault 5 which would not have made it up to the Pigeon Wood camp. At the breeding centre we bumped into another researcher, Stephen Rault, who was just going out.

'Aha!' Youseff congratulated him. 'A very nice new motor bike. So you are making some money at last.'

Stephen, who wanders around like some permanently distracted chess player, completely missed the point.

'It's not mine,' he finally answered.

'It's new!' Youseff insisted.

'It's the project's.'

'Well, someone is making some money,' Youseff insisted. 'It will be a new jeep next. Maybe you yourself will get a new jeep.'

'I don't need one,' Stephen said simply, 'I've got this motor bike.'

Youseff shrugged his shoulders with frustration. We went inside.

'Hi, Youseff!' someone greeted him. 'When are we going to Round Island?'

'Youseff! Have we managed to stop the new road?'

'Youseff! Have you done anything about the new bridge yet?'

Youseff pointed me in the right direction to find Carl and fled back to the sanctuary of his office.

'Now let's show you the factory,' said Carl. 'You've seen where the birds live. This is where they come from.'

The captive breeding centre is a series of cages and aviaries built in a circle around a tall tree. The open courtyard is criss-crossed with mud paths leading to the various cages.

'Let's start with the pink pigeons. There are fourteen pairs here. I keep Barbary doves as foster parents. They are brilliant foster parents, but they must have laid an egg at exactly the same time as the pigeons. They then feed the chick. Their milk crop changes – even by the day. I think it's something to do with the cells sloughing off their throat, but I don't know. So I take away their chick and give them a pigeon. Then off they go. That's the pigeons.

'The same with the parakeets. I've got four here, the only echo parakeets in captivity. I keep a whole lot of ring-necked parrots which are very good parents to feed them. I haven't had to use them yet, but it's important to have common birds around so you feel free to experiment with them. If you've just got your rare birds, you spend your life thinking "Jesus! I can't risk that!" You never get anywhere. Jersey was hamstrung like that for a while.

They're beginning to learn now.

'Now we've got the kestrels. I'm breeding about fifty a year.' We went into the office at one corner. A large deep-freeze blocked the entrance. A series of incubators lined the walls. 'In order to hatch, an egg must lose 15 per cent of its original body weight. It does this by letting the water evaporate out through the shell. So we weigh the eggs. If they're not losing enough water, we sandpaper the shell a little. If they're losing too much, we smear a little glue over one end. You may think I'm mad, but this gives me an 80 per cent success rate. No other bird breeder gets that.'

Outside the office was a line of open-faced nesting boxes. Each one contained six or seven young kestrels. They crowded at the back, bunched together. They looked clean and absurdly fluffy, as if they had just emerged from a spin-dryer, with sharp little triangular beaks sticking out.

'They're almost ready to be hacked out. I keep them here for thirty days. They mustn't be too old or they'd fly off straight away and get lost. Dead the next week. They must make exploratory flights first and keep returning to their boxes. We feed them for the first month as well with quails and mice.'

The quails were sitting in some comfort just around the corner. They busied themselves as we looked through the mesh.

'Why quails?' I asked on their behalf.

'They're a nice size. And they've got the right meat-to-fat ratio – a chicken is too fatty – and their bones are just right. Chewy but not tough. So quails it is.'

'Hard luck, chaps.'

We walked on.

'And there's mice.'

We went into a tiny room where little aquariums were crammed with progressively bigger white mice. Carl put his hand in amongst the larger ones and pulled out a wriggling handful. He arranged them by their tails, rather as one would arrange a hand of cards.

'Not squeamish, are you?' He grinned and stroked their soft skins. Their tails looked transparent pink against his knuckles.

'Not so much,' I had begun to say, but stopped when Carl

swung them once around like a handful of conkers and smashed their heads smartly on to the table.

'Grub's up.'

The mice dangled limp in his hand, blood trickling delicately from their thin noses.

'Let's feed Pink. He's my lover.'

I smiled indulgently, anthropomorphism with a passion.

Pink sat by himself. He saw Carl and swooped to the fence. Carl went inside and offered him a mouse. He sat on his hand, took it gratefully in one talon and bit its head off. Blood ran over Carl's wrist.

'Pink imprinted himself on me,' Carl explained. 'This is the danger of breeding. You have to keep away from the birds or they think of you as their mother. They imprint on to your face or your hand. He now thinks he's human so he won't touch the other kestrels. He thinks they're just a bunch of silly birds. Don't you, Pinky?'

Carl chucked him under the beak. Pink looked bursting with energy, his chest puffed out, his eyes jet black and unblinking.

'As he refuses to have anything to do with the other birds, he won't breed with them. So he breeds with me.'

I looked at Carl with fresh disgust.

'What do you mean?'

'He's my lover. He fancies me something rotten. When we need his sperm for artificial insemination, I put on this hat, it's like a bowler-hat with a rubber brim, and he flies down and fucks my brains out. When he ejaculates, we collect his sperm from the brim.'

'And he thinks you're his mother?'

'Perverted, I agree,' Carl admitted. 'Not how I'd treat my mother, but then I'm not a kestrel.'

Gerry and Lee and their collection of Malagasy animals had arrived the previous day. They were now ready to fly back to Jersey, and Carl and I set off to help them load the animals on to the aeroplane.

'I'll show you a kestrel on the way.' Carl stuffed some dead mice into his pocket. On the way to the airport, he parked on a stretch of road high up on a hill and walked around whistling.

'There he is.'

A tiny speck moved fast across the hill. A moment later a kestrel hovered over us.

'You see he can't hover for long. His wings are the wrong shape.'

The kestrel landed on a stump nearby. He looked expectant, correctly so. Carl fished in his pocket and lobbed a mouse high in the air. The kestrel watched it unflinchingly. The mouse turned over, its legs splayed out, and began falling. With a lazy flap of wings, the kestrel lurched off the stump. He swooped low, rose up and caught the falling mouse with his talons.

'Peculiar skill to catch a falling dead mouse,' Carl said with admiration.

'There can't be too many to practise on.'

'Are you taking the piss? Bloody writers. Gerry is always making crackpot comments like that. Now you just watch that bird. He'll fly low along the hill into the wind. Then come back to his nest downwind, flying higher.'

Sure enough the kestrel flew slowly upwind, making rather heavy weather of it, and then turned and went screaming back along the top of the hill before disappearing into one of the crags.

'He'll eat its head and give the body to his mate. He might come back for more.'

A couple of minutes later, entirely unannounced, there was a plumpf of wings and the kestrel was back.

'Here,' said Carl, 'just put this on your hand. Hold it out like a sugar lump.' He put a dead mouse in my hand. 'And for God's sake don't flinch.'

I held out my hand and watched the kestrel. It hovered above me and then disappeared from view. There was a rush of feathers, a light stroke across the palm of my hand and the mouse had vanished. The kestrel sat comfortably on its stump, the mouse in its talons. I looked down at my hand expecting to see blood. Unblemished.

'Quick, eh?' Carl said.

Mauritius Kestrel
"falco Punctatus"

'Yes,' I agreed, rather astonished. I felt as if I'd narrowly missed a fatal accident.

At the airport hotel Lee and Quentin were frantically trying to sort out the documentation for the animals. Gerry and I sat it out on a balcony. The plane was imminent. A couple of beers arrived. We toasted the journey ahead. In front of us the palm trees leaned over the beach.

'It's at moments like this that I long to recite *The Owl and the Pussycat*,' Gerry said, 'but flying by plane is so ghastly. I used to ship all my animals – a much better way to travel. We all had a chance to acclimatize ourselves as we went. I could spend more time with them and get to know them, and there wasn't so much stress.'

Lee flounced over and plonked herself down in a chair.

'Gerry, where are your trousers? For God's sake! We're leaving in five minutes.'

'Don't worry about my trousers, honey. Plenty of time. Trust women to spoil a good drink by fretting over a pair of trousers.'

The pandemonium compounded dangerously at the airport. Quentin and Lee vanished ahead with all the tickets to join the queue. When Gerry, Carl and I wandered in, a policeman pounced on Gerry and demanded to see his ticket.

'I don't have it.'

'Then I must arrest you,' was the dumbfounding reply.

'What are you talking about?'

'Come this way, please.' The policeman began to apply gentle pressure to Gerry's arm.

'You don't know who you're talking to,' Carl warned him.

I had a fleeting vision of Gerry being handcuffed. Gerry possibly had the same idea. He lifted his walking-stick.

'Get off me. I wouldn't have come to this airport if I didn't want to fly.'

'I'm sorry, sir.' The policeman was insistent. 'No ticket, you must come with me. Nobody flies wearing shorts.'

'You don't understand.' Carl laid a friendly arm on the policeman's shoulder. 'This man is a friend of the Prime Minister.'

The policeman looked disbelieving.

'Does this mean anything to you?' Carl produced a suitably impressive but totally irrelevant card and pushed it under his nose. The policeman looked askance and waved us on.

Lee and Quentin came over.

'We're off.'

Gerry struggled to his feet. 'Here goes.'

Carl and I waved them off. We then drove around the side of the terminal to retrieve the animals from the hanger and put them on the aeroplane.

It was considerably easier to get into the back of the airport than the front. We drove around the edge of the runway looking for the right hanger. It was deserted. We stopped outside and slid back the huge corrugated iron door. The wooden cages were piled in one corner. We peered inside. The bandros looked back rather nervously. The giant jumping rats were in windowless wooden boxes, and the reptiles and tortoises were travelling inside cloth bags which were nailed down inside a wooden trunk. An official materialized.

'You want the London plane?' he asked. 'The third on the right.' He waved us on.

There were a surprising number of planes lined up, their fins in the air like so many sharks. Several of them were beginning to rev up. They towered over us.

'Third on the right?' Carl said. 'It must be this one.'

We parked alongside and piled out. A gang of men in oil-stained dungarees crowded round us. The noise of turbo engines was deafening. The men heaved the cages on to a hydraulic hoist. We jumped on and rose up into the belly of the plane. We tried to wedge the cages in the back of the hold, but the ceiling was shoulder-high and the cages wouldn't all fit in. I caught a glimpse of the bandro cage with 'Edward and Araminta' written across it in Lee's handwriting. The men began peering inside.

'Animals?' they asked.

'Yes.'

They jubilantly banged on the tops of the cages to attract their attention.

'Stop it!' I yelled.

They wandered off and returned with a wooden pallet which they broke up by smashing it against the floor. Then they wedged the pieces between the cages.

We crawled out of the plane back on to the hoist.

'*Bon voyage*!' Carl shouted above the din. 'It'll be better in Jersey.'

In the calm of the departure lounge above us, Gerry and Lee would be sipping champagne.

The trip was over.

'The buggers,' said Carl.

SIX

INDIA

THE COMPOUNDING PROBLEM OF POPULATION – THE TEEMING COUNTRYSIDE – TEN INDIAN MINUTES AT THE MINISTRY – INVISIBLE POT-HOLES IN THE SKY – HARRY ANDREWS AT THE MADRAS CROCODILE BANK – FIFTEEN FEET OF POTENTIAL HANDBAG – BARBECUED RATS AND CROCODILE EGG MAYONNAISE – THE IRULA SNAKE CATCHERS AND TREE PLANTERS – PARAMANANDA ('VERY MUCH CHEERFUL') LAHAN IN ASSAM – THE 20,000 RUPEE NOSE – RIDING ELEPHANTS TO SAVE RHINOS – FOUR CARTRIDGES AGAINST THE KALASHNIKOVS – PARAMANANDA'S NOT SO VERY MUCH CHEERFUL OUTLOOK

Moving from Mauritius, a drop in the Indian Ocean which you can drive around in an afternoon, to India involves a quantum leap in numbers. Mauritius has a population of 1 million, 860,000 of whom are Indian. For every Indian in Mauritius there are 1,000 Indians in India. Only China has more people. Between them, India and China account for 40 per cent of the world's population.

But like the people involved, these figures are not static. The Indian population is growing by 2.5 per cent a year. This may not sound much, but the numbers compound dangerously upwards.

If the Indian population continues to grow at 2.5 per cent, it will double in thirty years and quadruple after sixty to 2.7 billion, equivalent to just over half the current world population. There is no reason to suppose this will not happen as the Indian population has been growing by 2.5 per cent ever since the first census in 1951. In the last ten years it grew by 162 million. To give a sense of perspective on these extra children who are now growing up in India, they represent two-thirds of the population of North America, or well over the population of Brazil, or the combined population of Britain, France, Spain and Greece. They are all under ten, and in five years' time they will start breeding themselves.

So much for abstract numbers. What this actually means in India is that outside the broad leafy boulevards of New Delhi, where roomy whitewashed houses sit back in large gardens and security guards doze comfortably at the gates, the rest of the country is a teeming crowd.

The cities are bursting with traffic and people, but you'd expect that in a city. The astonishing thing is that the countryside is exactly the same. However remote a place, there is always a crowd. On the main road in the most remote village people pass like the Christmas shopping crowds along Oxford Street.

Buses, trains, lorries, rickshaws, motor scooters and bicycles weave improbably around each other and are all chronically overloaded. A typical Bajaj motor scooter will be driven by a man with his son standing upright between his knees. His wife will ride side-saddle behind him with their daughter wedged between them, and a baby on her lap. Every bicycle carries two people, one pedalling, the other draped over the cross-bar, and often a third on the back. On buses so many people are squashed so tightly together that it looks like a clothes shop; you cannot believe people are actually living inside their clothes. The trains are not only equally crammed inside, but have people hanging off the doors and windows and sitting on the roof.

This crowd in India has reduced the country to a vast expanse of baked brown mud. There are no trees, no wild flowers, no hedges. There is no inherent moisture in the ground, it is either wet mud or dry mud depending on whether it is raining. An umbrella is essential. When it rains there is no other shelter; when the sun glares down there is no other shade.

I had come to India to meet two Jersey trainees, Harry Andrews, who works at a privately funded crocodile sanctuary in Madras, and P. Lahan, who had deprecatingly described himself as 'a middle-level functionary in the hierarchy of the Forest Department of Assam', but who turned out to be in charge of the game reserves which hold the last populations of Asian elephants and rhinos in India.

After looking at the small birds on Mauritius, the small animals in Madagascar and Brazil, and no animals in West Africa, I was looking forward to seeing Indian crocodiles, elephants and rhinos.

The first indicators that life in India is becoming untenable are the animals, and the most obvious animals are the large ones. Elephants used to live right across India. There are now only 15,000 wild elephants and these are marooned in heavily guarded government reserves. The Indian elephant population represents half the wild population of Asian elephants. The others are spread in small populations from Bangladesh to Vietnam. These populations have no possibility of meeting up, so they are at much greater risk of extinction than their total number, 30,000, suggests. There are twenty times fewer Asian than African elephants, yet there is much less concern about their future. Perhaps because Asian elephants participate so readily in public ceremonies, people do not consider them to be endangered. But Asian elephants rarely breed in captivity, so when the source in the wild dries up, the only elephants left in India will be depictions of the god Ganesh.

The other large animal which used to live right across east Pakistan, north India, Bhutan and Bangladesh is the great one-horned Indian rhinoceros, *Rhinoceros unicornis*. There are now 2 left in Pakistan (and reports that one of these has been poached), 375 in Nepal, 80 in Bhutan, none in Bangladesh and 1,200 in Assam of which 1,100 are trapped in one reserve. As their horns are small and rounded, they are not turned into dagger handles for the Yemenis but are ground into dust by the Chinese.

P. Lahan advised me that to visit Assam I needed a Restricted Area Permit which could be obtained from the Ministry of Home Affairs in New Delhi. I soon found out where most of the excess Indian population spend their time – in the internal machinery of the Indian bureaucracy. Like the bacteria which quickly infested my stomach, Indian bureaucrats infest the long corridors of bureaucracy, with the notable difference that they prevent anything from emerging at the other end.

The Ministry of Home Affairs is housed in a large blind brick building. The corridors are dingy, the walls brown with dirt apart from a waist-high stripe where people brush along them. Occasional red stains of betel juice spit run down the walls like blood from a stabbing attack. The corridors were lined with applicants. Men in dhotis squatted and chatted, one family spread itself comfortably out over the floor and drank *chai*. The air smelt of bedi cigarettes. There was no sense of urgency or impatience.

I finally ascertained that Mr Prakash Chander was the District Officer in charge of issuing permits to Assam. I pushed open the door to his office and found two holy men in saffron robes angrily berating an imperturbable Sikh who merely stroked his oiled beard smoother beneath its hairnet. One of the holy men was truly biblical with wild eyes and grey hair, stamping his staff on the ground between his sandals. He appeared to have painted the Japanese flag across his forehead. The other was young, blond-haired, blue-eyed and bearded. He kept whining in a soft Californian drawl 'What's he saying now?' The Sikh picked up his Dial-M-for-Murder bakelite telephone, pushed a couple of chrome buttons and chatted at length. He then abruptly swept out of the office. The two holy men scampered after him. I decided to wait where I was on the grounds that he must return sooner or later.

An hour later he did so and gave me a lengthy questionnaire which concentrated on my ancestry. 'Return to me in six days' time and I will have your permit ready.'

'Why do you need six days?'

'We have to check various references.'

'What, like my father's place of birth?'

'Just various references.' He refused to be drawn.

'Are you sure of this? I've got flights booked.'

'There will be no problem.' He wobbled his head encouragingly.

I wandered out feeling this was too good to be true. But then six days must be long enough. The rest of the applicants were still all dozing in the corridors. They clearly knew something I didn't. In the meantime I flew to Madras to meet Harry Andrews and look at crocodiles.

Nothing in India happens without a good deal of bizarre misadventure and breathtaking charm. The flight to Madras was no exception. On the way we stopped at Hyderabad. It may have been an unscheduled stop because we were all still drinking coffee when the plane veered to the left, dipped sharply and came screaming in to land. For a moment I thought it was a crash landing because we hit the tarmac with a bang which emptied all our coffee over our laps. We ricocheted off and crashed down again, jolting up and down with skull-shattering force until the pilot finally wrenched us to a stop.

Nobody either got on or off the plane, and in due course we took off again with much shuddering and heaving. After a beguilingly smooth climb, the plane fell fifty feet without warning and our freshly poured cups of tea again scalded our knees. The pilot's voice came over the loudspeaker.

'I apologize for such a bumpy landing and take-off at Hyderabad. It was nothing to do with my flying skills, it is just one of the hazards of flying in this part of the country. And as for the air turbulence we have now just suffered – as you know the roads up here in the sky are invisible and I cannot see the pot-holes to steer around them. We were meant to be flying at 30,000 feet, but somehow we never quite got that high, so we're flying at 23,000 feet. Thank you and please enjoy a pleasant flight.'

The Madras Crocodile Bank is forty kilometres south of Madras itself. The coastal drive down was slow and hot with the sun overhead and exhaust fumes heavy on the road. On the left the sea spread out, brown and uninviting. The countryside on the right was dry, flat, featureless and baked hard as brick. The crowd along the roadside walked under umbrellas. Brick and mud villages looked like ancient excavated ruins.

A metal signpost cut to form the silhouette of crocodile jaws pointed the way into the Croc Bank at Vadenemelli. Harry

Andrews came to greet me. He wore a blue-checked dhoti and T-shirt and had the fine pointed nose and narrow face of the Tamils. His head seemed only loosely attached to his shoulders and wobbled lightly like a ship's compass suspended on gimbals. Whenever he agreed with me, his head shook easily to and fro as if he was actually disagreeing but was merely too polite to say so.

We sat down and he called for two coconuts. The first thing I wanted to straighten out was his name.

'Well, you see, my grandfather adopted the surname Andrews when he was working with the Britishers in the 1930s. He became a Catholic because there were some Irish monks here. His real name was Amnuay Tetegri, an old Sanskrit name.

'So he converted and went off to England. All the family thought that he would come back with lots of money for them. In the event he just came back with a Rolls Royce for himself. Everyone was damned pissed off actually.

'And then he spent all day in the English club at Coonoor. Everyone thought he was doing business, so they again grew hopeful that he would make them a lot of money. But it turned out he was just drinking toddies all day. He never did any business so nobody got rich. Everyone was damned pissed off all over again.

'I was christened a Catholic and went to school in the Nilgiri Hills at St Joseph's. I then read engineering at Madras University. Then I gave up engineering to work at this place. My parents were very saddened because an engineer can earn as much dowry as a doctor or lawyer. But I'd met my future wife, Romaine, and we didn't care about that.

'It was a little rough here when I first started, there were no buildings or anything. I camped while she stayed in Madras. Now I've built our house and she works as the administrator in the office.'

We finished our coconuts and walked outside. I could see the sea through the trees. A series of low brick walls surrounded various pens and the smell of fish and fishy things hung in the air.

'When did you arrive here?' I asked.

'In 1982. It was very different then. There were no trees, we planted all these, and just 750 rupees in the bank. There were only 400 crocs.'

'Sounds quite a lot to me.'

'Well, we have 5,000 now.'

We set off through the shade to look at some of these 5,000 crocodiles. The Croc Bank is spread over forty acres of sand dunes, and the pens are enclosed by waist-high walls. We leaned over one. The pen was the size of a football pitch and was liberally coated with crocodiles, thousands of crocodiles.

They basked in the sun around the edge of the pool, their jaws gaping open and the corners of their mouths curled into satisfied grins. They lay collapsed over each other, sprawled anyhow with their heads resting on backs and their tails curled around their faces, soaking up the sun in companionable silence.

'There used to be three species of crocodile in India, two freshwater ones, muggers and gharials, and a salt-water one living off the coast. These are muggers. They used to be pretty much everywhere, but now they're pretty much nowhere. There is such pressure on the rivers for irrigation and washing and fishing that the crocs get killed off. They have nowhere to hide. We have over 3,000 muggers here, but there is nowhere to put them back. A while back we reintroduced 850 into some rivers in Rajasthan, but they were all killed. The Pakistan government has asked us for 1,000, but we won't release them because we know there is nowhere safe for them to go. So they stay here.'

'I don't blame people for killing them,' I said. 'If you were washing your clothes in the river and one of these popped up you'd be pretty frightened.'

'No, muggers never eat people. They just eat fish. What people don't understand is that crocs are good for the fish population. They prey on the predators, so the general numbers of fish increase. Without crocs, the predators grow too powerful and the fish get smaller. They also keep the river clean. When there were crocs in the Ganges, it was much cleaner. Now it is filthy and you get a good deal of cholera and bilharzia.'

We walked on to a small pen where a single huge crocodile lay slumped by the pool. At the sight of us he raised himself up on to his stubby legs and with a swagger of hips and a flick of his tail he plunged into the pool. About fifteen feet of prime handbag potential slithered over the edge and glided smoothly into the water. Two eyeballs remained bulging above the surface.

'He's a salt-water crocodile. They live down the coast and right across into Indonesia and the Pacific Ocean. They grow to twenty feet and weigh up to a tonne.'

'Why do you want a monster like this?'

'He's not a monster, he's wonderful. It is true that salties sometimes get the taste for human flesh and go out of their way to eat people. They tip over canoes and such like.' Harry made it sound rather playful. 'But there's no reason why we can't live together. These crocodiles have survived unchanged since the time of the dinosaurs. His direct ancestor was eating dinosaur flesh. They got to their perfect evolution before we even started on ours. So who are we to kill them off now?

'You should see the way crocodiles breed. It is very moving. The female lays the eggs in the sand and then guards them. When they are ready to hatch, she will dig up the earth if it is too hard so that the babies don't get trapped underground. Then if they haven't hatched by a certain date, she will gently break open the eggs to let the babies out. And then she carries them in her mouth to a safe place in the water where she or her mate protects them. It is a beautiful relationship. I defy anybody to say that crocs are monsters after seeing that.

'And another thing which is biologically fascinating is that the sex of a crocodile egg is only decided after forty-six days of incubation. It depends on the temperature at which the egg is kept. If it is hot they become males, if it is cold they become females. And the crocs can decide this by digging a deeper or shallower nest. Who knows? This may be a natural way of regulating the population. We're doing a lot of research on it here. Think of the implications if we can work out a link with the human reproductive cycle. We could go through a couple of generations where the population is mostly male. Population control could be much more subtle than offering free radios for vasectomies.'

Gharial
"gavialis gangeticus"

Modern crocodiles divide into two groups. One group, the *Crocodylids*, consists of crocodiles and alligators which are distributed in virtually all tropical and sub-tropical environments. They eat fish, large animals and carrion. The other group is the gharials, *Gavialis gangetius*, which are slender-snouted crocodiles. They only eat fish, they are virtually unstudied, virtually extinct and only found in India. There were eight in the next pen.

The gharials were yellowy-green in colour with smooth skins and long thin snouts bristling with sharp little teeth. 'Gharial' is the Hindi for pot, and the male crocodiles have a large round growth on the end of their noses which looks like a clay pot. It is hollow and amplifies their calls under water.

Harry hopped over the wall and walked down to the water's edge. After looking around carefully, I followed him. The crocs were quietly gliding about in the water. The females were only visible as two frog-like eyes moving across the surface. With their gharials, the males each looked like a Christmas pudding closely followed by a pair of frog-like eyes. Harry had taken a plastic sack sloshing with water from a keeper. He pulled out a large flapping fish which he threw into the water. The ripples faded away, and all that could be seen were a couple of Christmas puddings floating around – or so the fish might have thought. We sat on our heels by the edge of the pool and watched the green surface for signs of life.

Suddenly the water erupted as a few yards away from us a croc reared out. He stood on his back legs, thrashing his tail beneath him to keep his balance. The fish was flapping in his jaws, and he made a great show of juggling it around so it tipped further down his jaws towards his yellow throat. He lost his balance and crashed back into the water. A moment later he was up again, and the fish was manoeuvred further along his line of teeth whilst his tail whipped to and fro. He finally gulped down the fish, collapsed back down out of sight and the pool went quiet.

'How many gharials do you have?'

'Just 11 breeding females. We've bred 25 babies. That compares with the salties where we have 3 breeding females and have bred 264 babies.'

'So most of your crocs are muggers?'

'Yes, we have 560 breeding mugger females. We're producing 2,000 babies a year.'

'What are you going to do with them all?'

'Actually we're going to stop breeding muggers next year. We have enough and there is nowhere to put them back. So we've got some other projects on the go. They mainly concern a local tribe around here, the Irulas.'

'What do they do?'

'They catch snakes, rats and termites.'

'Nice. Anything else? Do they farm any greens to go with them?'

'No. They have no land. But you'll like the rats, we're going to eat some tonight. Come and meet everybody anyway.'

Before I could say I was allergic to rats, Harry had led me through the trees to the office.

The Croc Bank was set up by Romulus Whitaker, an American snake-catcher who arrived in India as a hippy in the 1960s and stayed. He set up a snake farm in Madras in the 1970s and then became interested in crocodiles. He bought the forty-acre site in 1980 when he saw how endangered the Indian crocodiles were becoming. He now spends most of his time in the Andaman Islands, where a number of aboriginal tribes are being exterminated by Indian settlers. The Andaman Islands were used by the British as a penal colony, and they encouraged Indians to settle there and log the forests. Many of the tribes have gone extinct.

'The Irulas are not unlike the tribes on the Andamans,' Harry explained. 'They used to be a nomadic tribe living off the forest. As there is no forest here any more, they have settled on the edges of villages, but they have never acquired any land so they often get moved on by the villagers. There are of course many tribes in India, but the definition I make is that the Irulas are more like Aborigines. They have no land. The villagers are like villagers everywhere in India. They are not rich, in fact they are often very poor, but they have their feet on the bottom of the ladder. They are part of Indian mainstream life.

'The Irulas know everything about the forest. They use herbs to heal, they eat termites and they are expert snake-catchers. They used to sell the snakes to the snake industry in Madras. Then the government banned the sale of snakes to the skin industry. A good move for snakes, but it left the Irulas without a job.

'Romulus suggested that they use their snake-catching skills instead to provide venom for anti-venom serum. So they now catch snakes – kraits, vipers and cobras – extract the venom and sell it to hospitals. We have set up the Irula Tribesmen Snake-Catching Co-operative and they keep the snakes here whilst they extract the venom.'

'So you have crocodiles and poisonous snakes.' I made a mental note not to go sleep walking. 'Where do the rats fit in?'

'Well, the Irulas are very good at catching anything which lives down holes. The paddy-fields are infested with rats which eat a good deal of the harvest. Sometimes you get 2,000 rats to an acre. The Irulas catch them for a fee from the farmers and sell them to us.'

'You must eat a lot of rats.'

'No, no, we don't eat them all. We feed them to the crocs. But we're eating some for supper tonight.'

Supper loomed unavoidably closer.

'So how do you like them?' Romaine asked prettily.

I looked down again at the tiny glistening bodies hunched on my plate. They had been skinned and barbecued. They looked like baby rabbits and were full of tiny splintering bones.

'Hmmm,' I said appreciatively, trying to sound amused and broad-minded at the same time. I dipped a slice of tomato into the bowl of mayonnaise to take away the greasy taste.

'You prefer the mayonnaise?' she said innocently. 'I made it myself.'

'Really?' I eagerly took another large dollop.

'Yes,' Romaine went on, 'with crocodile eggs. The very devil to beat you know.'

The tomato paused in mid-air as I digested the implications of crocodile eggs. The mayonnaise slipped off the tomato and fell splat on to my knee.

'Very rich,' she said.

I put the tomato slice into my mouth without mayonnaise.

'Very rich. Are there any other ingredients you need to warn me about? Cockroach fritters or headlice dal?'

'No, no. Just go easy on the mayonnaise. Think how much nutrition a baby crocodile needs to build him up.'

The next day Harry took me to see one of his own ideas. As the Irula women were left out of snake-catching, he thought they should be involved in something else so he has formed a tree-planting co-operative. The Irulas know a good deal about trees, so Harry has encouraged them to plant seedlings and look after them. He raised money from the local government to buy the seedlings and set up a tree nursery. He then identified tracts of wasteland which were not being used for anything else and got permission from the appropriate village chiefs to plant trees there. The arrangement was that the Irulas would plant the land with trees, and after three years the village and the Irulas would harvest some trees for firewood and sell the surplus wood with the profits shared equally. From then on they would extract timber as and when appropriate. All the villagers had to do was sit back and watch.

We went off on Harry's motor bike to see two sites, the first a new project, the second one where trees had been planted three years ago. We turned off the road and drove for twenty minutes into a complete wasteland, dry and rocky with no signs of life. Then in the distance I saw a cluster of huts. When we arrived we found a number of Irula men digging a well and building huts. There was a large roofed area where the seedlings would be stored. An Irula woman called Jagatha, who was in charge, came out to greet us. She was short, very dark and had thick curly hair. Women are better with trees than men because they stay and care for them rather than sloping off for a good snake hunt. With Harry translating, Jagatha explained what was happening.

The men help with the heavy work like building the well, and they also build up low mud walls around the hillside to stop the soil being washed away and to trap the rain water. They use no irrigation. Then the women take over. They organize themselves into groups of 200 and plant seeds just before the rains, 1,500 per acre so that after three years they can thin them down to 500 trees per acre. They plant a thorny hedge around the saplings to keep out goats and do not allow any grazing for the first two years.

Jagatha showed me into the huts they were building. They had mud walls which would then be covered with cow dung which is more hygienic as well as dust-free. The walls were smooth save that each one had a little alcove.

'What's that for?' I asked.

Jagatha giggled nervously, putting her hand over her mouth. She finally said something to Harry.

'It's a shrine for their goddess. They worship a goddess called Kaniama.'

'What sort of goddess is she?'

'She's the Goddess of Land and Animals.'

The next site we visited was three years old. Through a gate we entered a hedged-off area where some huts stood around a deep well with a windmill cranking up water. An Irula family emerged. They showed us around a tree nursery where in the shade of taller trees they have grown 10,000 saplings to sell to local farmers. Then we walked out into the 90 acres they had planted. The trees were 15 feet tall, and bushes which held the earth together had grown up around them. The fast-growing acacia trees had been thinned out earlier in the year. A family of partridge ran across the path in front of us.

'They've seen deer here as well,' Harry said.

It seemed a perfect project.

'Unfortunately not quite perfect,' Harry replied. 'You see the Irulas are still living here, but now the villagers want them to leave. We are not agreeing to this. But actually it is not Irula land, it belongs to the village even though it was wasteland before we started planting trees.

'At another site where we planted 200 acres with trees we had the same situation. The Irulas planted the trees, then the villagers wanted the Irulas to leave. So we gave them a 200-acre forest with about 100,000 trees. Guess how many trees were left after the villagers had taken possession?'

'I dread to think.'

'None. In one year they had cut them all down for firewood.'

It used to be thought that if Indian villagers were given enough money and left to their own devices, they would develop their local economy in a sustainable way. Any interference by the West was considered inappropriate as the West could not possibly appreciate the subtle ways in which the villagers understood their environment. From my limited experience I think this is like giving an unemployed skinhead in Telford a machete and £100 and letting him get on with his life.

Indian villagers have no concept of saving any of their inheritance for future generations. 'And why should they?' people ask defensively on their behalf. 'They can't afford to look beyond tonight's meal. It's only people in the West who can afford to care about the future. Spread enough of your wealth around and sure, the villagers will stop having fifteen children and start thinking about saving their country.'

Well, perhaps. Perhaps the Indian villagers who cut down a newly planted 200-acre forest were so desperate for firewood that they took the view that it was better to cut it all down in one year rather than keep it as a sustainable resource.

But another example of Indian village life made me realize that the villagers have no idea what is good for them. Harry and I went on a snake hunt with some Irula men. We met in their tiny huts on the edge of the village and walked off into the scrub. A crowd of long-legged villagers came to watch what we were up to. The Irulas walked slowly and pointed out where snakes had crossed the sandy path and where they had shed their skins. They each carried an iron bar with which they dug around the roots of various trees. They put twigs down the holes – if they moved then we had a snake on our hands. The first few holes were empty, then a twig twitched. The Irulas dug some more, then before I could jump out of the way a five-foot snake came hurtling out. One of them caught it deftly by the neck. It was a rat snake, thick as my arm and golden yellow.

Rat snakes are non-venomous and completely harmless – unless you're a rat. They are therefore extremely useful to have around. The villagers all pointed to this one and jeered. Harry explained that it was harmless. Everyone laughed in disbelief as the snake curled around the Irula's arm. Then, rather than put it back in its hole, the Irula put it into a sack.

'What is he doing?' I asked.

'He will release it somewhere safe.'

'But everyone knows it's harmless. And as it eats rats, it's good to have around the village.'

'The villagers would kill it as soon as we go.'

'But can't you educate them?'

'You've seen – I've shown them it's harmless but they would still kill it. And rats eat up to 20 per cent of their harvest. If they had more rat snakes, there would be less rats. Do you know that rats hoard grain? We've found rat holes with four kilos of grain inside. If we could solve the rat problem we would be farming our paddy-fields much more efficiently. But these villagers will not listen. They think all snakes are poisonous so they kill them.'

My last view of the crocodiles was the most dramatic. Harry took me to the large pen at night. The moon had not yet risen. I could hear a faint shuffling as the crocodiles moved around on the sand, but I could see nothing in the darkness. I just knew there were thousands of crocodiles immediately in front of me.

'Now put your torch up to your eyes and switch it on.'

When I switched on the torch, it lit up the gold and silver reflections of thousands of crocodile eyes. They gleamed back at me out of the darkness as if the lights of a city had been switched on all at once. For a while we stood there like children marvelling at fairy lights. Then I switched off my torch and they vanished into the blackness.

Back at the Ministry of Home Affairs the same people were lounging around the corridors. There were the same men in dhotis squatting along the walls, the same family drinking *chai*, the same feeling of suspended animation. Only the two holy men were missing. I retraced my footsteps to Mr Prakash Chander's office.

'Just one moment, Mr Whitley,' he cheerfully told me at 10 o'clock. 'We are just finalizing your application. It will be ready shortly. Please allow ten minutes.'

I sat and waited at Mr Chander's desk. He spoke at length on the telephone, then abruptly swept out of his office. I waited. I allowed ten minutes. I waited. I allowed another ten minutes, and then another thirty minutes. I waited until it became clear that he had sloped off for lunch and nobody else knew a thing about me or my application.

When he returned at 3 o'clock I was just finishing my book. He showed neither surprise nor remorse at finding me still at his desk.

'Please allow ten minutes, Mr Whitley.' He wobbled his head approvingly and stroked his beard. 'My secretary assures me it is now ready.'

He talked into the heavy bakelite telephone again whilst I struggled with the overwhelming impulse to bludgeon him to death with it. He then made a dash for the door. I remembered the holy men and scampered after him. I followed him around several corridors feeling rather foolish and wondering what to do if he was just going for a pee.

After chatting to a couple of other wandering civil servants, Mr Chander finally led me to an obscure back office and took a scrap of paper from a tiny man surrounded by large piles of folders – his secretary.

'Here you are, Mr Whitley,' he said magnanimously.

I read the three-line statement a couple of times. There was no room for ambiguity. The Ministry of Home Affairs had granted me permission to apply for a permit to visit Assam.

'What's this?' I flapped the paper in his face.

'You may now apply for a permit,' Mr Chander said graciously.

'But what have I been doing for the last six days?'

'We do not issue permits here. We only issue permission to apply for permits. You must go to the Foreigners' Registration Office to apply for a permit.'

'But I'm booked to fly up to Assam tomorrow.'

'Then I suggest that you must be hurrying. The office closes at 4 o'clock and it is now quarter to.'

The next fifteen minutes were spent in frantic negotiation. The rickshaw driver sensed I was in a tearing hurry and stopped halfway to renegotiate the fare. The doorman at the Foreigners' Registration Office told me that they were already shut. Barging through a succession of offices, I repeatedly had to reassure outraged civil servants that they could spare two minutes from their cosy chat over their cups of *chai* to sign my application and point me towards the next office.

At each stage I was saved from being consigned to the pending tray by producing P. Lahan's letter. It was a wretched crumpled thing by the time I had finished handing it around, but it had the vital letterhead of the Government of Assam. And when they read it, they came across P. Lahan's description of himself as a 'middle-level functionary in the hierarchy of the Forest Department of Assam.' Here was a kindred spirit. They stamped my forms, their lethargy almost kindled into a flourish.

I collected all the necessary stamps and signatures, presented my international driving licence, health certificate, four signed photographs and flight ticket as proof of identity and was finally given permission to go to Assam. In all their haste, I noticed that they had made a mistake – they had given me permission to visit the Manas Reserve, an important elephant sanctuary and World Heritage site which had been closed to tourists for two years because of rebel fighting.

P. Lahan was sitting on his veranda when I finally tracked him down at his home in Guwahati. It was Saturday morning and he was drinking gin.

'Mr Whitley!' he greeted me. 'I was not knowing when to expect you.'

'Didn't my telegram arrive?'

'No, I received no telegram. But kindly do not worry. We have been moving offices so everything is topsy-turvy. Do you drink gin?'

His cheerfulness was infectious and I felt my sweaty and tetchy mood which had accumulated during the five-hour flight and hour-long taxi ride begin to recede. I sank back into his bamboo sofa and gratefully accepted a gin.

P. Lahan is a remarkable-looking man. He has a bald and almost perfectly egg-shaped head and oval oriental eyes. His teeth protrude, splayed wide, so he always appears to be smiling, and he sports a magnificent moustache, twirled up at the ends. These ends gradually unravel until the moustache looks more and more ragged, like a prawn pinned to his face, at which point he senses something is wrong and twiddles the straggling hairs back up into a handlebar.

He commiserated with me over the episode of the permit.

'It is difficult to come to Assam because it is very violent. There are a lot of shootings and all that. We in Assam do not feel that we are part of India. Look at a map, we are right up by Nepal and Bhutan, we border Burma and Bangladesh and are joined to India by only a thread. Well, we want to be more independent. So we have the United Liberation Front of Assam, the ULFA.

'The trouble really started in 1986 during the election following Mrs Gandhi's death. The ULFA killed every one of the sixty Congress (I) candidates. So the Indian government put us under direct rule from Delhi and sent the soldiers in. There are countless soldiers here now, and they cause resentment.

'And then below the ULFA there are a host of other tribal problems. You will see people of all races here – there are refugees from Tibet and Bangladesh, descendants from Mongolia. I myself am from Thailand, my family moved through Burma until we reached here. So Assam is like a melting-pot of all these different races. The real trouble-makers are the Nagas and the Mezos and the Bodos. They all want their own separate homelands. Sadly you will not be able to go to the Manas Reserve because the Bodos attacked the rangers' camp and stole their rifles. They killed three forest rangers, stole forty guns and burned the place to the ground.'

'I was given a permit to go to Manas.'

'Really? That is highly unusual. It has been closed to visitors for a long time on account of the violence. I will take you then, Mr Whitley. You should not miss seeing it.'

'Great. By the way, please call me Edward.'

'Very well, Mr Whitley.'

'What's your Christian name? I've only ever seen you referred to as P. Lahan.'

'My name is Paramananda.'

'That's quite a mouthful.'

'Yes.' He smiled unexpectedly. 'It actually means "Very much cheerful". It is Sanskrit. "Param" means "very much", and "ananda" means "cheerful". Most people are just called "Ananda" but my parents went the whole hog.'

Paramananda had been the second trainee to go to Jersey.

'There was that fellow from Mauritius who was the first, then me. I stayed at a guest-house in Gorey, and William Oliver picked me up on his way to the zoo every day. I was always having to change rooms in the guest-house because other tourists were coming. There wasn't a proper course then. The zoo was very small. But all the keepers spent a good deal of time showing me how they looked after their animals.'

'If you didn't know I was coming, how will we be able to visit the reserves?'

'Do not worry on that account. You are fortunate. Next week is the Hindu New Year so there is a week's holiday.'

Over the next week Paramananda lived up to his name. He was indefatigably cheerful throughout the week we spent driving around Assam and staying in reserves. We set off the next day for the Kaziranga Reserve, a day's drive to the east of Guwahati.

Assam is a flat river plain bordered by mountains, the Himalayas to the north and the Meghalayas to the south. The Brahmaputra drains off the eastern end of the Himalayas in Tibet and flows west through Assam before turning south and joining the Ganges to form a massive delta in Bangladesh. 'Brahmaputra', Son of Brahma, creator of the earth, is the only male river in India.

'Perhaps it is male because people are so frightened of it,' said Paramananda. 'Every year it floods and many people die. In fact the floods used to be good as they brought alluvial deposits which made Assam very fertile. Now, because the Chinese have removed all the forest in the mountains, the river brings mud which silts up all the paddy-fields. Nepal has also cut all its forest, so the Ganges has the same problems.'

We travelled for a day through the flat muddy plain where the only signs of life were people. The roads were choked with them. We drove slowly, either stuck behind a procession of lorries or hooting our way through a crowd.

Before I had come here, I had imagined that the elephants could migrate between the thirteen reserves. But as we drove through the landscape I realized that this was impossible. Each reserve was little more than an island.

As we drove further east, we passed a group of Mongolian women. They wore separate skirts and shawls, and instead of a single plait hanging down their backs, they had great manes of unruly hair. Rather than walking demurely by, they waved as we drove past and their slanting eyes stared at me with undisguised curiosity.

The day was drawing to a close when Paramananda told me we were entering the Kaziranga Reserve. The road borders one side of it.

'We might see a rhino. Look to your left.'

And sure enough not 200 yards from the busy main road I saw a rhino.

It was as simple as seeing a cow. The rhino was chalky white against the marshy grassland, and as if that wasn't enough of a giveaway a couple of egrets perched on its back, their pure white wings clear as a rifle target. It was the most uncamouflaged animal I have ever seen. There it stood in bold relief, gently grazing as if it were of no more interest than a goat. My first reaction was what a magnificent sight it was, a prehistoric animal living amongst us. This is the uniquely privileged reaction of

One Horned Rhinoceros.

someone who can afford to visit India and travel around looking for animals like rhinos just to be able to marvel at them. The second, perfectly logical thought is 'There's 20,000 rupees sitting on the end of its nose.' And this would be the only thought of someone who has to live there and scrape together a living as a subsistence farmer.

I wondered whether the rhino was aware of this. After all, rhinos have now been poached for at least 300 years for their horns. The message might have started percolating through – *evolve into hornless rhinos*. But then they would need so much time to adapt to this, thousands of centuries, and the poachers are shooting anything with any horn at all.

And the more I watched him, the more I had the impression that he was indeed acutely self-conscious about his horn. I wanted to shout out 'Hey you! Cyrano!' to see if he reacted. But I knew he wouldn't. More's the pity. If rhinos would only get the message, they might not stand in full view of a main road where thousands of impoverished rice farmers walk to and fro every day.

When we reached the rangers' camp I began to appreciate that Paramananda was something more than a 'middle-ranking functionary'. At the sight of his benignly grinning face, every forest ranger or anyone else wearing khaki and flip-flops snapped into back-quivering salutes. Paramananda acknowledged these with a slow smile and a casual touch of his eyebrow.

'I used to work here,' he explained. 'From 1975 until 1979 I was assistant director. Then I went to Jersey. When I returned I was promoted to director and stayed until 1985. Since then I have been Chief Conservator of Wildlife. I think later in the year I will be transferred to the Manas Reserve as director.'

I was introduced to a line of men who had formed up outside the car. Paramananda gave some instructions to someone and then turned to me.

'I have ordered some food but I am afraid that it will be very basic, just some grub. Let us go to our rooms now to wash up. I will be sending you information when the grub is ready.'

The grub turned out to be a splendid meal of chicken korma, dal and chips laid out on an enormous table. Paramananda poured tomato ketchup on to his korma. A servant stood rigidly to attention whilst we ate, and pounced on any empty plates.

The next day we rode through the reserve on an elephant and I began to get a sense of the scale of the operation.

'The reserve is 420 square kilometres and we have 400 rangers. As there are 1,100 rhinos it means each man has 3 rhinos to guard. Last year we lost 27 rhinos to poachers. There is no other poaching of animals, only a few male elephants have tusks, and it is not worth being caught poaching a bush deer or something like that. People like to poach rhino because they can smuggle the horn fairly easily. We are quite close to Burma here, or they can ship it from Calcutta to Thailand. As soon as the horn gets into the hands of Chinese businessmen, they can get it to Hong Kong without difficulty. The Chinese grind it down into powder to make medicines. I suppose medicine is a better use than being made into dagger handles like the African rhino, but I can't believe it actually cures anything. After all it's just hair.'

The working elephants were saddled up and brought around to a raised platform. I walked up to one and patted her trunk, marvelling at her size. She towered above me. I felt her strength as I pressed down on her trunk with all my weight. She could have effortlessly lifted me off the ground. Her eye, almost hidden inside a ball of fluffy eyelashes, was set in the middle of a large expanse of cheek and looked strangely far apart from any other feature, a good yard away from her mouth, for example, and it was tiny in proportion to the rest of her face, like a whale's eye. Her skin was as dry as a reptile's but lightly covered with sparse hair. Each hair was set an inch or so apart from the next one and stood up three inches. This gave a slight haze to her outline. She explored me with the tip of her trunk, which was wet and pink, and then let it dangle.

'Give her this,' Paramananda whispered, as he turned to hide what he was doing from her. He pulled a banana from his pocket. I took it, but before I knew what had happened her trunk had snaked up and with a tiny twist she had slipped the banana out of my hand and lobbed it into her cavernous mouth. Her trunk then snuffled around me looking for more but I grabbed it and firmly swung it away from me. She bowed her head and looked rather miffed.

We walked up on to the raised platform and climbed into the padded saddle on her back. The mahout sat forward right on her neck, his bare feet pressed into the back of her ears which were mottled pink and grey and hung down in tatty fringes. He carried a short steel spike, turned at one end like a shepherd's crook, which he jabbed into raw patches on the top of her head to give her directions.

It was the first time I had ridden an elephant and I was surprised by the slow rhythm of her walk. We lurched off in a stately fashion. I looked around at Paramananda sitting behind me. He appeared so superbly pompous and contented that I almost howled with laughter.

'Because we are on an elephant', he said, 'we will get much closer to the rhinos.'

And we did. We could walk within fifteen yards of them. They were spread across the plain in groups of twos and threes, generally close to a pool of water. They would begin to sniff the air as our elephant approached, turning their heads this way and that to get a better perspective on the smell. Their eyes were tiny and clearly of no use to them until it was too late and we were too close. Then they would suddenly see us for what we were, three inquisitive men on an elephant rather than just an inquisitive elephant, and with a snort of disgust they would turn and trot purposefully into the shelter of some long grass.

Seeing rhinos at such close quarters I was impressed by how well put together they are. Although undeniably stout, there is something surprisingly delicate about them. They are not at all lumbering or clumsy. Their armour plating is a perfect fit like a well-tailored if rather severe suit, but when they trot off into the bushes they move with something of a swagger as if to imply that had their suits been designed by a French tailor things might have been different.

By the end of the morning we had seen around fifty rhinos.

'There are so many of them here,' I said to Paramananda. 'It can't be natural to have them so close together.'

'Well, perhaps not. But the reserve is 430 square kilometres.'

'But you have over 1,000 rhinos here, that works out at less than half a square kilometre per rhino.'

'We are working on relocating some of them in other reserves to broaden the gene pool and all that, but these things take time. Now as soon as our backs are turned doing something like that, the poachers will take advantage and come in and shoot some rhinos. Then word gets around that we have lost our grip, so more poachers come in and try their hand. So life becomes more difficult for us.

'You see we are in a war zone here. The IUCN (International Union for the Conservation of Nature) or the WWF can come up with all these proposals such as bio-genetic diversity and bio-spheres and all that, but that is all just jugglery with words. Here we are actually policing the reserve. We have 42 camps around the reserve with 400 forest guards, that is a camp in every 10 square kilometres. It is a full-time job protecting this reserve.

'We do the work on the ground without any help from the IUCN or WWF. They come in and because they are anxious to be seen to be doing something, they fly around in helicopters and survey the land. Then they write a report which tells us to do this, this and that. Well, all this is fine and dandy, but where are they now? They've gone off somewhere else and we're left here trying to run it.'

I asked Paramananda why he thought it was important to protect the rhinos. With such overwhelming pressure mounting from the growing population, it was surely a futile job. His answer was the best analysis of the problems of conservation I have heard.

'Well, people from outside look at the reserve and ask "Why can't we farm that land? What use are those rhinos? They are just taking up space which we could farm." My answer to that is that yes, of course they take up space. But if you don't like something, you can't just kill it off. We do not like mosquitoes because they are an irritant, but if we kill off all mosquitoes we have to think what will take their place.

'The rhinos are just as much part of the food chain and all that. We cannot decide whether they should remain alive or not, that is up to God. We cannot play at being God and making his decisions as we have only imperfect understanding and it would end in disaster. We must keep the world as he gave it to us. If we kill off things in the food chain, we may very well cause ourselves a good deal of damage.

'All around the reserve there are villages and we point our guns at them and say "Keep out of this reserve." They say to us "Why?" And we say "Because it is in your long-term interest." So they say "We need firewood to cook now. We need to eat tonight. So what if the whole world cares about rhinos? We don't." All we can do is point our guns at them and say "Believe us, this is in your best interests."

'We have to use force now because there is no time to educate them. In the troubles in 1986, the Forest Department was forced to vacate a reserve called Laokhowa because of fighting. The forest guards were attacked by rebels wanting their guns. Within two weeks all forty-three of the rhinos which lived there were poached. There were none left. Obviously over time perhaps we can educate people, but at the moment it is just a matter of controlling them.'

The next reserve we visited was Orang, a smaller reserve not favoured by tourists. In fact, because of the trouble in Assam, no tourist has visited Orang since 1986. It comprises seventy-two square kilometres and holds fifty rhinos. Despite being surrounded by villages, no rhinos were poached last year. When I joined the reserve's director, Bhuper Talukdar, on his early-morning tour I discovered why. Despite being a lowly paid government official in a reserve where there are no tourists to give tips and no obvious incentives to excel, Bhuper is completely dedicated to his job. We drove around and stopped at each rangers' camp. Bhuper knew all the names of the 220 rangers, and spoke to them all as individuals; he bossed some of them around, gently chivvied others and gave one or two a real bollocking.

'I know all my men,' he said as we bounced along the mud tracks. 'They all need different methods of management. I have built up the best team in the Forest Department. They all take real pride in what they do. We didn't lose one rhino last year.'

That evening I went on an anti-poaching patrol. We left at twilight, two elephants ridden by armed guards. The guards carried two sorts of guns, pre-war Enfield 303s and antique shot-guns. Despite their age, the bolts of the Enfields were smoothly oiled. I was a little alarmed to discover that they only had four cartridges each.

We set off through a marsh and then crossed a deep muddy river. As they hit the water the elephants' feet splayed out, cushioning their weight so they plunged slowly down. I wasn't sure whether they actually hit the bottom or not because we lurched through the marsh with a curious floating motion.

We saw a number of rhino, fifteen or twenty. Each time we approached them, I wondered whether the rhinos felt any particular rapport with the elephants. They have a good deal in common – they are both huge animals, docile unless provoked when they will blindly charge down their antagonists. And they are both unworldly in the sense that there is less and less room for them in the world which gives them less and less time. There is a touching symmetry that highly endangered elephants are helping protect the even more endangered rhinos from poachers. Here are two mighty animals, their physical supremacy unchallenged for fifty million years, now reduced to eeking out their lives in tiny reserves. They are both so vulnerable.

Riding around the reserve I soon ceased to be as impressed by the rhinos (it is astonishing how quickly one becomes accustomed to seeing the most extraordinary things) as by the wealth of other life we came across, all the ordinary small everyday animals which were actually extraordinary to me because I hadn't seen any of them since I had arrived in India. There were moorhens, bush pigs, marsh deer, cranes and fish eagles. Thousands of dragonflies zoomed over the marshes. At one point a flock of green parakeets which would take years to build up in Mauritius flew overhead. It was a huge flock and as they flew past they all dived in one direction as if someone had thrown a switch.

In the event I was pleased that we didn't meet any poachers. There had been a shoot-out last year when both a guard and a poacher had been killed. I was impressed that the guards had managed to kill anyone with such antique weapons, but I gathered there was some uncertainty as to whether one poacher had been shot accidentally by another – the poaching equivalent of friendly fire.

I took Paramananda to task over the matter of the weapons when I returned. He was sitting up on the elephant platform overlooking the reserve.

'Why don't the guards have better guns?' I asked. 'If they come across poachers, they'll be up against AK 47s with automatic fire.'

'This cannot be helped,' he said mildly. 'This is all we can afford.'

'But what about giving them more bullets? Four bullets doesn't leave much room for error.'

'No, enough is enough. If they can't shoot a man after four shots, they will never shoot him. It concentrates their minds. If they miss with the first, which is very likely in all the rush, and with the second, then they know they only have two shots left. If they miss with the third then they know they must get him with the fourth. It is good discipline. Anyway, most probably everyone is running like mad after the first shot.'

When we drove to the Manas Reserve the New Year celebrations were in full swing and bands of children were singing and dancing amongst the traffic. They surrounded each car and refused to let it move until the driver had given them five rupees.

After crossing the Brahmaputra we entered Bodoland. There were many more soldiers and checkpoints. Each bridge was guarded by piles of sandbags and mounted machine guns. Instead of 'Vote Congress (I) for stab(I)lity' (horribly ironic with hindsight), the walls all carried Bodo graffiti. The Bodo people were easy to distinguish from the Indians, for they had the flashing slanting eyes of Mongolians. The Bodo women wore yellow saris, 'their favourite colour', Paramananda said. At one point a very drunk Bodo fell across our bonnet and sang a long song with his nose pressed against the windscreen. I was about to give him the obligatory five rupees, when Paramananda burst into song at the top of his voice. A large audience gathered around us. The Bodo looked askance. There was a great cheer when he finished.

'What was all that about?' I asked.

'It was a Bodo song. They didn't expect me to speak Bodo.'

'What was it about?'

Paramananda looked embarrassed. 'It was about such-and-such a man from such-and-such a place, who smells like a non-person,' he finally admitted.

Set up in the foothills, Manas is much more wooded than the floodplain reserves of Orang and Kaziranga. As well as rhinos, there are elephants and tigers. But the closest we got to a tiger was a fresh paw print. We dismounted from the elephant to take a closer look. The tiger had been walking slowly and had apparently taken no notice of the little footprints of deer which criss-crossed the track. A great hornbill took off and flew slowly over the tree-tops.

'Do you have reserves like this in England?' the guard asked me.

'You mean with 400 square kilometres of forest?'

'No, with tigers and elephants.'

'No, we have no tigers or elephants.'

'What big animals do you have?'

'We have some wild ponies and deer. Otherwise it's badgers and foxes. There's a big campaign to save the field-mouse. And we spend a lot of money on donkey sanctuaries and saving stray cats and dogs.'

'What's a donkey?'

'It's like a yak.'

'So you save yaks? And cats and dogs?' He looked at me uncomprehendingly. 'So this is why the Britishers come to India,' he finally said.

It was hard not to feel foolish.

Indian Elephant.

Paramananda took me to the guards' camp which had been attacked by Bodos. They had come at night and had rounded up the guards at gun-point, broken into the gun-room, stolen all the guns and ammunition, and had then set fire to the buildings. A fight had broken out and three forest guards had been shot. The camp was now staffed by thirty soldiers as well as the forty guards. The remains of the burned-out buildings stood to one side. A new watch-tower had been built and was manned by two sentries.

'This is an extreme illustration of the battle,' Paramananda said. 'Normally people do not get shot and all that, but you must understand that there is a constant attack on reserves.'

'How long can this fortress approach last?'

'Well, people talk about education. This is the big thing at the moment, educate people to understand the long-term benefits of having a natural world and then we will all live in harmony with nature. We will not need to have watch-towers or armed guards.

'But I do not think it will ever work. In my experience I find that I can only talk to people of my class. If I say something, only people of my class understand it. Other people bring a different perspective to bear on what I say. They have different motives, they think I'm saying something else and so they hear something else from what I am actually saying.

'So I say to people here: if you have less children, we will help you set up your business. You will be better off. We have tried to do this for local people around here. We offered them help with their chicken farms and growing crops and all that. But the people do not understand. They either think we're interfering, or they only hear half the message. They think I've just said I'll help them with their business and they continue to live as before.'

'But isn't that because you have a strong caste system here?'

'That might be one reason. But ask yourself if this is not true the world over. People from different classes do not understand each other. They distrust each other.

'Here in India the poor people distrust us when we say "Have less children." And with good reason as nobody looks after them when they are old or sick so the family has to. And the more children they have, the richer they become. From the age of five, children bring in more money than they cost to feed.

'So it is our self-interest against their self-interest. If we want animals roaming around, then we have to pay for them to be protected. We have to pay for that land not to be developed.'

It was quite a shock to leave the Manas Reserve. I had grown used to exploring vast tracts of forest, riding through grasslands on an elephant, walking up the deserted banks of the river. Outside the gates to the reserve was a crowd of people. My first reaction was that they were queuing to get in. Then I realized that this was just the usual Indian crowd milling around doing nothing in particular.

But of course they *are* queuing to get in.

Some days later I left India and flew on to the Philippines. On the aeroplane I read a newspaper article which suggested that the world map should be redrawn to reflect the number of telephones in each country. Telephone bills are the key to real economic data. For instance, they show up all the drug-dealing activities in South America which otherwise never appear in the world economy. Telephone tariffs are the most accurate measure of the world's trade. The article caught my eye because it mentioned India.

India, shortly to host the world's largest population, has the same number of telephones as Central London. And as well as being left out of the world's communication revolution, 70 per cent of the Indian population have no access to the traditional forms of media, such as newspapers or television. If few people outside India know what is happening in that country, still fewer people in India know what is happening anywhere at all.

Like some yeast culture forgotten in a damp cupboard, India is festering uncontrollably. This is true of all the developing countries – nobody knows what is going on in Nigeria or anywhere in Central Africa, or in the sprawling suburbs of Brazil or Mexico or Indonesia. The population of all these countries is set to double in thirty years and redouble in sixty. But there is no access to these people. There are no telephones, no television, no press, so there is no way of infiltrating them, or educating them, or controlling them or even just helping them avoid disaster.

In the best tradition of science fiction movies where brainy professors with steel-rimmed glasses and portable telephones get swallowed up by some heavy spongy blob, the freedom and stability of the developed world will be enveloped and suffocated by the rest of the world's population.

Ask the rhinos. It's happened to them already.

SEVEN

THE PHILIPPINES

MARLYNN MENDOZA AND THE ECO-SYSTEM OF BUREAUCRACY – SIX YEARS' WORTH OF RAIN FOREST – CARMEN LEVISTE'S BROKEN CAMERA – MALENA FERNANDEZ, THE WALL STREET WHIZZ-KID – EYEBALL TO EYEBALL WITH THE MONKEY-EATING EAGLE – BEN SALARZA'S LEATHER HOOD – CLIMBING INTO THE LAST FOREST – THE APPROACHING CHAINSAW

I have always imagined the Philippines as a vivid caricature of the rest of the world. Everything which goes on in the world goes on more blatantly in the Philippines – the old dictator was not only corrupt, his wife also owned 1,300 pairs of shoes; the revolution which overthrew him elected a housewife, a real housewife, as president; the saintly head of the Catholic Church is called Cardinal Sin. It's like a pantomime. Not content with Easter eggs and bonnets, his congregation celebrates Easter with mass crucifixions.

So when I heard about the Philippine eagle, I expected something larger than life. Sure enough, it is the largest eagle in the world, with a wingspan of eight feet and talons and beak to match. It eats monkeys for its livelihood. It also eats bats, flying foxes and any bird smaller than itself (all of them). And it has recently been seen attacking dogs and baby carabao (a carabao is a sort of cross between a water buffalo and an ox). As far as I could ascertain, it had yet to start on humans.

But when a monkey-eating eagle starts attacking carabao there is clearly something wrong. Carabao must be horribly tough compared with delicious monkeys, but the eagles have no option. Each pair needs around 60 square kilometres of virgin forest to support it and the Filipinos have axed their forest so quickly a comprehensively that they have reduced it from 5 million hectares in 1970 to 600,000 hectares in 1991. There are precious few patches of 60 square kilometres left intact. The annual loss of 200,000 hectares has slowed recently, not because there is a move to save the forest, but because it is now reduced to such small pockets that commercial logging is scarcely viable. However, farmers follow the loggers and clear the remaining forest for their shifting agriculture. In six years' time there will be no original rain forest left.

There are now only twenty-three recorded nest sites of the Philippine eagle. And there is no room for doubt. Eagles do not flutter out of sight like little songbirds twitching around in the undergrowth to exasperate ornithologists. They soar imperiously overhead and when they swoop to attack, their wings blot out the sun.

So the Philippines seemed the perfect place to conclude my tour of inspection around Gerald Durrell's army. They combine all the national characteristics I had seen elsewhere on my travels – debt, poverty, corruption, bureaucracy, destruction and pollution. Four Jersey trainees are battling in the middle of all this, two working in the government, one working for the Philippine Eagle Programme and one fresh from four years on Wall Street.

Marlynn Mendoza was my first point of contact. Marlynn works in the Wildlife Assessment Section which has a staff of twenty-two and is one of three sections in the Wildlife Division, which is one of six divisions in the Protected Areas and Wildlife Bureau, which is one of three bureaux in the Environment and Research Office, which is one of fifteen offices in the Department of Environment and Natural Resources. She was due to meet me at the airport.

'You'll recognize her because she's small,' David Waugh had warned me. 'I mean all Filipinos are small, but she is particularly so.'

When I came staggering out of the airport I looked along the faces clustered by the arrivals barrier. I knew someone had recognized me because there was an unseen bustle, then a tiny rom beneath the crowd. I quickly discovered two Marlynn. She is indeed small (she came up to my she is a formidable organizer. Within moments of nds she had hustled away the crowd of pimps, ts and taxi-drivers, and with swift, thorough and ruthless negotiation had selected a porter and led me to the waiting minibus. A few minutes later we were well on our way into the Manila traffic.

Manila is a hopelessly unplanned, sprawling mess which can be topographically represented as a dumb-bell. At one end is Metro Manila. This includes Makati, the business area where everything is gleaming and chrome; Intramuros, the old walled city built by the Spanish; Malacanang Palace where Imelda Marcos's 1,300 shoes are on display; and various modern walled villages with their private armies and Beverly Hills mansions where the rich live. At the other end is Quezon City, a vast slum where transport, water and electricity occur sporadically and sewage flows the whole time. The only link between these two areas is the urban motorway, Epifanio de los Santos Avenue, 'Edsa'.

Edsa was now jammed with cars bumper to bumper. Beggars worked their way along the marooned cars, smearing their hands and faces along the windows. Every country has its own peculiar form of transport, and in the Philippines it is the jeepney, a spectacular sort of minibus. Jeepneys look something like Second World War trucks. They have vast square bonnets, mounted headlamps and canvas canopies. They are made of stainless steel, bright and shiny as Art Deco New York diners, and they are generally festooned with orange and yellow bunting. Until you get used to it, each traffic jam looks like a carnival.

Like four or five million other people in Quezon City, Marlynn lives with her parents, her brother and his wife and their children in a three-bedroomed house. She is thirty-five and single. The street is lined with open sewers and stalls selling fried food. There are frequent power cuts and the water supply is cut off from 10 p.m. to 5 a.m. and again from 10 a.m. to 5 p.m.

For the next three days Marlynn took me to work with her. We left the house at 5.45 a.m., caught a motor bike with a side-car down to a main road, and then took a bus. Everyone on the bus carried a handkerchief folded into a tiny neat square, to be held over the mouth or flapped at the exhaust fumes which poured in through the open windows. When we left the bus, we caught a jeepney to the government building. It was Monday morning, and the staff were lined up outside the building as if for a fire practice. They formed lines behind their team leaders and, on the stroke of 7 o'clock, they all held up their right hands and sang the national anthem.

The Protected Areas and Wildlife Bureau was on two floors of a nine-storey building. The office was open-plan, the ceiling was low, and the desks were set out as in an exam room. On Marlynn's floor I counted 120 people sitting at identical desks with piles of paper in front of them. There was a power cut, so everyone pulled out a battery-operated neon light and worked patiently in the buzzing grey light. The heat rose throughout the day. I had never worked in a government bureaucracy before, so this was a chance to get an inkwell's view of the inside.

Marlynn showed me her files, and I sifted through the work of the Wildlife Division. I came across a document which inadvertently revealed how difficult it is for the department to achieve anything. It was a brief history of the last few years of the department's development. It read as follows:

> The Department of Environment and Natural Resources (DENR) had its beginnings in the old Department of Agriculture and Natural Resources (DANR). In May 1974, the DANR was split into two departments in recognition that natural resources and agriculture were broad and diversified concerns. As such, the Department of Natural Resources (DNR) was mandated to ensure the conservation, optimal utilization, and programmed exploitation of the country's natural wealth. With the shift to parliamentary government in 1978, the DNR became the Ministry of Natural Resources (MNR)...
>
> The events of February 1986 brought radical changes that

> altered the character of the MNR. First, President Corazon C. Aquino created the Department of Energy, Environment and Natural Resources (DEENR). The DEENR, however, was again reorganized into the present Department of Environment and Natural Resources (DENR) in June 1987.

It seemed to me that the changing state of the department was of more interest to civil servants than anything happening in the world outside.

As the Philippine eagle has discovered, the 'conservation, optimal utilization and programmed exploitation of the country's natural wealth' resulted in the very quick, unsupervised and piecemeal destruction of the forest. Another document described the consequences of this destruction:

> Soil erosion is estimated to be about a billion cubic metres of material per year, or about 200,000 hectares of land at one-half metre deep. About 75 per cent of alienable and disposable lands are vulnerable to erosion and 13 provinces are already severely eroded.
>
> Deforestation, urbanization, industrialization, and improper land use all lead to accelerated soil erosion. In turn, soil erosion results in the loss of precious top soil, deterioration of prime agricultural lands, reduced water supply, increased occurrences of flooding and increased sedimentation of rivers, lakes and reservoirs.

So with all this going on in the world outside, what does DENR do on a typical day? The power cut seemed an appropriate metaphor. Everyone worked very hard, but in an entirely different world from that of real life outside. People spent a lot of time working through huge piles of paper stamping them and passing them on. A number of upright typewriters clacked away producing yet more paper. Marlynn fussed around, handing out papers to all around her and gathering them back in again.

'What are you working on?'

'I'm writing the wildlife briefing paper,' she said. 'It tells everyone in the Wildlife Division what we do.'

It was an eight-page document. I read the lengthy functions of the Wildlife Division, all of which sounded formidable, like the titles of particularly ambitious Ph.D.s. Here is an example from the Wildlife Assessment Section:

1. Formulate policies, guidelines, plans and programs for the conduct of studies in wildlife, including game fishes and their habitat;
2. Conduct measures in the biology, ecology, population dynamics and utilization of rare and endangered wildlife and those with potential for trade including other species of fauna and flora;
3. Generate technology for the captive breeding of rare and endangered wildlife and those species with trade potential;
4. Formulate guidelines on the harvesting and utilization of wildlife species.

I looked around at the comfortable, plump middle-aged ladies working with Marlynn.

'Do you do all this?'

'Yes, we try. We have a great deal to do.'

'Do you think it's achievable? There's no point setting yourself incredible targets if you're never going to get remotely close to achieving them.'

'No, we do achieve them. Take the generation of technology for the captive breeding of rare and endangered species. I'm personally doing that.'

'What, here?' I gestured at the open-plan office sprinkled with battery-operated neon lights.

'No. We have a captive breeding centre up at the University of the Philippines in Los Banos. I'll show you.'

She then introduced me to one of the charming plump middle-aged ladies.

'This is Marie-Anne. She is the Treasurer of the Section and Head of the Applications for Special Projects.'

'What have you done today?' I asked this lady with a fearsome job title.

'Today I went to cash a cheque to pay some staff. The bank is a long way away so it took me most of the day. But now I'm looking through these applications.'

The application on her desk was from the Asian Waterfowl Census, which wanted permission to count migratory birds.

'What will you do with this?'

'Well, I'll read it and pass it on to Marlynn.'

'What will you do with it?' I asked Marlynn.

'I'll read it and send it to other colleagues who have comments on it. Then I'll gather all the comments and send them to my boss.'

We found Marlynn's boss, a kind, mild-looking man.

'What will you do when this proposal arrives from Marlynn?' I asked.

He frowned at it with a practised worried expression.

'I will consider it, then I will pass it to my colleagues for any comments. Then I will hand it to my boss,' he said after some consideration.

'Can we see your boss?'

'He is a very busy man.'

'What will he do?'

'He will look at it, then if I have recommended it, he will stamp the proposal and pass it back to me.'

I looked around the office floor.

'So most of these people will have seen it by the time the proposal is approved?'

'Yes.'

I thought of a trading floor in an American investment bank, of much the same size, with just as many people, but each trader buying and selling millions of dollars' worth of shares at his own discretion. If each trader had to submit every proposal he received for joint scrutiny by every other trader, the market would seize up. Much the same has happened with the regulation of the environment. The regulations and directives are clearly unworkable. The DENR has no authority as long as it continues to circulate paper for its own consumption.

Marlynn leaves work at dusk. The traffic is equally bad, but at least it is impossible to see the clouds of exhaust fumes sweeping across the roads. I could only tell how smoky the air was because it was hot and gritty, and every now and then I choked.

Every weekend Marlynn takes a four-hour bus ride up to Los Banos in the hills. I joined her to see how she enacts Directive 3 of the Wildlife Review, the generation of technology for the captive breeding of rare species. Marlynn studied at the university in the Forest Ecology Research Department, a decaying building on the edge of the campus. She led me to her project, the flying lemurs. There were five of them hanging upside down in a large square cage. They are not actually lemurs but flying foxes. As they are nocturnal, they just hang around during the day looking like broken umbrellas.

'I'm analysing their diet,' Marlynn said. We went into the cage and she showed me a clothes rack with a line of nails along the beam. 'We tie different leaves along here, and then I see what they have eaten. I tabulate everything so we can see what vegetation the flying lemur prefers. And I watch them all night through the observation window. One of them has a baby, the first flying lemur born in captivity. She carries it around inside her wings.'

Marlynn and I watched the flying lemurs through the night. We sat on folding chairs in a little concrete hut by the cage. As it grew dark, Marlynn switched on red lights. The flying lemurs didn't do much through the night either. Marlynn made copious notes of every movement and watched intently as at about 3 a.m. they lugubriously swung themselves towards the clothes rack and started feeding.

Marlynn's hut had a concrete floor, a table and chair, a metal filing-cabinet, a fridge and a fan. When we finally went to sleep, she pulled out two plastic camp-beds from behind the filing-cabinet. As I tried to sleep with my legs sticking out over the end of the bed and a puddle of sweat sloshing around beneath me, the shadows of the flying lemurs moved across the wall above me like vampires' wings.

I realized why Marlynn comes here every weekend. It is her

privacy. Away from the office, away from her family, away from the traffic, she sits in her tiny concrete hut writing long observations of flying lemurs which no one ever reads. Amongst all the nonsense of the paperwork and the hyperbolic prose, none of which will ever contribute to the safety of one tree or animal, this was one woman's happiness.

I left Marlynn to try to get a step closer to what was really happening on the ground. I went to the large island of Palawan, the most westerly in the Philippines. Carmen Leviste had been a Jersey trainee in 1985. Jersey had not been able to contact her since she left, but Marlynn was certain that she still worked at the DENR regional office. I arrived at Palawan unannounced and made my way into the tiny town of Puerta Princesa. The local offices of the DENR are called PENRO, an acronym of 'Provincial Environment and Natural Resources Office'. I found PENRO easily enough. It was a wooden building set on the high street. Inside, sixty people were all sitting at desks sifting through papers. The boss, Vincente Canabara, told me that Carmen Leviste worked at the community office of PENRO, CENRO. He seemed very suspicious that I should arrive unannounced to see a junior worker in the community centre, but he sent me by car to CENRO, an eight-mile drive through coconut and banana plantations.

CENRO was a square building in an expanse of wasteland. When I walked in I found a replica of PENRO, a team of eight people sitting in an empty office. But here they had no papers and no typewriters. They were just sitting there in silence as if they were schoolchildren being punished.

Carmen Leviste looked embarrassed to see me. She looked even more embarrassed when I explained why I had come.

Yes, she admitted, she had been to Jersey in 1985. She had been sent by her boss and she had had an interesting time. But she had not been in touch with Jersey since then. The camera they had given her to photograph her peacocks, the endangered Palawan peacock, had broken and she couldn't afford to mend it. She didn't like to tell Jersey this. Would I like to see her peacocks? She was in charge of the captive breeding programme.

She took me to a wire cage at the back of the office. Two small peacocks scratched around in the earth. They had laid one egg last year, but nothing this year. She fed them rice. I looked down at them and thought of all the chickens scratching around the villages, breeding and producing eggs every week.

Back at her office I asked what she did in a typical day.

'Nothing at the moment. You see we have no money. We are paid 100 pesos (£2.40) a day for our salary. But there is no money to do any projects. And we have no telephones here and no post.'

'So you're paid to do nothing?'

'Yes. We do nothing. We cannot do any research, we cannot travel anywhere, we just stay here. Sometimes we are paid late.'

Carmen had nothing more to add. When I realized that I had exhausted the extent of conversation, I made my excuses and left. She showed no surprise that I had come halfway round the world and had only spent an afternoon with her.

'There is nothing to see here. We do nothing.'

Back in Manila I called up Malena Fernandez. She was leaving for Jersey in two days' time. She gave me directions to her house in Dasmarinas Village, one of the private fortified compounds. The security to get into Dasmarinas Village was so tight that the taxi-driver was only admitted when he surrendered his driving licence. Inside, the verges along the broad streets were like croquet lawns. Sprinklers jetted, bougainvillaea cascaded over the hedges and guards sat by the embossed gates. Large villas and embassies were set amidst green lawns.

Malena's bungalow had no windows facing the road. Inside it opened up like cloisters with windows overlooking a courtyard. I waited for her in a room full of deep white sofas and ancient sculptures. She charged in wearing jeans and a T-shirt like all the other people on the streets outside.

Malena had been at high school and Smith College in the

United States, then joined Chemical Bank where she traded for four years on Wall Street.

'I was trading currencies. It was tough, a real man's world. Most women would call it a zoo, but I've worked in a zoo and I'd say that traders are the real animals.'

She went to business school to do a two-year MBA, but then decided to work in conservation.

'I just thought that I could easily have continued to make money. Everyone else in my family has made money apart from one brother who became a monk. We're all bankers so I knew how to do it. But then everything in the Philippines is getting destroyed so fast that I thought this is both more important and more of a challenge.

'I left business school three months back, and then heard about Jersey. It seemed perfect for me. I've always been interested in animals. When I was at high school I used to work at the marine park in my spare time.

'At Smith College I studied Economics and Zoology, so I've always oscillated between the two. And one of my aims is to make conservation or zoos more profitable. There's no reason why they should always think of themselves as a charity and go around with a begging bowl, unable to afford to expand. They should look at themselves as a business. They're in the business of saving animals, and people want to help them and it costs money so let's not shirk from this. They can be too discreet about it all.'

'Everything seems such a mess here,' I said. 'I spent a week with the DENR and still couldn't understand how anything they did related to anything else.'

'Frigging politicians,' Malena snorted. 'They just mess up everything in this country. And all the bureaucrats just go around working out whose butt they should be kissing instead of doing their job. And then they work out how much cash they can earn on the side.'

'What does your father do?'

'He used to be Governor of the Bank of the Philippines. He was put in by the IMF to control Marcos, but it was too late. Marcos had squirrelled away his cash by then. We think about $15 billion. Not bad when the national debt was $28 billion. My dad stayed on with Cory Aquino until October 1990 when he retired.'

'What does he think of you doing conservation work?'

'He's rather shocked. But he thinks that if I can do it well, then it's a job worth doing.'

'How will you do it well?'

'I don't know yet. That's what I'm hoping to find out in Jersey. But I'll go in and knock some heads together. I'll eventually have to work with the government because you need legislation behind you. In fact there is quite a lot of legislation there, it's just that nobody takes any notice of Cory Aquino.

'For example, she put a total ban on logging. Excellent. No more trees to be chopped. Then suddenly twenty-five companies were exempted from the ban! Why? Because they were the biggest! They had got together and bought off enough senators and, lo and behold, they can continue logging. Well, they'll put themselves out of business at the rate they're logging – but they'll put the rest of the country out of business along with them. It's like that here. If you don't know how to play the game, you should get out of the ring. People cannot expect conservation to be anything other than a bloody hard fight. And because it's all about money, you have to use tactics which you learn at business school, or even better on the streets.

'If I can change the attitude of the heads of the top twenty companies in the Philippines, I would make an enormous impact. Take San Miguel, the brewery, one of the largest companies in Asia. Now the president of San Miguel has done everything – he's built up the company and so just making more money isn't an incentive for him. But if I can point out that he could be responsible for a huge change in the way people in the Far East look at the world, then maybe he'll be interested. This is his chance for immortality. The middle managers will just go trucking along unless they get a directive right from the top. A number of companies in America and Europe are really changing. The chairmen are thinking that unless they change now, their products won't be selling in twenty years' time. I hope they're right.'

My last trip in the Philippines was to a private operation which Jersey has supported by training one of the staff, as well as providing an egg incubator. This is the Philippine Eagle Conservation Programme. It is based on Mindanao, the most southerly island of the Philippines.

Domingo Tadena, the Jersey trainee who works at the aviaries, was away at the Peregrine Fund receiving further training, so I met up with Denis Salvador, the project director.

The project is based at a camp outside Davao. The camp has twelve eagles. It also has a rather scruffy collection of other animals and birds – a crocodile, some monitor lizards, an Indonesian cockatoo, a blue macaw from Brazil, a pair of bear cats and civet cats, various other eagles and some songbirds. The Philippine eagles are set apart from the rest of the animals.

'Why do you have these here?' I pointed at the motley collection.

'Education. We need to educate the Filipinos about the wildlife of the Philippines.'

'But cockatoos don't even come from here.'

'They were a present from the Indonesian ambassador.'

'But you have no signs or anything to tell people what these animals are.'

'We're working on it.'

We walked up to where the eagles are housed. They were awesome birds. Standing so close to one I felt horribly like something they would eat without a second thought. They looked at us through the wire mesh with supreme dignity.

'We have two pairs together and eight separately. We have imprinted four of the birds and hope to breed with them soon. You must meet Ben Salarza.'

Ben Salarza looked an ordinary sort of bloke. Only his leather jacket, which had a hood that made him look like a tadpole, gave a hint of what he did for a living.

Ben's job is to be fucked by the largest eagle in the world. He has spent two years courting this eagle and now, in the breeding season, he goes into his cage whereupon the eagle leaps on to his shoulders and fucks his head. It is the same technique as that used by Carl Jones with Pink, but here a bowler-hat would be something of a nicety. This Philippine eagle, named Junior, weighs twenty pounds and has massive talons which rake Ben's shoulders. Ben grabs Junior's penis and collects the sperm in his hand. He then dashes out of the cage and syringes it up.

Meanwhile another eagle keeper, Mang Gone, is conducting a love affair with a female eagle called Diola. He has gone through the same process of going into her cage until she considers him her mate. He spent long hours sitting in the nest while she circled him, enduring several vicious attacks and bringing her food like any eagle mate would, before she allowed him to touch her. Now that they have been bonded, his job is to masturbate Diola every day during the breeding season. Once Junior has ejaculated into Ben's hand, Mang injects the sperm into Diola who invites him to copulate with her by lifting her tail.

I was in no position to judge whether this was serious science or a sick joke. Certainly it hasn't resulted in any more eagles being born.

Ben went into the cage to bring Junior out for closer inspection.

'It's alright,' Denis said. 'You can go closer.'

I approached warily. When I got to within two feet of the biggest eagle beak in the world, I took a closer look at it. It was a terrifying piece of equipment, the size of my hand and curved round to end in a sharp spike. Had Junior so wished, he could have stabbed through my skull and sliced out most of my brains. But with a bit of luck, I reasoned, perhaps he was just dreaming about his next copulation with Ben's head. His eyes were bright yellow with tiny black pupils and when our eyes met he looked straight through me. He abruptly opened his wings, and although I was standing two feet away, they enveloped me completely. The wing feathers were chocolate brown, and underneath his chest and inside his armpits were beautiful soft white feathers like duck down. He flapped again.

'I'm sorry, Junior,' I ducked out, 'I've got a headache.'

The Philippine Eagle Programme used to receive an annual grant of $50,000 from the DENR to supplement its income. This was stopped in 1986 following its repeated failure to breed any birds. For a private project to succeed, as Carl Jones drummed into me in Mauritius, it needs to produce results and have a good relationship with the government. It can then begin to influence the world outside its aviaries in both managing the wild population of birds and promoting public education. At the moment the project is moribund; there are just two eagles who spend their time having sex with men. I went into Domingo's office. It was empty save for a certificate from Jersey on the wall and the egg incubator, which has remained unused. As the forest disappears around them, the eagles in captivity become increasingly irrelevant – there will be nowhere left for them to live.

The only known nest sites of the Philippine eagle are all on Mindanao and the only pockets of forest left are on the tops of mountains. To get there requires a good deal of planning. I talked it over with Denis. It would involve a day's jeepney ride followed by a brief walk. We would camp at the top of the mountain and walk over to see the eagles' nest the next morning. Denis gave me a guide from the eagle camp, Eddie Juntilla, and together we stocked up at the market with rice, dried fish and dried squid.

The next day we set off at 5.30 a.m. and took a succession of jeepney rides deeper into the middle of the island. I was again struck by something which had become increasingly apparent during my travels – there are no more remote places left in the world. Here I was bumping along a dirt track in the middle of a remote island in the Philippines, and there were people all around me. Scrubby plantations of banana trees and paddy-fields spread out on either side of the track. The occasional jeepney came the other way and everyone ducked into their handkerchiefs to avoid the dust. There was not a hint of a forest anywhere, the landscape was stripped bare. There were no trees, no marshlands, no copses. No shelter.

Eventually we were the only passengers left in the jeepney. The track began to climb up into some hills and soon the jeepney stopped. It would go no further. We shouldered our packs and set off. Because the jeepney had let us down, the walk was longer than Eddie had bargained for. It turned out to be a five-hour walk.

We climbed higher and higher along the track which was sprinkled with small wooden villages. At the top of one hill, I had my first glimpse of forest – a dark green line on the horizon with some straggling green patches immediately below it.

We descended into a valley, forded a river and started our climb up the other side. We were now walking on footpaths and the sharp-edged grass which lined the track scratched my legs. Three hours later I was reeling along like a drunkard. My legs were moving extraordinarily slowly, my eyes were swollen and sore from salty sweat and I kept falling over. We were walking up cleared hillsides and the ground was covered with a slippery floor of vines. My boots had no grip on this and I continually crashed into the undergrowth. Eddie strode calmly along in his flip-flops. Sometimes we walked along felled tree trunks which were laid end to end. I counted ninety paces along one majestic trunk. The black conical remains of charred trunks stood upright amongst the vines.

'Last year all this was forest.' Eddie gestured at the ruined hillside.

'Who's doing it?' I was puzzled because we had only passed a few houses, hardly enough to lay waste to hundreds of acres of forest.

'People come from very far. They burn here and then hope to come and live here. But then sometimes they don't come, they find other jobs instead.'

We came to another hamlet of three wooden huts with neat little gardens outside. Various families came out to see us and stared with interest at the red-faced white man gulping for breath. Any girl with breasts carried a baby. The sun was going down and we pitched camp on a flat piece of ground. Eddie produced a Second World War bayonet and cut two V-shaped poles and a cross-bar to make my tent. We bundled undergrowth around the sides to keep out the dew. After spending an hour chewing through the dried fish and squid and another hour dental-flossing it out of my teeth, I wriggled backwards into the tent and slept right through until the first cockerel at 4 a.m.

The next morning word had got around that a red-faced white

man was climbing up to see the eagles' nest, and a small crowd of children and assorted men joined us. We set off up the mountain with quite a throng running behind us. I suddenly realized that we were now in real forest. The track climbed sharply and we hauled ourselves up on the roots of trees. The air was cold and misty. Wild orchids grew out of the mossy branches overhead.

We reached a ridge where a small look-out point had been cleared. Eddie pointed across the top of the forest canopy which stretched out unbroken over the valley in front of us.

'There's the nest.'

I followed his finger towards an unusually large tree with a forked trunk. There was a platform of branches in the fork the size of a tree-house, and sitting there was an eagle chick. I say 'chick', but through the binoculars it looked about four feet high. It stood ankle-deep in the twigs, occasionally walking around the nest, but showing no inclination to fly. Its parents were nowhere to be seen.

We sat and watched it for about an hour. A number of thoughts went through my head. First of all it seemed so solitary. Everything else in the forest was teeming with life. The tangle of vegetation growing up all seemed mutually dependent and right under my nose a line of ants carried fragments of leaves to and fro, each greeting the others as it passed; clouds of mosquitoes settled on our legs. I thought about the larger animals such as monkeys and flying lemurs which lived in colonies, and of course humans as well. But this baby eagle was entirely alone. It just sat up above the forest canopy and waited to be brought food.

Following a train of thought I had started in India, I again wondered why all the animals which thrive with us are so objectionable. Rats, cockroaches, ants, cockerels, dogs, goats – these are all man's familiars. We may admire all the magnificent beasts like elephants, rhinos, eagles and whales, but we kill them off and are left with this ghastly menagerie.

As we sat there, the silence was broken by the noise of a motor bike. The shrill roar rose clear above the roof of the forest, insistent as a drill.

Philippine Eagle
"pithecophaga jefferyi"
'91

'What is a motor bike doing here?' I thought angrily. 'They get everywhere.'

Then the engine seemed to get into trouble. The high-pitched squeal deepened as it sank into something. It sounded as if it was stuck in a bog. Then it cleared and shrieked again.

'Chain-saw,' Eddie said.

Chain-saw. So even as we looked down at this eagle, the forest around it was beginning to fall. The eagle could certainly hear this noise, but it had no concept of what it was or what it meant. From its perspective looking out from the nest, it would assume that the whole world was one big forest. That was all it could see and it had no reason to suppose that it didn't continue indefinitely. Perhaps the noise of a chain-saw was such a consistent background noise that the eagle thought it was a form of cicada; perhaps it hadn't noticed that the noise crept closer every week.

When the eagle chose to fly, it would soar up above the valley and see the wilderness outside. Then it would be too late. In six years' time there will be no forest left in the Philippines.

I noticed that the children who had come up with us were getting rather bored with the eagle. They sat on their haunches and started whittling away at the branches of trees with their knives. They neatly stripped the bark off saplings and trimmed their offending shoots. When the saplings were reduced to nice whippy raw yellow stumps, they chopped them down and threw them carelessly into the undergrowth. I was about to tell them to stop but I didn't know what they were hacking down. They might have been useless weeds or they might have been ten-year-old hardwood saplings waiting for a gap in the canopy above.

There were seven or eight children, each armed with a small knife. Eddie looked down at them and smiled. All Filipinos love children, and these were charming, smiling and attractive. But I felt a tremendous and irrational loathing for them. Why were there so many? Where did they think they were going to live? What did they think they were going to eat?

Then the chain-saw struck up again and I realized exactly where they were going to live.

EPILOGUE

TOADS CRAWLING THROUGH COTTON WOOL

When I had finished this book I visited Gerry in France where he was writing *The Magic Finger*, his account of the trip to Madagascar. We swapped manuscripts, argued over who had won the games of Scrabble and draughts in Morondava and covetously eyed up each other's metaphors. We then settled down to talk about my tour around his army of trainees.

When I started my travelling, the destruction of the forest had seemed a containable problem. My first trip had been to St Lucia where everyone knows exactly how much forest is left and the arguments over its future are well-documented. The St Lucian parrots are still rare, but they will not go extinct through negligence or the piecemeal destruction of the forest. I had walked through the forest in an afternoon. I was surprised by how tiny it was, but St Lucia is a small island. I had expected that when I reached places like Brazil or Madagascar, I would find large tracts of forest which would be able to take care of themselves and dwarf man's attempts to destroy them.

But wherever I went, I found that the original forest had been reduced to pocket-sized reserves. I climbed a hill in Brazil and looked over the entire lion tamarin forest; there were just thumbprints of forest left in Madagascar. No matter how remote the place looked on the map, when I arrived there I found people in jeans and flip-flops busily clearing trees to make room for more banana plantations, cattle grazing or paddy-fields.

In Nigeria I saw a truck with the slogan 'King of the Forest' painted across its headboard. Until I saw its load, I would have associated the expression with some magnificent creature like a jaguar or an eagle. The truck was carrying vast tree-trunks.

The more I travelled, the more I saw that the destruction is completely out of control. The forest is supremely vulnerable. It can be attacked from all sides by insidious invasion. The more the forest is opened up, the more edges appear and the easier it is to get inside and clear the trees. Farmers follow up the inroads made by the big logging companies; because the soil is so poor, the destruction becomes self-perpetuating as more forest has to be cleared when the crops fail. Once cleared, it doesn't grow back. My last sight of a forest was in the Philippines where I had seen an eagle chick almost ready to fledge. Even as I watched it, I heard the distant squeal of an approaching chain-saw.

The cumulative effect on me of seeing this destruction in every country was one of anger, panic and depression.

'Everything is desperately urgent,' Gerry agreed. 'The destruction of the world is progressing at the speed of an Exocet, whereas conservation struggles along at the speed of a horse and cart. It is tempting to try to do everything at once. I hear of all these wonderful projects which need to be done, but I can't do them all. I have to limit myself to what I can achieve.

'This is why I have kept our projects small and long-term. I want the work of the Jersey Trust to be an example to the rest of the world. If the lion tamarin project works and the tamarins and their forest are saved, then it can be used as a model for other larger problems like the Amazon rain forest. People can see what we have done in Mauritius where we have saved two birds from certain extinction and are now advising the government on the creation of the first national park. They can see how the mechanics of conservation actually work.

'The beauty of the Training Centre is that it is a catalyst. It enables us to reach out and influence people and governments without us having to spend thousands of pounds, which by the way we haven't got.

'So far we have had 300 trainees through our hands from every part of the world. You have obviously not seen all of them, but you have seen enough of a cross-section to realize that we have our successes and our disappointing failures. The funny thing is that even the failures teach us something. Perhaps we chose the wrong candidate, or taught them the wrong things. Or maybe we simply underestimated the difficulties they would face back home. Too many people assume that when you're dealing with animals it's all like Squirrel Nutkin – but as you've seen, it's a battle out there and we have to fight very hard.

'Having read your manuscript I want to introduce some teaching of initiative into the training course. I want to show people how to achieve things when confronted by a brick wall of impoverished bureaucracy. It makes me sad to hear of that girl sitting in an office in the Philippines with nothing to do and thinking that there's nothing she can do. Even with no money you can achieve things – ask my bank manager how much money I've had for most of my life. If we could teach her how to achieve little things, like how to influence people in the way that Ernest Lamptey does for his zoo in Ghana, then she could be heading upstream rather than drifting uselessly.'

Another problem which became increasingly obvious as I travelled around was that destruction is simply more profitable than conservation. If a family wants to become richer or a company wants to maximize its profits (which shareholders expect), then they are better off chopping down forests to plant crops, or taking out the timber or minerals in the most brutal way. As a well-fed foreigner who could afford to visit their country and spend 60 pence on a meal at a restaurant, I felt unable to tell people to shun this wealth. Confronted by such financial pressure, I asked Gerry how he thought that conservation could succeed.

'There are two approaches,' he said. 'The first is that if you want conservation you have to pay for it. If we want to see green forests and animals, which are still seen as a luxury by short-sighted people, then that costs money. So we could buy tracts of land and keep them intact. But if the human population continues to grow, ultimately the land will be overrun. So although it buys time, this is not a long-term solution.

'Another way of paying for conservation is by helping the poor countries develop to a stage where families don't need fifteen children to secure their future. Our record at this is very bad. If there's a famine, we just bale them out with shipments of grain without providing the training or the means to farm more efficiently so that they produce more grain in the future and do not need to plough so much land. Once they've developed to a stage where their population stabilizes, we can see what's left of the forest. But we must tackle this population growth or it will kill us all.

'The second approach involves learning a different philosophy. The trouble is that money is the only currency for so many people. What I try to show people, both my readers and my trainees, is how to realize their full potential.

'We all walk around so clenched up the whole time, particularly if we're working in a bureaucracy where we spend our lives worrying about who will kick us in the teeth or stab us in the back. I want people to have confidence in themselves. It's like the yoga I used to do before my hips ran out on me – it released my mind and gave me the courage to try all sorts of things I would otherwise have avoided.

'People often tell me that they wish they had lived a life like mine. I say "Well, why didn't you? All you had to do was to live it." They then look rather abashed, and mutter about how they had a mortgage and were saving up to buy a bigger house. The truth is that they never had the confidence to take the risk. The worst thing in life is to have reached the end of it and wish that you had lived it differently.

'All this sounds rather an abstract philosophy, particularly to an African or Indian fighting against starvation. But we have to get away from money as a yardstick of success and recognize the wider beauty of life. Everyone in the world, from princes to peasants, needs to understand some basic lessons of ecology, of how the planet works. People in both rich and poor countries are equally ignorant, but in different ways. The rich people are making money and polluting, the poor are trying to keep their huge families one step ahead of starvation, but nobody thinks ahead to what it all means for the future of the planet.

'You can't constantly tinker with a watch and then expect it to tell the correct time. You can't keep cutting down forests or polluting the air and water and expect the earth to stay fruitful. The soil is bound to wear out and wash away, crops fail and the climate change. Once people understand these things, then conservation will have a chance.'

Unlike many conservationists who concentrate on the 'environment' or 'development', Gerry takes animals as his starting point. In many of the countries I visited, animals had come at the bottom of the list of priorities. In Gambia the Fulah name for wildlife is '*suvo*', meaning 'meat'; and in Madagascar they eat rare lemurs because they taste almost as good as cats. Even the government officials ostensibly involved in conservation are often so preoccupied with their own welfare and their careers that the animals are disregarded. On several occasions I felt embarrassed about taking such a keen interest in the welfare of animals when so many people are so impoverished. But Gerry's life has been committed to animals and his philosophy goes deeper than merely looking after the cuddly ones.

'People are so blind about animals,' he explained. 'It is as if we have forgotten where we belong in this world. People tend to look at animals and say either "Oooh, isn't he cute?", or "Yuk! How ugly!" We think that a dog is intelligent because it fetches sticks, that a cat is cute because it purrs, that a sloth is mentally retarded because it's so slow and that a slug is simply disgusting.

'But these are human judgements which separate us from animals. We admire them if they show signs of behaving like us, but if they get too close, like apes or chimpanzees, we laugh at them. The very expression "to ape someone" is interesting because it is complimentary to the animal in getting that sophisticated, but at the same time it's firmly derogatory and puts them in their place – they're just animals, we're *humans*. But we've hardly made such a success of the world that we have a right to hold ourselves up as this paragon of intelligence.

'If only we thought of ourselves as animals, we would solve the root of our problem. If the Indian villagers realized that they were animals, just like that rat snake you saw, they would see that Nature has created a place for both of them and they can help each other. But no – yuk! It's a snake! No matter that it's entirely harmless and could help them control the rats, they kill it.

'I'm quite prepared to spend an hour on a bench with a slug and see how it lives. Maybe it's got something to teach me, maybe I can see another part of the jigsaw. Many people think that conservation is just saving fluffy animals – what they don't realize is that conservation is a war to prevent the human race from committing suicide.

'Most of all, I want people to realize how wonderful it is to live in this world surrounded by all these extraordinary and beautiful creatures. Even as we're talking now I'm aware of the swifts up there, and the lizard in the tree behind you and the bees in the lavender. People don't open their eyes to the world around them, they just crawl through it like toads crawling through cotton wool.'

My travels have left me swinging between despair and hope for the future. On the one hand, nobody thinks that they can do anything to stop the destruction. People vaguely look to politicians, who are after all running our countries with our money, but they are too obsessed with being re-elected to make the necessary changes. They would never dare to quadruple the price of petrol or ban the use of private cars for example. There is no formal organization which can take a leading role in conservation. In each country I visited I saw apathy, ignorance, corruption and above all vast numbers of impoverished people walking across an increasingly impoverished landscape.

On the other hand, when I think of the Jersey trainees I visited I feel hopeful. I remember Rhema's conversation with the Rastas who hunted the coney; Claudio Padua who gave up a lucrative career to study Brazilian primates; Germain Rakotobearison's giant tortoises and Paramananda Lahan's ration of four cartridges for his elephant patrol against poachers. If I had visited Mauritius ten years ago, the island's condition would have seemed as desperate as that of the Philippines now. So across the world there are glimpses of hope as people begin to work together to protect the forests and explain the consequences of their destruction.

My best analogy of what then happens is with Eastern Europe. All the governments said that it was impossible to change, so we dutifully bowed our heads and lived with that ghastly system for forty-five years, thinking that we couldn't do anything about it. A few people got shot going over the Berlin Wall, but otherwise we all kowtowed to the Kremlin. But all along a child could have told us that it was wrong to have a wire fence running through the middle of Europe.

Then suddenly it was overthrown. People just decided that they had had enough. I don't know what chemistry triggered that, but that's where the hope for conservation lies.

Any child can tell us that it's wrong to destroy so much of the world, yet governments make only the most feeble efforts to change anything. If you asked children whether it's right to destroy a quarter of all species living on earth in the next twenty-five years, they would be horrified. Ask any businessman and he will shrug his shoulders and think about how to tweak his profit margins. The world population is set to double in the next thirty years and double again in sixty years. It destroys everything it touches.

When we realize that we ourselves may be one of the species which will go extinct – we are after all just another animal – then we will do something about it. If we want something badly enough, we generally get it. That's when the chemistry changes. What we must realize now is how badly we should want it.